Buffalo Bill Cody

ALSO BY LEW FREEDMAN
AND FROM MCFARLAND

Cy Young: The Baseball Life and Career (2020)

Ernie Banks: The Life and Career of "Mr. Cub" (2019)

*Connie Mack's First Dynasty:
The Philadelphia Athletics, 1910–1914* (2017)

*Baseball's Funnymen: Twenty-Four Jokers,
Screwballs, Pranksters and Storytellers* (2017)

The Boyer Brothers of Baseball (2015)

Joe Louis: The Life of a Heavyweight (2013)

*DiMaggio's Yankees:
A History of the 1936–1944 Dynasty* (2011)

*The Day All the Stars Came Out:
Major League Baseball's
First All-Star Game, 1933* (2010)

*Hard-Luck Harvey Haddix
and the Greatest Game Ever Lost* (2009)

*Early Wynn, the Go-Go White Sox
and the 1959 World Series* (2009)

Buffalo Bill Cody

*The Man Who Shaped
the Wild West Legend*

Lew Freedman

McFarland & Company, Inc., Publishers
Jefferson, North Carolina

LIBRARY OF CONGRESS CATALOGUING-IN-PUBLICATION DATA

Names: Freedman, Lew, author.
Title: Buffalo Bill Cody : the man who shaped the wild West legend / Lew Freedman.
Description: Jefferson, North Carolina : McFarland & Company, Inc., Publishers, 2020 | Includes bibliographical references and index.
Identifiers: LCCN 2020036781 | ISBN 9780786499533 (paperback : acid free paper) ∞
ISBN 9781476640068 (ebook)
Subjects: LCSH: Buffalo Bill, 1846-1917. | Buffalo Bill's Wild West Show—History. | Entertainers—United States—Biography. | Frontier and pioneer life—West (U.S.) | Scouts (Reconnaissance)—West (U.S.)—Biography. | West (U.S.)—Biography.
Classification: LCC F594 .F685 2020 | DDC 978/.02092 [B]—dc23
LC record available at https://lccn.loc.gov/2020036781

BRITISH LIBRARY CATALOGUING DATA ARE AVAILABLE

ISBN (print) 978-0-7864-9953-3
ISBN (ebook) 978-1-4766-4006-8

© 2020 Lew Freedman. All rights reserved

No part of this book may be reproduced or transmitted in any form or by any means, electronic or mechanical, including photocopying or recording, or by any information storage and retrieval system, without permission in writing from the publisher.

Front cover: William Frederick Cody, 1892
(Harvard Theatre Collection, Harvard University)

Printed in the United States of America

McFarland & Company, Inc., Publishers
 Box 611, Jefferson, North Carolina 28640
  www.mcfarlandpub.com

Table of Contents

Introduction	1
1. Becoming Buffalo Bill	5
2. The Codys of Iowa	15
3. The Pony Express	26
4. Wars	40
5. Cody and Custer	47
6. The Mrs.	62
7. The Persuasive Mr. Buntline	70
8. Medal of Honor	77
9. Rodeo and Wild West Beginnings	91
10. The Wild West Goes Wild	103
11. Sitting Bull	112
12. Annie Oakley	123
13. Love 'Em and Leave 'Em	131
14. The Wild West Is the Toast of Europe and Everywhere Else	138
15. Indians	153
16. A Congress of Rough Riders	163
17. Divorce Trials	173
18. Cody, Wyoming	180
19. The Death of the Great Showman	190
20. Buffalo Bill's Legacy	205
Chapter Notes	219
Bibliography	227
Index	231

Introduction

Buffalo Bill Cody is one of my favorite Americans. During his lifetime he was the most famous and most photographed man in the world. For five years I lived in the community in the northern Rocky Mountains in Wyoming that he lent his name to and wrote for the newspaper he founded in 1896. I lived only a few miles from the Buffalo Bill Center of the West, the multifaceted museum founded to honor him following his death in Denver in 1917, a month shy of his seventy-first birthday. I have met and conversed with descendants of the great cowboy, once casually chatting about Medicare at a flu shot health clinic with one of his great-grandsons.

In my possession I have cardboard cartons of background information about the man christened William F. Cody in Iowa in 1846. The great western novelist Larry McMurtry contended that Cody and his expert markswoman show business partner Annie Oakley were America's first superstars. It is an easy point to agree with since they predated Babe Ruth in baseball and Red Grange in football, and presidents of the United States were not really lumped in with celebrities of their day. There are scholars who have invested lifetimes in studying Buffalo Bill's varied life, seeking to prove facts muddied by dime novelists whose works more resembled comic books than noteworthy serious examinations of the most influential man who swayed public perception of what the Old West was truly about.

There are many Cody stories. Unequivocally he did some things. Some things he might have done. Others he most assuredly did not. The stories all clung to him, and he did not care to issue corrections. No one will ever go wrong describing Buffalo Bill as colorful. If he lived in the present day, Cody would have eighty million social media followers.

Once, I did ask Bruce Eldredge, the now-retired CEO and executive director of the Buffalo Bill Center of the West, what Buffalo Bill might think about nearly fifteen years into the twenty-first century. Stressing that Cody was forward-thinking, Eldredge suggested the man who was

A sculpture of Buffalo Bill Cody stands by the front door of the Buffalo Bill Center of the West in Cody, Wyoming (photograph by the author).

born to be photographed aboard a stallion would be driving a hybrid automobile. And, oh yes, he would be pushing for the museum named for him to evolve into a more interactive experience. Cody was very much an interactive kind of guy. Anyone who asks me what made him special I urge them to read his Wikipedia page and dare them to come away unimpressed. Indeed, over the last couple of years, Eldredge's successor Peter Seibert has moved the museum in the interactive direction.

Without offering a nudge either way on yeas or nays about truth or fiction, here is a short list of accomplishments: rode for the Pony Express, fought for the Union Army in the Civil War, was a Cavalry scout, was a bison slayer as a hunter, won the Medal of Honor, turned his Wild West exhibition (always refusing to call it a show) into a stunning entertainment spectacle that toured the country and the world, and, after going to war with them, became the best friend the Plains Indians had by providing good wages in employment and offering travel to places they otherwise could never dream of visiting. In an era before the airplane, somehow he transported his Wild West exhibition, sometimes four hundred people and four hundred animals strong, across the ocean to dazzle the queen of England or the elite of France, hunted with the prince of Monaco, and influenced many thousands of young boys who wanted to run away and join the Wild West exhibition more than they wanted to run away and join the circus.

Cody was friends with Wild Bill Hickok and knew George Armstrong Custer and Sitting Bull, generals, presidents, and just about every other famous person who overlapped his lifespan. He was heroic and flamboyant, but was very much a man of flesh and blood, with a long but unhappy marriage; he suffered tragedy with children dying young and faced battles with booze. When he was in his right mind, he was a king-sized personality and generous to a fault, though he may never have truly been in his sharpest mind when making business investments.

Whenever I read about another Buffalo Bill escapade, it makes me smile. There are many books that highlight narrow aspects of his life, and there are full-fledged, quite well-done biographies that set out to prove something. My goal in producing a newer Buffalo Bill Cody biography was to thread together tales so the reader had a rollicking good time traveling from one end of his life to the other, exploring the occasional mystery surrounding his exploits and very much reminding those schools that have shied away from educating young students about this most extraordinary man that they should reenter the world partially created and partially imagined by the most singular western figure of them all. In some ways, when I was a resident of Cody, Wyoming, Bill's town, I interacted with Buffalo Bill every day. The Cody Country Chamber of Commerce sign welcoming visitors to the city of nearly ten thousand people features a picture of Buffalo Bill. Just across the street is the five-museum center. One wing is devoted to the life and times of Buffalo Bill.

William F. Cody died in January 1917 while visiting a daughter's house in Denver, some five hundred miles from Cody. In January 2017, I attended a commemorative wake in Golden, Colorado, on the grounds of the Buffalo Bill Museum and Grave. There is a long-running rivalry between the Cody museum, which is much larger, and the Golden museum. The Golden museum's trump card is its claim that it is the burial site of Buffalo Bill. This is a dispute I have stuck my nose into several times seeking to prove whether his remains lie in the ground in Colorado or were really kidnapped to the location in Cody where he stated he wished to be buried.

In August of that same year, still linked to the 100th anniversary of Buffalo Bill's death, the Center of the West put on a world-class symposium with experts in several fields and from several countries participating, each focusing on different Buffalo legacies and influences. The breadth of the topics was breathtaking. Talks ran right through lunches and dinners and energized and exhausted listeners for thirty-six hours. So it is no exaggeration to say that at any given time I was engulfed by Buffalo Bill lore.

On the very day I sat down to write these words, I visited the Buffalo Bill Center of the West. At the entrance to the Buffalo Bill wing, the traveler is greeted by a Buffalo Bill hologram. Dressed in a gray, three-piece suit, a blue tie with white polka dots over a white shirt, and knee-high, black leather boots and a pliable cowboy hat, Buffalo Bill speaks. This actor, a prominent Cody and Wyoming figure in his eighties named Pete Simpson, has Buffalo Bill's late-in-life, flowing, white hair and grown-out, white beard pointed at the end.

"Ladies and gentlemen," Buffalo Bill's greeting begins. "Permit me to introduce myself. I am William F. Cody. But you probably know me as Buffalo Bill. I am fortunate to know the West as few people dead or alive."

That is true, even more than a century after his death.

1

Becoming Buffalo Bill

It was a catchy nickname, the label bestowed on William F. Cody during his buffalo hunting days. It was so memorable it stood out to contemporaries and has stood out ever since, through the annals of history. Just plain old Bill would not have done it. Nor would have Will, as family members called the boy in his youth and throughout his life if you were a sister. Interestingly, Americans' propensity to refer to the king of the Great Plains as buffalo rather than bison—the scientifically accurate name for the 1,500-pound-or-more beasts—benefited Cody. Somehow, "Bison Bill" does not carry the same ring.

It is the rare set of parents who would dare to introduce a child to the world with a birth certificate shouting the name "Buffalo Bill Cody," and Cody's father Isaac and mother Mary Ann did not venture down such a path. William Frederick Cody is how the document read when the boy was born on February 26, 1846, in rural Iowa. He had to work for and earn the Buffalo Bill nickname. Like so many of the fascinating tales attributed to writers and Cody's own mouth, this one was a doozy. Whether every single detail of the setting and the result—which has traveled more miles than Cody did on horseback—are accurate, the core of the story of how Cody woke up one day called Bill and fell asleep the same day forevermore called Buffalo Bill, is tinged with legend.

After a childhood spent in Iowa and a few other states, after a stint with the Pony Express, and after time spent representing the blue side in the Civil War, Cody signed on for a new job on the frontier. Over an eighteen-month period in 1867 and 1868, Bill Cody's assignment was to kill buffalo to provide meat for the workers of the Kansas Pacific Railway. It was a federally chartered railroad that opened up settlement in Kansas and transportation to Denver, before later being absorbed by the Union Pacific. At least one report indicates Cody was required to kill twelve buffalo a day, which indeed could represent a full day's work. The pay was supposed to be $500 for each day of fulfillment, most assuredly big money

It is easy to come across images of Buffalo Bill Cody in the city he helped founded in Wyoming. Here his face adorns the Cody Country Chamber of Commerce sign (photograph by the author).

in the nineteenth century. The hunting challenge, coupled with the risk of being killed by Indians, would have accounted for the high rate of pay. It is unlikely one hunter could deliver that bounty every single day. The buyers figured on paying just one cent per pound for the meat acquired—as opposed to the Native American custom, which called for salvaging every bit of the animal for different purposes.

By then Cody was not a complete novice as a buffalo hunter. Dating to his scouting days earlier in the 1860s, Cody was based at Fort Hays, Kansas, where his prowess as a buffalo hunter won much approval. This was a proving ground for him in this realm. The second day into a march, Major William Royall urged Cody to hunt some buffalo meat for their Fifth Cavalry. Cody asked for some wagons to transport the dead animals back, but Royall, signaling a wait-and-see attitude, told Cody to kill the buffalo first and then he would get the wagons. Stung by the rebuff, Cody promptly headed out and killed six buffalo, fulfilling his command.

The next day Royall repeated his order for Cody to go kill buffalo to feed the men. This time Cody did not ask for wagons, but resorted to a different strategy to prove his point to the major. "Coming up with a small herd," Cody said he chose not to kill them on the spot. "I managed to get seven of them headed straight for the encampment, and instead of shooting them just then, I ran them at full speed right into the camp, and killed them all, one after the other, in rapid succession." Royall was taken aback and Cody said, "I didn't care about asking for any wagons this time, so I thought I would make the buffaloes furnish their own transportation."[1] Those soldiers who witnessed the operation did not underestimate Cody again.

Cody was a formidable shot and was armed with a state-of-the-art .50-caliber Springfield Model 1866 rifle that the government supplied to him. Unlike the muzzle loaders of the past, this was a fast-shooting gun. His fancy clearly taken by the equipment, Cody gave his rifle a nickname, calling it "Lucretia Borgia." Borgia was a real-life Italian–Spanish woman of noble heritage who lived between 1480 and 1519. It was claimed she was a member of a status-seeking clan who kept arranging marriages for her because her husbands somehow kept dying. The family was plagued by rumors of incest, murder, and poisoning involving Borgia, whose actual first name was spelled "Lucrezia."

Over the centuries since, playwrights and authors have fabricated epic tales with Lucrezia at the focal point of nefarious plots. At the time Cody named his rifle, a Borgia opera was playing. It is easy enough to see how he could make the connection between this so-called murderess and his deadly weapon. Mostly, it is just one indicator of Cody's early sense of showmanship, not yet tapped in any manner that would lead observers of the period to view him as one of the greatest showmen in American history.

Much of Old West mythology has been constructed on a foundation of exaggerated claims. In the case of feared outlaws and gunfighters, there was no clearing house to register kills, so word of mouth accounted for dead bodies more than reality. Whether it was Billy the Kid or someone else, legend spread fantastical figures about how many men bit the dust because of encounters with bloodthirsty villains, or even lawmen.

In the case of Cody and buffalo, there was an accounting. The Kansas Pacific Railway needed meat, and Cody supplied it, one dead buffalo at a time. During his year and a half procuring the meat, Cody and his team of Lucretia Borgia and horse Brigham were credited with the deaths of 4,282 animals. This was, of course, a significant number. However, claims from the occasional Cody-hater blaming him for single-handedly wiping out the Plains buffalo are absurd. Cody hunted so others could eat. The policy of the U.S. government to eradicate the forty to sixty million buffalo roaming the land was a specific plot aimed at driving the Plains Indian tribes onto reservations and eliminating them as a war-like threat to settlers stealing their lands. Destruction of the buffalo population was a by-product of the federal government's genocidal tactics with the ultimate goal of disarming all Native Americans, forcing them off their historic territories, and then training them to be farmers.

When Cody was hunting, the U.S. government's strategy to essentially eliminate the species was not publicly known. There were millions upon millions of the animals and no big-picture analysis of the harm being done to their future. In addition to the meat harvested, buffalo hides were desirable for robes, buffalo skulls were churned into fertilizer, and bones were part of refined sugar and used in making china plates. Germans created a method to convert buffalo hides into leather items. Concurrent with the rather devious governmental policy, there was also profit to be made.

Those same railroad workers nourished by buffalo meat moved on to the next job, the next construction. But the now-functioning transportation system was able to freight the hides and bones east for processing and manufacturing millions upon millions of products for sale. No authority existed to suggest that the pace of buffalo slaughter slow down for the survival of the species. The only advocates were Native Americans who considered buffalo holy or sacred and animals to be revered. But the Indians were powerless and seen as the enemy, regardless of tribal affiliation, during this time period.

Bill Cody was not privy to crystal balls or what the future might hold for the territory he shared with those mighty animals who could not outrun him and his horse. Like so many thousands of men mustered out of the army at the end of the Civil War, he needed a paycheck. He possessed a marvelous aim and a spectacular, instinctual horse that gave him an edge over most hunters, so he gained a local reputation. His sharpshooting led to many calling him Buffalo Bill, and the notoriety appealed to his vanity.

It is said that the first time the appellation Buffalo Bill appeared in a publication applied to Cody was in the November 26, 1867, issue of the newspaper *Daily Conservative* in Leavenworth, Kansas. The reference seems casual, noted in connection with a humorous hunting incident when Cody encountered a gaggle of cavalrymen who seemed to believe they were superior buffalo hunters. According to the report, Cody was in the field doing his job when he met up with five officers stationed at Fort Hays, a captain and four lieutenants. The soldiers were not terribly impressed with the comparatively ragtag Cody who was riding Brigham without even a saddle for assistance. Those men, seemingly feeling sorry over the likelihood Cody would be shut out, generously offered to share buffalo tongues and some tenderloin from their bounty and allowed him to follow along. Cody issued no hint of his expertise in such matters, but simply took them up on their offer. Talk about underestimating the

1. Becoming Buffalo Bill

opposition by the Fort Hays men. What ensued was the type of outcome that sticks to a man's reputation. It was no contest—Bill Cody shutting out the officers, and no doubt shutting their mouths. Sorry, boys. According to Cody,

> There were 11 buffaloes [no bison mentions by Buffalo Bill] in the herd and they were not more than a mile from us. The officers dashed ahead as if they had a sure thing on killing them all before I could come up with them. But I had noticed the herd was making towards the creek for water, and as I knew buffalo nature, I was perfectly aware that it would be difficult to turn them off their course. Thereupon, I started towards the creek to head them off, while the officers came up in the rear and gave chase. The buffaloes came rushing past me, not a hundred yards distant, with the officers about three hundred yards in the rear. Now, I thought, "it's time to get my work in," as they say. I pulled the blind bridle from my horse, who knew as well as I did we were out for buffaloes, as he was a trained horse.[2]

Buffalo Bill Cody was known for riding large, white horses on the prairie and in his Wild West exhibitions (courtesy of Park County Archives).

Cody's lavish praise of Brigham always made the equine animal sound like a wonder horse. Cody obtained Brigham from Ute Indians and always said Brigham was the fastest horse he ever rode, and apparently rated remarkably high in the IQ department. One 1868 newspaper report cited in a biography said that "Bill Cody has made a match to run the Brigham pony ninety miles in twelve hours. Brigham is to tote 175 pounds."[3]

Meanwhile, Bill Cody versus the cavalry was enough of an achievement. What commenced was a tour de force performance by hunter and horse, a remarkable display of pursuit, shooting accuracy, and marksmanship. Cody unleashed Brigham's speed, and the horse sprinted ahead, bringing him adjacent to the unsuspecting buffalo. Balanced on his steed, Cody called upon Lucretia Borgia and, combining the rifle's power and his own skill, quickly overcame the buffalo.

"I fired and killed the animal at the first shot," Cody said of reaching the first buffalo. "My horse then carried me alongside the next one, not ten feet away, and I dropped him at the next fire. As soon as one buffalo would fall, Brigham would take me so close to the next that I could almost touch it with my gun. In this manner, I killed the eleven buffaloes with twelve shots."[4]

It was the kind of effort that smacks of exaggeration in the retelling, but Cody was not alone on the Plains, not on stage solo for his act. There were witnesses to the result of this shooting showdown, several of them of reputable character, hardly in cahoots with him. The soldiers were mere bystanders drawn into the play by chance. They were transformed from doubters to believers, mouths dropping in astonishment. They had thrown down a challenge and been topped, not necessarily in such a way as to almost be humiliated, but at the least overwhelmed by a superior talent. It was as if some unwitting soul had sauntered up to basketball Hall of Famer Michael Jordan and said, "Hey, buddy, how about a one-on-one game to twenty-one?"

Since Cody had killed all the buffalo in the group, there was nothing for the cavalrymen to shoot. In a tweak, no doubt smiling wryly, he offered them tongues and tenderloin—the same offer they made to him. This colorful occurrence was described in Buffalo Bill's first autobiography—he more than once wrote about his life—and it was this occasion that gained mention in the Leavenworth newspaper. It is not clear if Cody's nickname was mentioned to the reporter by the soldiers or if it was just beginning to spread at that time.

Certainly, "Buffalo Bill" was not yet universally attached to Cody. In Major League Baseball history, the pitcher of all-time is Cy Young. Cy was short for "Cyclone," and today it would be unthinkable to christen another hard-throwing hurler Cyclone. Some may recall that the birth name of the great slugger "Babe" Ruth was George Herman. While there were some other Babes through the decades in baseball, such a bestowing of the same nickname now would be seen as audacious, even sacrilegious. However, at that time, in the post–Civil War 1860s, another hunter was at large in the same region, who by chance was also bestowed with the first name of Bill. Bill Comstock, who like Cody had been a scout and admired hunter and who, as part Cheyenne, had interpretive skills, was also widely known and referred to by his clique as Buffalo Bill. This was a bit confusing, and the men agreed it just would not do to have two Buffalo Bills soaking up the attention for the same type of buffalo-killing feats.

Comstock was then employed as chief of scouts at Fort Wallace in Kansas, and he had been involved in buffalo hunting longer than Cody. The soldiers stationed at that fort had great confidence in Comstock, and they felt he was the most deserving of being called Buffalo Bill, though he was more commonly referred to as Billy "Medicine Bill" Comstock, much the same as the buckskin-wearing scout affiliated with Fort Hays was still more often called Bill Cody. But both men coveted the attention and recognition.

This led to an arranged contest to settle the matter, and it was pretty clear after this one-on-one event that only one man would be worthy of the Buffalo Bill designation. The man who killed the most buffalo in one day would get to keep the name Buffalo Bill. The loser would basically be too embarrassed to continue using it. It is not clear if those terms were an official part of the bargain, but it sounded as if they were, in addition to $500 going to the winner. By then, Cody had done enough to convince Fort Hays soldiers where to put their money.

The matter sounds like a duel in the city, with seconds at hand monitoring the rules, but it was closer to a party on the prairie with all of the pressure on two men as others whooped it up. There are some researchers who state this intimately described battle between Cody and Comstock never happened. Or at least some say if it happened, it happened at a different time.

Above all, it is a delicious tale, and Cody relished telling it. According to Cody (and meshing in others' commentary), the Cody–Comstock affair played out under some basic terms. Competition was set for 8 a.m. and was to continue for eight hours. At 4 p.m., the Buffalo Bill who had killed the most buffalo remained Buffalo Bill. The contest was supposed to happen within thirty days of the initial challenge.

Cody wrote that the match took place about twenty miles east of Sheridan, Kansas, and it had been well-advertised. He said an excursion train (vacationers sampling the West?) made its way from St. Louis, carrying the well-dressed and the wealthy who were well supplied, or plied, with champagne. His recall suggested about one hundred people made that journey. Cody clearly places the events later in time than some others because he said he was married and his wife Louisa attended with his baby daughter Arta.

Under the parameters of the hunt, Cody and Comstock were followed by referees armed with an abacus or something to total up the kills. He said the buffalo were plentiful in the region, so there was no reason for them to split up into different hunting areas. They followed the same herd. Spectators who traveled so far to see this expert shooting were handicapped in their viewing, only permitted to come into the vicinity by wagon or horseback so they did not spook the buffalo.

In his recounting of the affair, Cody said he brought great confidence to the match. "I felt confident I had the advantage of Comstock in two things," he said. "First, I had the best buffalo horse that ever made a track." That, of course was his prime partner Brigham. "And second, I was using what was known at that time as the needle gun." That was his trusty Lucretia Borgia Springfield.[5]

Comstock's weapon of choice was another notable rifle, a Henry. When the competitors set off after the buffalo, the herd split. Comstock pursued the group running to the left, and Cody went to the right. Cody set forth a specific strategy to corner buffalo with the aid of Brigham, and anyone who saw him hunt that day had to agree he knew what he was doing.

"My great forte in killing buffaloes from horseback was to get them circling by riding my horse at the head of the herd," Cody said. "Shooting the leaders, thus crowding their followers to the left, till they would finally circle round and round." Cody said he observed Comstock taking a different approach. "Comstock began shooting at the rear of the herd which he was chasing and they kept running straight on."[6]

During this initial morning run, Cody killed thirty-eight buffalo. Comstock did okay, but was far behind, with twenty-three kills. Cody said his approach was like playing billiards, lining up the next shot when he pressed the trigger. The buffalo he killed were clustered fairly close together while Comstock's were spread over a three-mile distance. That meant more work for the referees in accounting for the downed beasts. During the intermission that followed, the revelers from St. Louis imbibed their champagne—the pause that refreshes.

Perhaps wiping sweat from his forehead, having some liquid refreshment (there is no mention of Cody's intaking any booze in the midst of the event), and discussing the doings, Cody and Comstock's supporters took note of another approaching herd of buffalo. So the men revved up again. These animals were calves and cows, not as large as the adult buffalo previously confronted. Nonetheless, Cody said these smaller buffalo moved more swiftly and had that going for them. Cody and Comstock resumed the contest. The score of this second round was Cody eighteen, Comstock fourteen. Billy was not closing the gap on Bill. The overall score was fifty-six to thirty-seven, a good solid margin in Cody's favor, although the day was not over. The revelers opened more champagne, and all, including the shooters, adjourned for lunch.

Part three of the day-long hunt began with the search for a new buffalo herd since another was not dumb enough to walk into the men's sights. The next group of animals was found three miles away. Cody was getting a bit smug about his big lead and decided to show off for the ladies from St. Louis, promising to pursue the big-headed, shaggy creatures while riding his star horse without saddle or bridle. While this seemed to excite many of the spectators, some did try to talk him out of the endeavor. Comstock's opinion was not recorded, though he could not have appreciated the showy maneuver.

"That's nothing at all," Cody responded to those expressing concern for his well-being. "I have done it many a time and old Brigham knows as well as I what I am doing, and sometimes a great deal better."[7] Perhaps Brigham was so talented he could have fired the rifle, as well. Cody stuck with his announced plan of leaving those usually crucial pieces of gear behind with his fans and once more went after the buffalo, seeking to clinch the championship.

But that was not enough for Cody. He sought to make an even stronger impression, particularly, it seems on those spectators of the female persuasion, his wife's presence notwithstanding. He continued his frantic pace of shooting and staying well clear of Comstock, but added one last trick to solicit oohs and ahhs from the gallery. Cody was up to a kill count of a dozen during this round when he went after one final animal, "which I had driven down close to the wagons where the ladies were. It frightened some of the tender creatures to see the buffalo coming at full speed directly toward them. But when he had got within fifty yards of one of the wagons, I shot him dead in his tracks."[8]

That was Cody's grand finale, bringing the curtain down on his performance with sixty-nine kills in one day. Comstock shot quite well and definitely was no idle challenger, but his final total was forty-six. Who was most worthy of the nickname Buffalo Bill was settled. Henceforth, Buffalo Bill Cody was the one and only Buffalo Bill of public fame and acceptance. The name stuck forever, but once he completed his contract feeding the railroad workers, Cody was pretty much finished with buffalo hunting as a job. The experience and stories clung to him, but buffalo hunting more lingered in his past rather than as a long-term profession.

For that matter, buffalo hunting was soon no longer a career for anyone. The hunted-out species driven to the edge of extinction barely escaped becoming a species that joined the dinosaur as something great that once walked the earth. There were sometimes exceptions to Cody taking to the Plains again for hunts, though not as an individual being paid for providing meat. Buffalo Bill as a name stuck like glue and spread, so Cody was called up to lead the rich and famous on buffalo hunts as a guide. This was a far cry from his early days as an individual buffalo hunter for wages. He was as much a celebrity as the people seeking an authentic western buffalo hunting experience.

It was not as if Cody was advertising buffalo hunts in the pages of newspapers or by word of mouth. The name Buffalo Bill wooed the clientele, people he knew who were really asking for favors and trying to impress other prominent people. Those who sought out Cody immediately thought of Buffalo Bill first when they were trying to entertain special individuals. Buffalo Bill, always a schmoozer, who had a habit of making important friends, was always glad to provide when his skills were in demand for a major hunt. Individually, these occasions were auspicious enough. Together they continued to enhance his fame and popularity, and perhaps one day he would be able to call in favors in crucial situations simply because he had taken a gang out on a buffalo hunt and provided a memorable experience.

Buffalo Bill Cody may have been accidentally famous in the first place, but for all the fictitious adventures ascribed to him, his rise from deprivation and tragedy and his genuine talents as a guide, scout, and shot stood up to scrutiny in his being the real deal.

2

The Codys of Iowa

The LeClaire, Iowa, house of William F. Cody's youth is a small wooden structure covered in yellow paint. The building still exists, a testament to his famous name's pull, but it does not stand in the small community along the Mississippi River where he once resided. The building was actually forfeited by his hometown for lack of interest, picked up whole, and transported by train to Cody, Wyoming, where it now stands in the Cashman Greever Garden belonging to the Buffalo Bill Center of the West.

This structure is referred to as Buffalo Bill's boyhood home, although he was born in a log cabin on a farm on February 26, 1846, about two miles away and the family moved into this house in 1849. There were other childhood moves, as well, but unlikely as it seemed, the house moved, too. Indifference by LeClaire residents marked the availability of the house, and it was sold to the Chicago Burlington and Quincy Railroad in 1933 and relocated next to the Burlington Inn in Cody, Wyoming. This made some sense since the railroad was still operating train tours to nearby Yellowstone National Park. However, by 1947, interest in rail tours into the 2.2-million-acre national park was waning, train travel losing out to the rise of automobile traffic. At that time, Cody's niece, Mary Jester Allen, was in charge of the Cody museum built in his honor. She was able to secure the house, and it has lived on the center's grounds ever since.

In his youth, Cody and his family were on the go often enough. Bill, or Will, was seven years old in 1853 when the Codys moved to Leavenworth, Kansas. This was not the final move of his childhood, either. The Codys had always been a mobile clan. The first Codys in the United States arrived before there was a United States, embarking in the Massachusetts Bay Colony in 1698. Family members emanated from the Isle of Jersey near Normandy. After crossing the Atlantic Ocean, Codys dispersed through New England, into Pennsylvania, and into Canada near Toronto. These days there are Cody family descendants not only in Cody, Wyoming, but also in several other countries.

Will's immediate family included his parents and seven siblings. The children consisted of five girls—Martha (from his father's first marriage), Julia, Eliza, Laura (who at times went by Nellie and others Helen), and Mary (or May)—and three boys, Samuel, Will, and Charley. Will was the fourth oldest. Later in life, after his parents and brothers Samuel and Charley had passed away, the famous brother was a devoted sibling who was generous to his sisters and helped take care of their families, often financially. They were fiercely loyal to him.

Many members of the Cody family that spread out from Massachusetts became Quakers, and as such they held strong views against slavery, the hottest political (and human rights) issue for most of the nation's first hundred years. Cody's father Isaac was steadfast in his opposition to the evil practice that led to the near-unraveling of the nation and the outbreak of the Civil War. The best-known story about Will's father Isaac stems from his vocal challenge to pro-slavery figures who stabbed him for his views, a wound that ultimately led to his death and a drastic change in Cody family circumstances. But that came after the Codys changed domiciles a few times.

When Buffalo Bill penned the autobiography that first appeared in 1879, he got his own birth date wrong in the opening sentence of the book. It read, "My debut upon the world's stage occurred on February 26th, 1845."[1] However, he was born a year later on that date. He should have asked his mother Mary Ann.

Cody portrayed his young self as somewhat roguish, always getting into trouble, taking risks, but emerging from scrapes fortunate to remain in one piece. "Even at that early age my adventurous spirit led me into all sorts of mischief and danger," he wrote, "and when I look back upon my childhood's days, I often wondered that I did not get drowned while swimming or sailing, or my neck broken while I was stealing apples in the neighboring orchards."[2] It might be said that Cody was equally lucky to escape from many more risky escapades during the following decades of his life as well. Whether he merely liked the sound of his self-analysis, or he really was a bit of a trouble-seeker as a kid, Cody did not seem to mind portraying himself as something shy of a choirboy in behavior.

In addition to years spent in LeClaire and in Leavenworth, during a second stay in Iowa the Codys lived in Wapsipinicon Valley near McCausland. Isaac Cody built the larger and sturdier home that is now referred to as the Buffalo Bill Cody Homestead, and it was added to the National Register of Historic Places in 1974.

Cody moved about sufficiently enough that the modern-day traveler is likely to stumble upon several houses, museums, and statues of him spread around the Plains states and the West. Even though LeClaire city founders

2. The Codys of Iowa

once pretty much let his early home get away, the community of approximately four thousand people now houses a small Buffalo Bill Museum on the banks of the Mississippi that splits its contents between highlighting the man's life and local history. A visitor to the inside of the museum can see a notice about a fundraising campaign to build a replica of Buffalo Bill's

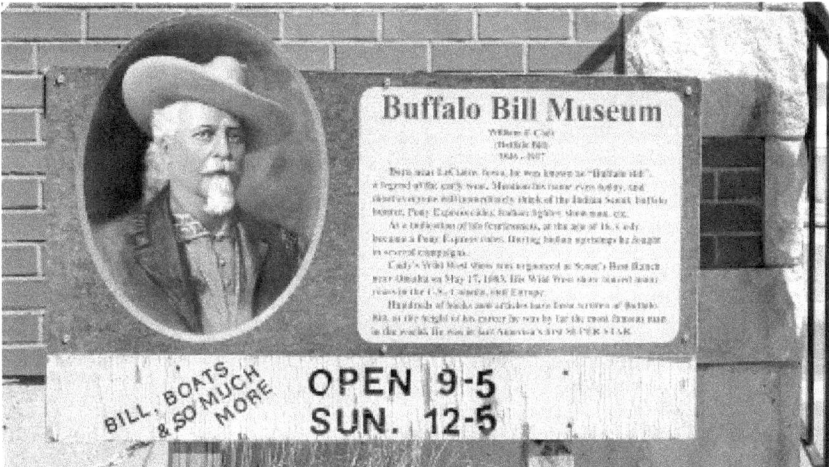

The Buffalo Bill Museum is located in LeClaire, Iowa, commemorating his birth in 1846 and early life (photograph by the author).

A plaque commemorates William F. Cody's birthplace in Iowa (photograph by the author).

boyhood home. There are apparently regrets about the sale of the old house, but the Buffalo Bill Center of the West is apparently not giving it back.

While Bill placed his name upon a few books during his lifetime, sister Nellie, as he referred to her, was probably the real writer in the family. Twice married, to Alexander Jester and Hugh Wetmore, she worked for the Duluth, Minnesota, newspaper, set up in business by her famous brother, and she published an admiring book of him called *Last of the Great Scouts* under the name Helen Cody Wetmore. Born four years after Bill, Helen/Nellie spoke of their Iowa days fondly—at least initially.

An exhibit inside the LeClaire, Iowa, Buffalo Bill Museum (photograph by the author).

Her memories of the limestone and wooden Iowa home her father built are sweetly portrayed. "A pleasant, roomy farmhouse, set in the sunlight against a backdrop of cool, green wood and mottled meadow," she wrote. "This is the picture that my earliest memories frame for me."[3] She gets Buffalo Bill's birth year right and refers to herself in the first chapter as Helen, even if Bill called her Nellie. Also, in typical confusion about Buffalo Bill's life, she neglected to mention brother Charley, born in 1855.

Bill, who as an adult sat astride horses in regal fashion, as if born to the saddle, recalled engaging in his first horse ride in LeClaire and recounted being thrown off and spraining his arm. Nellie refers to his first equine trip on the back of a pony. Cody said his father nearly fled to the gold fields of California in 1849, but his traveling partners backed out on him before they went too far. Bill said he attended school in Iowa for a short while, though he expressed no enthusiasm for the commitment and thought his parents just wanted him in a controlled environment for a

2. The Codys of Iowa 19

An additional exhibit inside the LeClaire, Iowa, Buffalo Bill Museum (photograph by the author).

chunk of the day. Whether it came naturally, or he learned it in school, William F. Cody had marvelous penmanship, fortunate for those later in the century who sought his autograph and for twenty-first-century autograph collectors.

One defining moment of Cody's childhood—and for his whole family—was when his brother Samuel, twelve, but five years older than him, was killed riding a horse in 1853. In Bill's description, the two had departed the farm to round up some cows, Samuel defying their mother's order not to ride the horse he chose. When they were returning past the local school house, Cody said, Samuel went into show-off mode; the horse reared back and fell on him, the incident killing him from internal injuries. Samuel was buried in Scott County, Iowa, and his grave site is considered to be a stop on the Cody Trail, named such for the future renown of his brother. Cody portrayed his father Isaac as overcome by grief and said Samuel's death provoked the sale of their farm and the move to Kansas.

Charley, the youngest, was born after the Codys left Iowa for Kansas. However, he was just a baby when Isaac's controversial public appearance at an event provoked his death, a delayed murder of sorts, in 1857. When Charley died from an illness in 1865, that left Will the only male member of the family. He was just eleven years old, and the tenuous financial circumstances led to him joining the work force at that young age.

William F. Cody sits with three of his sisters (left to right: Julia, May, Helen) in the early 20th century (courtesy of Park County Archives).

Strong belief in right and wrong was Isaac Cody's undoing. His view of slavery as an abomination was not the majority opinion in his part of Kansas. Sentiment over the issue boiled in the North, where the anti-slavery stronghold lived. Sentiment of mind-your-own business was prevalent in the South.

Kansas was still a territory in 1857, and small-scale slavery existed there as the combustible issue moved toward provoking conflict. Each territory bucking for statehood recognition was the object of great attention from the North and the South. Isaac Cody had his beliefs, but as a Free Soil Democrat, they held some complications. He was against slavery, but that party also stood for keeping African Americans from settling in Kansas. That was not good enough for pro-slavery adherents, some of whom were his neighbors and whom he soon learned resented him. The elder Cody joined with some to create the Salt Creek Squatters Association. However, he was a minority member. The group quickly adopted a platform supporting pro-slavery immigrants.

On July 4, 1854, an Independence Day party was thrown. Food was freely served, and members of local Indian tribes attended, some performing dances. But numerous residents of nearby Missouri attended, and they were pro-slavery individuals. Indeed, Missouri was a slave state until 1865, after the Civil War, when the practice was abolished. Will Cody and his older sister Julia attended the activities that day.

Feelings escalated from there, with the Squatters Association becoming more strident and with Isaac becoming an outcast. The strong opinions and anger forced the Codys to depart the Salt Valley. On September 18, in a meeting that included discussion over a dispute involving Isaac, a man named Charles Dunn, who was pro-slavery, lost his temper, rushed Isaac Cody, and stabbed him in the side.

He was grievously wounded, and family members rushed Isaac to the home of his brother Elijah in Weston, Missouri. Refuge and treatment aided Isaac, but his recovery was halting and he never recovered his strength 100 percent. At the time, a local newspaper, which favored slavery, reported on the attack, but with an edge, essentially editorializing that the assailant should have done a more thorough job. The article calling Isaac "a noisy abolitionist," in part read, "Cody is severely hurt, but not enough, it is feared, to cause his death. The settlers on Salt Creek that his wound is not more dangerous, and all sustain Mr. Dunn in the course he took."[4]

The point of the knife did touch one of Isaac's lungs. Julia said he was never strong enough to walk anywhere on his own again. Will, eight years old at the time, was outraged and emotional, and talked of revenge. "I wish I was a man," he said. "I would just love to kill all of those bad men who want to kill my father, and I will when I get big."[5]

The assault on Isaac Cody seemed to inflame his foes rather than satisfy them. This was a time of violence, political upheaval, and rigidly held opinions. Rather than view him as a weakened enemy no longer worth the time, the pro-slavery crowd seemed to look upon Will's father as a target. These men were on the prowl to finish him off, according to family lore. Fearing for his life, Isaac went on the run, only periodically visiting his family. It was the right move. In his original autobiography, Buffalo Bill wrote of vigilantes coming to the Cody home and demanding family members turn over his father. They stated clearly and unequivocally they were there to kill him.

When his mother opened a window to confront the group and shouted, "Who are you? What do you want here?" their response confirmed their attitude. "We are after that old abolition husband of yours," someone yelled back to her. Playing her role dutifully, but intelligently at the critical moment, Mrs. Cody retorted, "He is not in this house and has not been here for a long time." The argument ricocheted back and forth with a man replying, "That's a lie! We know he is in the house and we are bound to have him." Again, Mrs. Cody said, "My husband is not at home, but the house is full of armed men and I'll give you two minutes to get out of the yard. If you are not out by the end of that time, I shall order them to fire on you."[6]

This was a bold bluff because Mary Ann Cody was not backed by an army at all. Will had returned home in the company of a herder, the only other young male around—he later said he thought they mistook the herder with him for his father and spies had alerted this lynch mob. As a subterfuge, his mother called upon the herder to call out names of non-existent warriors, as if positioning them to shoot. Will, his sisters, and the herder stamped their feet to mimic the sounds that might be made by shooters deploying around the house, and Mrs. Cody then shot an old rifle into the air. The villains departed without further incident.

It is somewhat surprising that this bunch melted away without an exchange of gunfire because the men seemed determined to do in Isaac. "The next morning we accidentally discovered that they had intended to blow up the house," Will said. "Upon going into the cellar, which had been left open on one side, we found two kegs of powder together with a fuse secreted there. It only required a lighted match to send us into eternity."[7]

Nor was this the end of sustained threats on his father. One day, sick and weak, Isaac returned home to see his family and try to recuperate. An intoxicated man Will already considered an enemy came to the house, declared he was there to kill Isaac and then entered and demanded to be fed dinner before searching the house. Isaac was home. Galled by this intrusion and intimidation, the youngster Will grabbed a pistol, cocked it, and plunked his bottom down on the top of the stairs leading to where his father was prone and unable to move. However, the man backed off, Cody's theory being that he was under the influence and grew too dizzied to carry out his mission.

This tenuous existence for the Codys continued for some time. Meanwhile, Will was growing up—a bit, at least—and developing his horsemanship around cattle, accepting more serious schooling, and enjoying his first puppy love with a gal called Mary Hyatt, a name he remembered decades later. The way he recalled his courtship was that he built her a playhouse demolished by a rival bully named Steve. He came out on the losing end of the subsequent fight, badly beaten, he said. Then the teacher whipped both of them for fighting. A day later, the stubborn Will rebuilt the playhouse, and Steve knocked it down again. Cody dove for his throat, and they tumbled to the ground. Cody had a small knife with him, it fell from his pocket, and he grasped it and stabbed Steve in the thigh. Steve and other kids were yelling Cody had killed him, so he ran for it.

Will informed his mother of what had happened and of an offer from one of the freight drivers they knew to take him on a road trip to Fort Kearney for forty days while the heat cooled. He even got paid for the journey by Russell, Majors and Waddell. Indeed, upon his return, Will learned peace had been brokered between his family and Steve's, and there were no more confrontations between the boys. Interestingly, this was the same freight company that some years later started the famed Pony Express.

Often on the move, Isaac Cody returned to the family home, once again suffering from an illness. He had been to Cleveland and said he caught a cold, but this seemed too simplistic a diagnosis. The weight of his injury debilitating him over the last few years, coupled with this illness, led to his death in April 1857. Will said the cause of death was kidney disease. Born in 1811, Isaac was only forty-six years old when he passed away, leaving his family in a dire financial situation and without a breadwinner.

A month after his father's death, Will, just eleven, entered the working world, accompanying a herd of beef cattle on the road to Salt Lake City where it was to be delivered for military consumption—shades of his future buffalo hunting days. It was on this journey that Will Cody claimed to have killed a man for the first time, a member of a Native American raiding party that came after the cattle well into the trip. There is no genuine proof either way except for Cody's word and the subsequent retelling of a version of the tale by sister Helen Wetmore, and some doubt whether this incident actually happened.

The way Cody told the story in his autobiography, the outfit was camped some thirty-five miles west of Old Fort Kearney with the cook making dinner. Shots were heard from the direction where the three lookout men were left with the animals. Those in camp could hear the whoops of the raiders and saw the cattle being driven off. The Indians came after the well-armed cowboys, who fired upon them and then ran for it and ducked behind an embankment on a slough.

Without horses and transporting a wounded man, the leaders declared they were going to follow the water on foot back to Fort Kearney, a decidedly lengthy walk, while at the same time repelling attackers taking potshots at them. Referring to himself as the youngest and smallest of the escaping party, Cody said he fell behind the group to a point where he was walking alone in the night. Spotting an Indian pursuer looking over a bank at him, Cody said he quickly fired his pistol. The Indian fell dead over the bank into the water.

"I was not only overcome by astonishment," Cody said, "but was badly scared, as I could hardly realize what I had done. I expected to see the whole force of Indians come down upon us."[8] That did not happen. Instead, the other cowboys returned to his side, questioning what happened. Once they reached the fort the next day, Cody said the cavalry mounted up in pursuit of the Indians. The herders rode with the soldiers, and he reported that three of their men first killed had been scalped and mutilated and most of the cattle had fled.

Upon returning to Leavenworth, Kansas, with the rest of the men, Cody said a newspaper reporter got wind of his shot, and he was interviewed for the first time in his life. Will said he was called "the youngest Indian slayer on the plains."[9] He did not name the newspaper in which this appeared, however. Much later, when one of his sisters said he was in school with her at the time, he did not contradict her. Later record-checking indicated Cody was unlikely to be present during this real conflict. Maybe the great storyteller got an early start.

Cody mentioned in recounting the start of the fight that this type of thing—the threat of him being killed by Indians—is what most worried his mother on the job. Helen commented in her book that the sisters all fretted about the same thing, worried he would be scalped. She commented they were all crying upon his departure for Utah. Wetmore also detailed a completely different involvement between Will and other Indians, asserting his courage resulted in his safely shepherding home a wounded companion.

However, while Cody was away, Martha, his sister from his father's first marriage, suffered heartbreak in her own marriage from an unfaithful husband and died. At the funeral, Wetmore wrote, young Bill, who believed the man responsible for Martha's death because of his treatment, stood up to the husband, calling him "Murderer." He continued, "one day you shall answer to me for the death of she who lies there."[10] That was twice a youthful Cody was reported to make such threats, once aimed at his father's attackers and now to the face of his sister's widower.

Before he was into his teens, the boy who would become Buffalo Bill Cody, gaining world renown, had lost a brother, a sister, and his father and was soon to lose a second brother. Cody family lore has it that his mother Mary and one sister were on a trip to an unspecified southern city when mom consulted a fortune teller. She returned to Kansas telling other family members the seer predicted great things for her son, saying one day he would become very famous and accomplish much.

The story seems too glib to be real, even if opening this fortune cookie of sorts ended up being an accurate prophecy long before anyone had heard of Buffalo Bill. Whether it was retroactively imagined by Cody sisters after Will did become quite famous or not, like so many tales ascribed to his life, it made for lighthearted and colorful reading.

3

The Pony Express

He rode like the wind, doing a man's work, his horses flying like Pegasus, with the stamina of a marathon runner. Or maybe the story was too much like Pegasus, mythology revisited, perhaps revised.

After his father Isaac died, Will Cody was in need of employment. His father had been a freighter, transporting loads between Davenport, Iowa, some fifteen miles from LeClaire, and Chicago. The family was in the good graces of Russell, Majors and Waddell, and the company they ran. It moved goods west to supply soldiers who were making the region safe for settlers and farther west, where in 1849 gold was discovered in California.

These were the men who were soon to create the bold venture of moving mail to the Pacific Coast by fast horse relay team. At the time, it took fifty-three days to send a letter across the country, moved by steamship. The freighters dreamed up the Pony Express, with their method promising six-day delivery. The Pony Express had a remarkably short shelf life of less than twenty months, but it is one of the best-remembered ventures that helped open the West to development.

How Cody came to be employed by the Pony Express was a multistep process. In 1857, three years before the Pony Express mail system came into being, Cody's mother Mary Ann approached the freighters to see if they could put her boy Will to work doing something. She had nothing elaborate in mind, just steady employment where he could bring home steady wages. A two-month cattle drive paid handsomely, Cody collecting $50. He wrote that he received "the sum all in half-dollar pieces. I put the bright, silver coins into a sack, which I tied to my mule and started home, thinking myself a millionaire."[1] Who wouldn't?

Will drove some wagons locally, short distances, and brought the money home to his mother, who was trying to keep the family afloat by renting rooms to boarders while his sister Julia handled the farm work. Eventually, Will got hired on as a messenger for the company. But this was petty stuff for Russell, Majors and Waddell. Their money was made from long-haul wagon-train journeys. That was work for grown men, though, not boys who had yet to reach their teens.

The company paid well for the time, partially because the work could be dangerous and not every man was cut out for it. The way Cody remembered the situation, there were almost always openings if a man, or a boy, was willing to take short-notice jobs filling in for drivers who became sick. When they recovered, this fill-in relinquished the reins again. When not steering the wagon, the employee would ride a mule.

There was another catch about the opportunity. It was not a local job, but one that required long trips through hostile country. Cody wrote in his memoir that his mother did not like this work very much because he could be gone for months and she wanted to keep him nearby. The path might cross those of Indians upset over the influx of whites to their lands, and there was violent unrest in Utah from the Mormon settlers trying to establish themselves. A freighter might well get shot.

This matter arose after Will had roamed the Plains and was caught up in his first battle with Native Americans. He said his mom did not want him to risk his neck again. The freight company owners pledged to Mrs. Cody they would take good care of her son, look after him closely if they were stranded in the mountains over a winter, and bring him safely home. For a mother, this was definitely a leap of faith trusting the semi-strangers with her boy, especially after she had lost her husband and two other children. The clinching assurance seemed to be a promise Will could change his mind at Fort Laramie and join a return freight train to come back early. Mrs. Cody remained reluctant, but in the end gave her blessing. The bosses also agreed to send Cody's pay directly to her. Thus, young Will became closely acquainted with Russell, Majors and Waddell and their operations.

Shortly before the railroad altered the landscape, these were impressive wagons and wagon trains of freight. Oxen hauled each sturdily built wagon with a capacity of seven thousand pounds of goods and supplies. But this wagon train's twenty-five wagons were packed with six thousand pounds each, not the maximum. A wagon master was the trail boss who called the shots, and he had a chief deputy.

The scope of Russell, Majors and Waddell's freight business was staggering. Cody recounted statistics illustrating what a big deal they were. The company, he said, owned 6,250 wagons, could run 250 trains, controlled 75,000 oxen, and employed 8,000 men. Another historian lowered some figures to 45,000 oxen and 6,000 employees, still huge.

The journey began smoothly, and Cody said he gradually got to know his companions. One man in particular stood out. The man later called Wild Bill Hickok became friend to and protector of the boy if he was threatened by bigger and older men. Hickok was ten years older than

Cody and took on a big brother role on this journey. From his later writings, after becoming famous, Cody revealed how impressed he was by Hickok. He called him a "tall, handsome, magnificently built and powerful young fellow. He was generally admitted to be the best man physically (in the company)."[2]

In his early twenties, Hickok was still unknown on the frontier, though like Cody destined for much greater fame. The Hickok history came to know was a man who was a crack shot with a pistol or rifle, a dashing man who sported a fantastic mustache, and a man who was a legendary lawman fighting off desperadoes in wild towns. He and Cody forged a friendship that lasted for Hickok's lifetime, and they crossed paths several times in the future. History has summed him up as an honest man of great courage and integrity whose one big mistake led to his demise at thirty-nine in Deadwood, South Dakota, shot in the back of the head by an enemy who sneaked behind him while he was playing cards. The rare occasion when Hickok did not follow his policy of sitting with his back to the wall cost him his life. But that unhappy development lay years in the future.

As for Cody, he always appreciated Hickok's efforts to help him and teach him on that early freight run. While they were both traveling men who often thrived thousands of miles apart, their friendship was dead solid and locked in. "You who live your lives in cities, or among peaceful ways, cannot always tell whether your friends are the kind who would go through fire for you," Cody said. "But on the Plains one's friends have the opportunity to prove their mettle."[3] Hickok proved himself a true friend to Cody.

From the first, Hickok was a savior on the freighting trip. Under the command of Lew Simpson, Cody felt the surly man was difficult to deal with and was quickly proven right. Calling him "an overbearing fellow" who "took particular delight in bullying and tyrannizing over me," Cody said one day Simpson ordered him to do something, and when he did not move quickly enough to satisfy the man,

> he gave me a slap in the face with the back of his hand, knocking me off an ox-yoke on which I was sitting, and sending me sprawling on the ground. Jumping to my feet, I picked up a camp kettle full of boiling coffee which was setting on the fire, and threw it at him. I hit him in the face and the hot coffee gave him a severe scalding. He sprang for me with the ferocity of a tiger and would undoubtedly have torn me to pieces had it not been for my newfound friend, Wild Bill, who knocked the man down.[4]

It was a feisty enough response from a youngster, but Cody was likely correct that the enraged stronger man would have beaten him up if not the for unexpected intervention of Hickok. His reputation in the future notwithstanding, Hickok was always on the side of right, and he stood up when others would have ignored the fracas. Simpson asked why he bothered, and Hickok, Cody said, uttered a little speech about justice. "It's my business to protect that boy, or anybody else, from being unmercifully abused, kicked and cuffed, and I'll whip any man who tries it on. And if you ever again lay a hand on that boy—little Billy there—I'll give you such a pounding that you won't get over it for a month of Sundays."[5]

Cody indeed proclaimed that was the beginning of a beautiful friendship. Hickok was already an adult, Cody a boy growing up fast, but the relationship forged on the trail lasted as they went their separate ways at various times, but also overlapped periodically in many ways and in many venues. In 1857, on a wagon freight train, they were still nobodies in the eyes of history, but this intersection of Buffalo Bill Cody and Wild Bill Hickok, neither yet given such audacious nicknames, was a worthy quirk of fate to note.

This was a personal matter between Cody and Simpson that could have escalated to destroy morale on the wagon train, and it did alter chemistry so that Hickok emerged as the alpha personality and at the time Batman to Cody's Robin. While the occasion was of great import to the two young men, it was not the defining incident of the journey. The wagon train faced other challenges as it rolled west. Cody said the train reached the North Platte River, where he had become embroiled with Native Americans on his prior cattle trip, and they were surrounded by buffalo. The animals were then still plentiful on the Plains. Ahead of the holocaust to come for their species, the wagon men could hunt for a ready supply of meat without uselessly decimating herds.

A comparatively easy day of supplying meat turned harrowing, however, when a wagon train heading east from California, spotted the buffalo and in its enthusiasm stampeded the herd right at the Cody–Hickok train. The buffalo, Cody said, ran roughshod over some wagons, crashing into others and damaging some. The normally placid oxen hauling the goods panicked and, mustering their strength, tried to run away while still attached to wagons. Cody described a stupefying scene of tangles, shouting, snorting, cattle breaking free, wagons being buffeted, and men trying to regain control. One tremendous buffalo broke a chain and yoke and ran away with them attached to his body. When the considerable dust and noise subsided, the scene resembled the aftermath of a tornado. The mess was sorted out, and the next day the wagons returned to their route.

That night, Cody reported, he, Simpson, and another man led their cattle to water, but were intercepted by twenty mounted and well-armed riders. They were not cordial, and their leader seemed to know Simpson, and not as a friend. Still, Cody did not initially realize they were in danger until their weapons were demanded. The leader was Joseph Smith, who had spied on the wagon train and then returned with back-up. These were some of the Mormon believers who were fighting U.S. soldiers in Utah. Their goal was to destroy the supply wagons heading for the troops. They were not so ruthless, though, as to kill the freighters. Simpson negotiated an uneasy bargain. Smith's men burned the wagons, but let the men go with some weapons for protection and with a single oxen-pulled wagon containing enough supplies to return to Fort Bridger. This was one of three wagon trains similarly assaulted, dismembered, and its occupants sent back to the fort where all were stuck for the winter. It truly was still the Wild West, with no safe passage guaranteed on the rugged Great Plains.

Come spring, the freighters began their trek home. Simpson was boss of two trains, but travel was via worn-down mules. The trains were moving fifteen miles apart, and Cody said one day Simpson ordered him and his deputy to join him seeking out the lead group of wagons. Before they could link up, the trio was waylaid by a band of forty Indians with no hint of wishing for a parlay. Running for it as the Native Americans got within three hundred yards, the three freighters halted and set up fortifications. There they made a stand. Although the odds were stiff, few of the Indians had guns, and shooting into the crowd the men swiftly downed three attackers.

George Wood, Simpson's second in command, was hit by an arrow in the left shoulder. Surprised by the resistance, the attackers backed off for a bit, discussed matters, and charged again. Once again repelled, the Indians held back and formulated a new plan. Cody said their foes tried to burn them out, but the grass was too short to threaten them. The Indians waited overnight, charged one more time, and when rebuffed, formed an out-of-range circle. The plan now seemed to be to starve the men. The attackers, who may have thought this trio represented stragglers from the first wagon train, did not know a second wagon train was on its way.

Startled by the approach of a large party of reinforcements, the Indians took one last run at the entrenched trio, and when it failed, dashed away before the wagon masters arrived. The wagon train had caught up just in time to save Simpson, Cody, and Wood. That was the last of the major incidents afflicting the journey, and the train returned to Leavenworth, Kansas. Cody said his bond with Hickok grew stronger over the winter stranded in Fort Bridger when he told the older man all about his family. Indicating this friendship was a two-way street despite the spread of years, Hickok followed through on his pledge to visit Cody's home.

Rather remarkably after his adventures, at his mother's urging, Will gave school another try. He lasted two and a half months before setting off for prairie learning that differed greatly from penmanship (which he did excel at), arithmetic, and the like. He had proven himself a reliable hand to

Russell, Majors and Waddell, and someone connected to the firm always seemed ready to give Cody a job.

Taking on a brazen challenge of trying to improve on the post office's service, these men sought to corner the market with faster mail delivery when they created the Pony Express. It was an idea whose time had come, but whose time would be fleeting. The Pony Express relied on hardy men, worthy horses, a spirit of adventure, and a commitment to a task never tried on a large scale. Early advertising in New York announced letters and other messages could reach the West Coast in unheard-of time. "Ten Days to San Francisco," an ad read under the larger letters stating who was going to perform such a feat: "Pony Express!"[6]

The California Gold Rush and the swift expansion of the population was the impetus for the start of the Pony Express. People clamored for better communication with the East. U.S. Senator William McKendree Gwin, born in Tennessee and transplanted to California, pushed the idea and proposed an overland routine to William Russell.

Russell embraced the idea, but his partners, Alexander Majors and William Waddell, at first declined, believing the plan unprofitable. Then those freight entrepreneurs of the Plains changed their minds. While that advertising surfaced in New York, the real mail service proposed by the Central Overland and Pike's Peak Express Company using riders on swift steeds began in St. Joseph, Missouri, and ran to Sacramento. The businessmen did not anticipate the quick arrival of the telegraph and the Transcontinental Railroad, but were responding to the demand of the moment.

The Russell, Majors and Waddell partners hoped to make their enterprise indispensable. In some quarters they were viewed as crazy for the attempt. Some said the plan was impossible. When they announced they were open for business, the Pony Express rulers set their opening price at $5 per half ounce of mail. Five bucks was a hefty sum in 1860, but the operational costs were formidable. Traveling light was essential, and no one envisioned customers shipping large boxes.

Organized to begin riding on April 3, 1860, the Pony Express captured the fancy of many—a feeling that really has never abated among students of the Old West and grew until it encompassed 120 riders, 184 stations (ten miles apart), and 400 horses, as well as hundreds of other support personnel. The men thought big, and they knew they had to act big to gain trust and provide top-notch service. Their ultimate goal was to win a U.S. government mail contract based on their ability to do a superior job. That never happened, but the Pony Express was quite a ride while it lasted.

The founders mapped out a 1,900-mile route from Missouri to California and constructed relay stations where riders could exchange horses and mail pouches, or mochilas, and hand them to fresh riders. The route followed the Oregon Trail and California Trail to Fort Bridger, Wyoming, and on over the Mormon Trail to Salt Lake City, Utah. The direction moved northward to Carson City, Nevada, and crossed the Sierra Mountains into Sacramento, California's state capital.

The Pony Express needed riders on the front lines and advertised for help this way: "Wanted: Young, skinny, wiry fellows not over eighteen. Must be expert riders, willing to risk death daily. Orphans preferred."[7] The wages were either $25 a week or $50 a month, depending on different sources, and if you lived to tell about it. Oh, the applicants were not supposed to weigh more than 125 pounds either.

Once hired, the riders were required to take an oath devised by Majors. It read: "I (name) do hereby swear before the great and Living God, that during my engagement, and while I am an employee of Russell, Majors & Waddell, I will, under no circumstances, use profane language; that I will drink no intoxicating liquors; that I will not quarrel or fight with any other employee of the firm, and that in every respect will conduct myself honestly, be faithful to my duties, and so direct all my acts as to win the confidence of my employers. So help me God."[8] It sounded more as if the company was advertising for choirboys rather than derring-do lads.

The first mail heading west originated in New York City and Washington, DC, and was transferred to the railroad and deposited in Missouri. A ceremony kicked things off on April 3, including speeches from Russell and Majors and M. Jeff Thompson, the mayor of St. Joseph. The first rider left St. Joseph at 5:15 p.m., delayed by the late arrival of the train from the East, and the mail arrived ten days later, as promised, though technically it was clocked in at 1 a.m. on April 14. William Hamilton made the delivery on the West Coast. Also on April 3, a rider left Sacramento heading east, and the mail made it to Missouri in ten days, again as pledged. From there, those letters entered the U.S. mail system for delivery to eastern cities.

One reason the venture was dubbed the Pony Express was because the owners sought smaller horses, weighing about nine hundred pounds because they considered them fast runners. Probably the most enduring phrase associated with the Pony Express, the employment advertisement featured the words "Orphans Preferred," as a job qualification. Indeed, a 2003 book about the Pony Express incorporated that phrase into its title.

The first riders were hired and away they went, charged with fulfilling the pledges of the new business, hoping to dodge trouble in the way of robbers and unhappy Indians resenting more and more each day the white man invading their territories and stealing their lands. Most Pony Express records vanished or were destroyed, so it is unclear who was the very first Pony Express rider heading west once those introductory speeches were concluded. Researchers lean toward a Johnny Fry riding between St. Joseph and Seneca, Kansas.

One of the untrue legends that stuck to Wild Bill Hickok for a time was that he was one of the first Pony Express riders. He was not. Hickok, who was twenty-three when the Express was born, was bigger than the prototype rider, as well as older. However, Cody's old pal was a wagon driver and guard for Russell, Majors and Waddell. On one of those driving trips, Hickok was attacked by a bear. While he managed to fight it off, he was injured. In response, as Hickok healed, in 1861, the company transferred him to its Rock Creek Station in the Nebraska Territory.

Once, Indians raided the Plant's Station in Wyoming, stealing all of the horses and mules, a severe handicap for a relay station on the route. Some believed the party was led by the famous warrior Red Cloud. Hickok was assigned to lead a recovery posse, and the group caught up to the thieves at Clear Creek, beyond the Powder River. After dark, they retaliated, creating confusion, reclaiming the lost animals, and stealing about a hundred Indian ponies as a bonus.

That was probably the highlight of Hickok's connection to the Pony Express. However, he and his old friend Will Cody did overlap again during their employment for Russell, Majors and Waddell. Will was still only fourteen years old when the Pony Express was founded, though a veteran of some wagon transport and work as a messenger for the company. Despite his youth, he mostly fit the profile of the young people being hired, though due to the paucity of records from those days leaving little beyond entertaining family lore and Cody's own words, there are some who suggest Cody never rode for the Pony Express. Others say he made the single greatest ride in the short history of the Express. And others, more in-between in their thinking, think he probably did some riding, but recorded nothing epic.

Always with Cody, the tale telling is as entertaining as a Broadway show, and those who get the most enjoyment out of the announced exploits are willing to suspend disbelief. Did he or did he not ride? Did he or did he not thrive? The dichotomy is so often there with examination of William F. Cody's life. For the hard nosed who wish to separate hard reality from gussied-up story, good luck. For those who like big fish stories, what the heck. It may be in the case of the Pony Express and Cody the label should read something like a Hollywood adaptation, "Based on a true story." Maybe.

The big deal over Cody as a Pony Express rider, due to his later fame, was also the story that has lingered when the boy, blossoming into manhood but still very much a teen, was credited with making the single most distinguishing ride in the year and a half the Express was in business. No less than Majors, in his late-in-life autobiography, said Cody was the protagonist in the drama of the ultimate Pony Express ride. "This round-trip of 384 miles was made without stops except for meals and to change horses and every station on the route was entered on time."[9] Majors aside, another version of the midnight ride of Will Cody marked 322 miles next to his name, lasting 21 hours, 40 minutes, while taking a toll on twenty different horses.

That was the ultimate Cody-does-the-Pony-Express tale. Majors recalled that adventure and in his autobiography also spoke highly and adoringly of Cody as a youth. "Nearly forty years ago in Kansas," Majors wrote, "a handsome, wiry, little lad came to me, accompanied by his good mother, and said that he had her permission to take a position with me as a messenger boy. I gave him the place, though it was one of peril, carrying dispatches between our wagon trains upon the march across the Plains, and little did I then suspect that I was just starting out in life one who was destined to win fame and fortune."[10]

First came the messenger job. Then came the wagon train job. This was before the Pony Express began operations in 1860, when Cody was still just fourteen. Of Cody in the Pony Express, Majors called him, "the Pony Express rider of the overland, and as such he faced many dangers, and overcame many obstacles, which would have crushed a less strong nature and a brave heart."[11]

That certainly was an endorsement of the mettle of Cody as a Pony Express rider, a rebuttal of sorts to those who asserted it was unlikely he ever rode at all for the mail service such as author Jim DeFelice in his Pony Express book. In referring to a specific day, DeFelice said of Cody that maybe he even saw a rider, "assuming Cody stopped mucking the barn long enough to take a look." He added, "it's not clear Cody was mucking a barn, or even doing anything at all for the Pony, that day or any day."[12]

The issue of Will Cody's connection to the Pony Express has floated around discussion of the short-lived horseback mail delivery line at least since 1879 when his autobiography was released. All those who would have firsthand knowledge of what Cody did or did not do for the Pony Express have, of course, long since died. Official records of the Express do not survive. And few others with critical involvement with the Pony Express and Buffalo Bill left written records saying yea or nay to his relationship. Majors, one of the founders, raves about Cody. Cody relates stories of the Pony Express in his autobiography. Helen Cody Wetmore talks about her brother aligned with the Express in her book.

Cody wrote that he came across George Chrisman, a wagon master for Russell, Majors and Waddell, when the Pony Express was just revving up. He already knew Chrisman, who was an agent for the Express with the power to hire. According to Cody,

> He hired me at once as a Pony Express rider, but as I was so young he thought I would not be able to stand the fierce riding which was required of the messengers. He knew, however, that I had been raised in the saddle—that I felt more at home there than in any other place—and as he saw that I was confident and could stand the racket, and could ride as far and endure it as well as some of the other older riders, he gave me a short route of forty-five miles, with the stations fifteen miles apart, and three changes of horses.[13]

Since this was an endeavor based on high speed, Cody said the requirement called for covering fifteen miles per hour. But he said he did so with ease on these assignments. He made an impression on others, if not by name, but by being called the youngest rider on the road. Cody spoke of fulfilling this role for only two months before going back home to Kansas because his mother was ill. Although he referred to it as being a Pony Express rider, this messenger job was not being a full-fledged, long-haul Pony Express rider. After an intermission and after his mother recovered from illness, but against her wishes because she thought his goals were too dangerous, Cody said he went to see Russell for a real Pony Express riding job.

Carrying a letter of recommendation from Russell to another agent, Cody hooked on as a regular Pony Express rider attached to the station called "Three Crossings of the Sweetwater" in Wyoming. Cody offered the story of his claimed 322-mile ride, which he said unfolded by accident. Cody returned from another trip to Three Crossings. Once there, he learned "the rider who was expected to take the trip out upon my arrival had gotten into a drunken row the night before and had been killed, and that there was no one to fill his place. I did not hesitate for a moment to undertake an extra ride of eighty-five miles to Rocky Ridge, and I arrived at the latter place on time. I then turned back and rode to Red Buttes, my starting place, accomplishing on the round trip a distance of 322 miles."[14] No doubt, Cody's butt and back would have hurt mightily, but he made no to-do about that.

Wetmore wrote of her brother being a messenger for three months, not two, and she told of an attempted robbery by a highwayman whom he outwitted as the gun-wielding man reached for the saddle bags. He spurred his horse into the man, and the animal knocked him over. The tale goes Cody leapt down and disabled and tied up the would-be thief, then raced for his home station, bringing in the man as evidence of why he had slowed down.

Additional testimony regarding Cody, not only as Pony Express rider, but also as the one who completed a 300-plus-mile ride, was ferreted out by biographer Don Russell. Edward E. Ayer, a wealthy man from the Midwest, founded the American Indian collection at Newberry College in Chicago. By his accounting, in the early 1860s, he was crossing the Plains in wagon trains and regularly saw Will on his Pony Express rounds, and said he actually shouted news to the travelers. Some years later, Ayer said, he met up with Cody at a banquet, reminded him of their passing acquaintance, but then said Buffalo Bill's math shorted himself in the story of the fill-in ride. Dissecting the distances between stations, Russell wrote, meant Cody really rode 384 miles. Russell felt Cody did not do much better in remembering accurate dates as in handling addition. "There is circumstantial evidence that is conclusive," Russell wrote of the 384-mile distance.[15]

Another rider, Bob Haslam, was credited with a 380-mile ride, and Howard R. Egan was credited with a 330-mile ride. Cody did not claim to make the longest-ever Pony Express ride. Majors did so on his behalf, and Russell's research supports that statement. However, not all other Cody biographers buy into the veracity of those most vivid Pony Express tales.

Cody wrote of Indian raiders stealing the horses from stations and of being pursued by Indians, though stating he outran them on a fleet Pony Express horse. These were the types of threats that most worried his mother and sisters. While once in a while in print he mentioned being scared by the circumstances, his pen mostly shied from discussing emotions. His chapter titles more often referred to "adventures" than close calls.

Majors knew Will Cody as a young lad, but he did not write about him until after he became Buffalo Bill and was world famous. He dedicated his 1893 book to Cody—and Cody wrote the preface. Majors did not stint on praise of Cody, expressing admiration for Cody's devotion to his mother and sister, and saluting him for the type of man he grew into. "Courtly by nature, generous to a fault, big-hearted and brainy, full of gratitude to those whom he feels indebted to," Majors wrote, "he has won his way in the world and stands today as truly one of Nature's noblemen."[16]

Majors was also exceptionally proud of the Pony Express, even if its mission did not last long. More than forty years after its demise, Majors held a special place in his heart for the operation as he wrote his memoirs, especially for the young men who peopled the ranks of the riders. "The men were faithful, daring fellows, and their service was full of novelty and adventure," Majors said. "The facility and energy with which they journeyed was a marvel. The news of Abraham Lincoln's election (to the presidency in 1860) was carried through from St. Joseph to Denver, Colorado,

3. The Pony Express

665 miles, in two days and twenty-one hours, the last ten miles having been covered in thirty-one minutes."[17] It was Haslam, whose nickname was "Pony Bob," who bore the news.

As the Pony Express's short run was ending, James Butler ("Wild Bill") Hickok resurfaced in an episode. In July of 1861 Hickok was assistant stock tender at the Rock Creek Station under chief agent Horace Wellman. The Pony Express at first leased the property from owner David McCanles and then cut a deal to buy it. However, Russell, Majors and Waddell fell behind on payments. McCanles grew angry and gave notice to Wellman he was going to shut down the station. He was said to be a short-tempered man and a bully who had bad relations with Hickok; it was suggested they may have been interested in the same woman.

On July 12, McCanles showed up with a shotgun, friends James Woods and James Gordon, and his 12-year-old son William. A confrontation at the door ensued with McCanles berating first Wellman, then Wellman's wife, and then Hickok. McCanles entered the house, brandishing the shotgun, and Hickok drew a pistol and shot him. Woods and Gordon heard the shot and barged into the building. Hickok shot both of them, though they were still healthy enough to flee. Mrs. Wellman caught up to Woods and pounded him to death with a garden hoe. Gordon was pursued and killed with the shotgun McCanles brought. Hickok and Wellman

A stone and plaque mark the tiny relay station that was a stop for the Pony Express in Gothenburg, Nebraska, in the 1860s (photograph by the author).

(but not his wife) and Doc Brink, another station employee, were tried for murder, but acquitted.

The incident became inflated. Some claimed Hickok shot and killed up to ten men. His reputation as a gunfighter became wildly exaggerated beyond reality, even if he was an especially quick-draw man. Some say that this particular encounter is what truly established Hickok with the nickname "Wild Bill."

The Pony Express was soon eclipsed as a communication option in efficiency by the telegraph and the railroad. The stations closed, fell into disrepair, were torn down, and were replaced by other structures in towns that grew up around the route. It has been nearly 150 years since that mail service ceased. As short as the operation was, it would have been easy for it to slip from memory, but rather its story has persevered through history. If tourists wish to see one of the last remnants of the Pony Express days, in addition to a museum in St. Joseph, Missouri, where the runs all began, they can stop in Gothenburg, Nebraska, a community of 3,500 people, where there stands a small wooden cabin serving as a mini-museum and gift shop. The remaining station was moved to the site in 1931 and has been open to visitors since the 1950s.

While the facts engulfing William F. Cody's links to the Pony Express

A marker in Gotehenburg, Nebraska, observes the establishment of the famous Pony Express mail delivery system started by a freight company in 1860 (photograph by the author).

remain murky in many eyes—whether he rode fast horses for the brazen company or not, whether he amassed well over three hundred miles at a sitting or not—the truth is that far fewer Americans would remember the mail service's existence if he did not include reenactments of its role in his touring Wild West exhibition, seen by millions upon millions around the world for thirty years. Young Will, grown into famous Buffalo Bill, gave the Pony Express new life through show business and made it immortal.

4

Wars

Freight messenger at eleven, Pony Express rider at fourteen, Will Cody morphed into an adult just as the United States was splintering itself, tearing apart at state borders, the lines between North and South never more pronouncedly divided. The Civil War began as the Pony Express died. True to his nature, Cody wished to be part of the action, even if there was nothing romantic about the bloody battles raging.

Since his father Isaac essentially gave his life, if only in slow-motion deterioration, to the cause against slavery, it was appropriate, even if he was living in Kansas where minds and allegiances were split, that Cody signed on for the Northern side. His father's memory was one thing, but his mother's presence, and her beliefs, which mirrored his dad's, were strong and also expressed to his face. "The Civil War had broken out, and excitement ran high in that part of the country. My mother, of course, was a strong Union woman, and had such great confidence in the government that she believed the war would not last over six months."[1]

Would that it had been true. Mary Ann Cody drastically underestimated the carnage. The war began on April 12, 1861, and ended on April 9, 1865. Arms laid aside, or not, some contend the South has never stopped fighting it. Some 625,000 Americans died in the conflict over the four years between Fort Sumter and Appomattox, but when it ended, the United States was still a country of United States and slavery had been abolished by President Abraham Lincoln's Emancipation Proclamation of January 1, 1863.

Starting in 1854, Kansas had basically been gradually overrun by pro-slavery Missouri factions and was described as "Bleeding Kansas." Not only did the Cody clan lose its father, but ultimately, its home, as well. Cody numbered himself among Free State supporters, who wished to see Kansas emerge from the conflict unencumbered by slavery and with his family's prospects brighter than they had been for years. As the battles raged in Pennsylvania, Virginia, Tennessee, and other eastern/southern states, like-minded Kansas men took up arms to invade Missouri. Seeking revenge against their neighbors, a leader mustered a company of twenty-five men, which Cody joined in 1861. The group began by stealing previously identified horses from Missourians in Westport and herding them back to Kansas.

The campaign lasted for several months, with Kansas riders pilfering top horses and entering into minor running shootouts with the men from Missouri. Cody did this on the sly, but his mother discovered his involvement and talked him into giving it up. Concurrent with this development was Wild Bill Hickok's shootout in Rock Creek Station, which gained great notoriety, and which young Cody, still fifteen, heard about. Hickok had taken on a job driving oxen-led wagons with supplies, and Cody bumped into him in Leavenworth, Kansas, just as he was about to leave for Rolla, Missouri, to start a train. Hickok offered Cody a job as his assistant, and Will joined up, partners with Hickok once more. However, with both men betting all they could afford on a horse race, as well as the horse itself, their animal, with Cody aboard, lost. They staggered away from the situation broke and unemployed.

Hickok promptly got himself a scouting job for the government, but Cody was rejected as being too young. Hickok raised enough money for Will to obtain a steamboat ticket back to Leavenworth. When the Civil War broke out, Cody wanted to go to the fight immediately because "there were many of us in Kansas with old grudges to settle. I, for one, remembered my father's suffering at the hands of the Pro-Slavery Party, and I was eager to enlist."[2]

Soon after, however, Cody was able to find a messenger job for the army. He had proven himself quite able at this task for Russell, Majors and Waddell. He said he made his first delivery within Kansas in the fall of 1861, but by the spring of 1862 was ranging wider. Attached to the Seventh Kansas, Cody seems to have been worked as a scout for the first time, investigating the paths of Kiowa and Comanche Indians near the Arkansas River.

Later that year Cody became a full-time scout, a member of a band of fifty to one hundred men called the "Red-Legged Scouts" financed by the governor of Kansas. They were abolitionists working against the South. Many of the group's or individuals' assignments were secretive, sometimes minor harassment, and other times related to spy work. This led to confrontations with outlaws, at first amounting only to skirmishes in Cody's parlance. The name the scouts took is open to question, but two possible explanations have been offered, each mentioning an occasion where the men procured red cloth to wrap around their legs to keep them dry. Things escalated to more war-like actions, and the Red Legs invaded and torched small Missouri towns, sending slaves to freedom and across the Kansas border. The stalkers were feared and accused of committing violent crimes, although they viewed themselves as men defending their home state and exacting revenge for Missouri men's brutalities. Cody rode with these men into 1863.

Although some time had passed since orphans had been preferred by the Pony Express, Cody became an orphan on November 22, 1863, when his mother, who had been sickly off and on for some time, died. "Thus passed away a loving and affectionate mother, and a noble, brave, good and loyal woman," Cody said. In his 1879 autobiography he wrote that he "loved her beyond all other persons."[3] Mary Ann Cody had made arrangements for Julia, the oldest sister, who had married, to become the guardian of the other girls. Will was not about to settle down into a parental role, as she well knew. Indeed, after she died, he was very much at loose ends, not sure what was next for him as a seventeen-year-old, or where he should go. By his own admission, he hung around Leavenworth for some time, his later self-analysis of the next two months being a harsh one, associating with "gamblers, drunkards and bad characters generally" while living in a "dissolute and reckless" fashion.[4] No one ever denied Cody liked to take a drink, but this was more depression drinking than party drinking.

This was an intermission in Cody's life, where the grieving over his mother interrupted his riding with the Red Legs. But there was no break in the Civil War. The South was far more resistant and resilient than Mrs. Cody ever imagined, and Lincoln and his generals were still strategizing to gain the upper hand in 1863. The Seventh Kansas Cavalry was regrouping as a true regiment for the Union Army right in the neighborhood. Cody did not intend to enlist as a full-time soldier. Nor did he write out much of a detailed description initially for his autobiography on how his situation played out. He basically said he was under the influence of bad whiskey and woke up one day as a soldier. By early 1864, after Cody turned eighteen, his Kansas bunch was roaming through Tennessee and Mississippi. Will's background was in fighting off Indians or outlaws challenging freight wagons, or hit-and-run battles for the Red Legs. He admitted he was ignorant about this type of face-to-face warring between troops and that he was not especially well-suited to it. He moved into scouting, something he did know about and which historians indicate time and time again over the coming years was something at which he excelled.

Shortly after the Kansas group hooked up with General Andrew J. Smith in Memphis, Tennessee, Cody, a private, was summoned to meet with the troop leader. He was surprised to be singled out for an assignment. Smith told him he needed to learn more about the whereabouts and movements of the Confederate Army. While Union troops were turning the war, and other deployments gained the upper hand in some areas of the South, General Nathan Bedford Forrest was making the most of limited resources and was pecking away at Smith's army, standing in the way of victory. Smith wanted to get the jump on Forrest.

The meaning of what Cody was being asked to do slowly sunk in. He was to go undercover, out of uniform, to obtain information. In other words, he was going to become a spy. "If I were caught, I should be hanged," Cody said. "It was a risk no man cares to take. To be shot or cut down in a cavalry charge is one thing. To die by hanging is quite another. But it was service for the Union, so I accepted the mission."[5] In his writings contained in a 1908 book, Cody did not make it clear if he actually did have any choice but to accept. He was talking to a general. A time would come when he was a better-known scout with a track record and generals did discuss plans with him and ask for his opinion. At this time he was practically a junior varsity scout, and very much a novice soldier with the lowest rank.

In Cody's retelling of the meeting, he said before he could depart Smith's tent, soldiers brought a Confederate spy to the general who had just been captured. When Cody's sister Helen wrote about this moment in her book later, she said the young man was named Nat Golden. He listened as the young man was questioned and had Union maps and plans confiscated, and then he did advance an idea. Not many privates would speak up to a general. Some might wonder if Cody was relaying fantasy in this entire discussion, or if, given the nature he displayed in the future as someone who knew how to wrangle fame, he was merely bold.

It was Cody's scheme to alter those maps and plans so they became uselessly incorrect and then for him to carry them directly to Forrest as a misinformation trick. Changing out of uniform and into neutral civilian clothing, aboard horseback, Cody rode straight for the South's encampment. Stopped regularly by sentries, he told his armed interceders he was bearing important information for the general. Cody at last wrangled his way into Forrest's headquarters and began talking fast, something he had a talent for. He gave the name Frederick Williams and told Forrest he was an old acquaintance of the Kansas spy (the one Smith had in custody), and this friend entrusted him with these papers before being captured. Ironically, Cody had recognized the young man as a Kansas native who had chosen the gray side, not the blue. Forrest was a bit suspicious of Cody's motive and asked why he had taken on such a dangerous task. Cody acted the role of an innocent hungry for work, saying, "Well, sir, I thought maybe if I did you the favor maybe you'd give me a job in your scout service. I'm a plainsman and used to scouting."[6] When he was only a little bit older, Cody was critiqued as being a terrible actor, but this was one time he would have had to dig deep for an award-winning performance.

Cody said he was subjected to the third degree and intense questioning, but he appeared to pass Forrest's test and was sent to join the other scouts. The first part of his mission was accomplished, infiltrating the enemy behind the scenes and apparently gaining the trust of an important personage. For three days, Cody picked the brains of the other scouts, amassing the kind of information he was sure would be beneficial to General Smith back at the blue headquarters. However, to get that information out of his head into the hands of Union commanders, he could not hang out indefinitely in the woods. When sent out on duty for the Confederates, Cody planned to flee. There was no indication, though, he was about to be sent anywhere on assignment, and Cody was itching to ride. He felt strongly it was time to go, before he was either accidentally discovered and charged as a traitor, or what he learned died on the vine because it was out of date.

Patience was needed, and Cody did not husband much of that. His hand was forced, though, on his fourth day in camp when he witnessed the same Kansas young man he had last seen as a prisoner with his Union buddies being hustled out of Smith's tent. Had he escaped? Whatever happened, the Kansan was a distinct danger to Cody. Cody watched the returned individual step into Forrest's tent. It was obvious within minutes Forrest would mention his Kansas friend who followed through with the papers Cody brought. Cody swiftly sidled over to his horse, saddled it, and galloped away. Each time he reached one of the guard stations he waved a letter in the air, saying he was being sent to deliver it. No one questioned him closely until he was nearly free of the Confederate lines. Only as he was almost in open territory did the sound of pursuit reach his ears. He heard shots fired and horses' hooves. He made like a Pony Express rider and rode like lightning. At one point he ducked to the side of his horse, Indian style, as he put it, and dodged a bullet. While the men chased, he outran them, regaining the safety of the Union fortifications.

Helen added a complication to her take on the escape, saying his ride brought him right up to six Confederate soldiers guarding two Union prisoners. Employing quick thinking, he created a diversion, shouting, "Men, a Union spy is escaping! Scatter at once and head him off. I'll look after your prisoners."[7] Of course, what he said was true and sounded believable, although it was he who was the object of the manhunt. He cut the ropes binding the prisoners and set them free.

This all very much sounds like the type of episode that would be recounted and played out in a western movie. The tale was told by Cody himself about Cody himself, and there were no other handy witnesses as he pretended to be someone else in the clutches of the enemy and his quick thinking and quick action saved his life. In 1864, with only a handful of people involved in an exercise, and even fewer of them likely to chronicle a small-scale event, there was no ready supporter to verify Cody's enterprise. There was no one wielding a cell phone to snap a picture, and there was no internet to spread the story of his clandestine deed.

Nor was another incident readily verified. Back to work as a scout, Cody said he spent weeks in the field as his outfit engaged in back-and-forth conflicts with Confederate General Sterling Price. One day, while riding ahead, he came upon a farmhouse. Cody wore a gray shirt and what he called Missouri jeans, so he must have most resembled a Confederate. A man was seated at a table eating when Cody entered. Shockingly, the man smiled and said, "You little rascal, what are you doing in those 'seecsh' (or secessionist) clothes!"[8] It was Hickok, also dressed in garb that would identify him with the South. Cody joined Hickok at the table for bread and milk. Afterward, Hickok paid their hostess, and they went outside. Hickok was also spying for Union generals and obtained the kind of information about Price Cody was seeking. Hickok told Cody what he knew and asked him to deliver a package of letters to General John McNeil. The friends again separated.

The Civil War continued, and Cody played no major part in its deciding events. He just brought home war stories. Before mustering out at the end of the war, Cody was assigned to a military headquarters in St. Louis. It was there he met his future wife, Louisa Frederici, and his courtship of her began. When Cody was discharged from the service, he was like many thousands of other men. He was unemployed with few prospects, and while he seemed to be a man of great resourcefulness, his talents seemed best applied in only a few professions. One of those was freighting, driving those oxen-powered wagons ferrying supplies west to settlers or those troops who remained in uniform to keep restless Indians under control. So there was Cody, once again, a wagon master hauling goods across the Plains, a task he kept up through 1866.

Blinded by love, around that time he convinced himself he was finished with freighting and its nomadic lifestyle. He decreed he was going to get married and settle down. No more roaming the prairie. Will Cody may have meant it when he said it, but the retrospective review of his decision can be summed up in one word: Ha!

As the United States began rebuilding during Reconstruction, Cody was really just another guy. The war produced heroes and villains, depending on which side you were on, and the most famous of the generals for the South like Robert E. Lee gained lifetime respect from residents of that part of the country. As for Northern leaders, many became honored career military men of great influence like William Tecumseh Sherman, or presidents, like Ulysses S. Grant. Abner Doubleday was credited with inventing baseball, even if he really had nothing to do with it.

There was another general whose name emerged from the conflict, a general who became one of the most famous, General George Armstrong Custer. As his life progressed, Cody came to know, or at least meet, almost every famous person in the country and throughout the world. However, he was friendlier with and spent more time with Custer than most of the others.

As exciting and as dramatic a youth Cody had lived, even if only half of what he highlighted was true, the reality was he was just getting started recording one of the most singular lives in American history. Maybe he did accomplish great things for the Pony Express. And maybe he spied for the Union cause during the Civil War. But for all of that, William F. Cody had yet to really splash his name on the national and world stages. To his closest family relatives, Cody always remained Will. Many friends called him Bill. The universe writ large was soon in on the trendy, known-to-one-and-all name of Buffalo Bill.

A statue of Buffalo Bill Cody stands behind the Buffalo Bill Center of the West in Cody, Wyoming (courtesy of Park County Archives).

5

Cody and Custer

One of the most controversial figures in the West during the second half of the nineteenth century was George Armstrong Custer. Called the boy general for his exploits during the Civil War, Custer continued his military career as a cavalry officer during the Plains Indian Wars. So many years later he is best remembered for his manner of death, the massacre of he and his men at the Battle of the Little Bighorn in Montana in 1876 by a vastly larger body of Indians under the command of Sitting Bull.

William F. Cody and Custer were friends, men of great egos and a select amount of charm who admired one another after crossing paths in the field, and elsewhere, over the years. Their relationship began in the spring of 1867. Although Custer, who attended West Point for officer training (and finished at the bottom of his class), had reached the rank of general in the Union Army, it was a temporary, or brevetted, title of brigadier general. Even so, Custer proved himself more worthy on the battlefield than he had in the classroom, and promotions had come rapidly from second lieutenant, the usual rank bestowed on West Point grads. He distinguished himself leading troops several times in critical situations, sometimes at the head of a column, a saber waving about his head, with displays of courage. Custer's swift ascension, combined with his key roles at various times, brought him his first publicity. Confederate General Robert E. Lee's first flag of truce was given to Custer and he was present at the cessation of hostilities when Lee surrendered to Ulysses S. Grant in Virginia.

At the end of the Civil War, Custer was still in his twenties, and his permanent rank in the standing army dropped to lieutenant colonel. General Philip Sheridan provided Custer with a command in Louisiana and Texas as part of Reconstruction. Again, as part of the volunteer army, Custer had the rank of major general. For different periods, Custer was out of the army, but on July 28, 1866, Custer became a lieutenant colonel at the head of the new Seventh Cavalry Regiment, based in Fort Riley, Kansas.

It was in Kansas where Cody and Custer met. Despite the changing nature of Custer's rank in the records on paper, when he mentioned his name, Cody always referred to Custer as general. For that matter, a present-day review of Cody's military affiliations and official titles can also be confusing. He served for the Union Army and with irregulars during the Civil War. He was a scout on the Plains for cavalry detachments, sometimes as a member of the army and sometimes as an adjunct. Later, he was called colonel because of an honorary rank in the Nebraska National Guard. For sure, it was difficult to keep up with Cody. What no one denies is that he was a scout par excellence.

Custer was commanding his crew at Fort Larned near the Arkansas River, and Cody was scouting out of Fort Hays. Custer showed up with his riders and informed the commandant he wanted a guide ready to help him the next day. Cody was chosen and ordered to ready the best mount available. However, many of the best horses at the fort were worn out at the time, Cody said. He knew the best traveler was a mule, and he selected that beast for the task.

The next day, Cody's mount did not make a good first impression on Custer, and the general said so. "Captain," Custer said to the fort commander, "I haven't got time to dilly-dally along the road. I want him to have a horse, and a good one." Cody said he assured Custer the mule would not fail him, and the captain explained about the other horses being somewhat down and out. Custer replied, "Well, if that is the best you have, I will have to put up with it."[1]

A long ride commenced, Custer setting a relatively quick pace. Cody stayed up and the men talked, the general peppering him with questions about the terrain and the Indians in the area. During a short period, when the men were not together, Cody said he put his spurs to the mule "a little to wake him up."[2] After some distance, Cody, who had faith in the animal, noticed some horses were showing signs of fatigue, but the mule was not. Cody engineered a stop by telling Custer they had reached the last water available for forty-five miles and it might be best for the horses to pause and drink and the soldiers to replenish their canteens.

They entered sandy terrain, which for lack of firm footing slowed down everyone. Wishing to prove his point to Custer, Cody said, he would sometimes give the mule a spurred boot and the animal surged ahead. Playing with the circumstances, Cody would then tell the mule to slow down. His trick worked to the point Custer began praising the mule as a pretty fast horse, after all. "Oh, he isn't warmed up yet, General," Cody said. "He doesn't go good until he gets his second wind."[3]

This little ride turned into a battle of wills and surges, Custer refusing to allow Cody to pull away from his favorite horse. Still, Cody reported, he

5. Cody and Custer

did once move far enough ahead that he had to wait for Custer, who discerned what his scout was doing. He half-laughed it off, but also refused to allow his horse to be shown up, so kept pushing it. The last of the journey went on like this until they were at Fort Larned. Cody said Custer's horse died that night from its exertions. Custer responded, "Well, I will never say anything against a mule again."[4]

Starting that year, Cody said, he and Custer embarked on many hunts for game, buffalo, antelope, deer, and turkey. During the hunts, and in the years that followed, when the two men got together after an absence, Cody said, Custer brought up the mule. Clearly, he never forgot the incident or how he met Cody. "The general was full of life and was a splendid entertainer in camp," Cody said, "besides being quite a practical joker. He liked to play practical jokes and delighted in taking certain tenderfeet out for a night's snipe hunting."[5]

Apparently snipe hunting goes back in time much earlier than the twenty-first century hunter might think. Always employed as a practical joke, a neophyte is duped into standing alone and waiting to have snipes driven his way by others in the group. Snipes, being nonexistent, never show up, and the victim is made a fool. Some date snipe hunting to the 1840s, but it was obviously around by the 1860s if Cody and Custer ganged up on the occasional unsuspecting character. "I have known tenderfeet to stay and hold the sack all night before tumbling to the fact that they had been sold," Cody said.[6]

Cody said that when he fulfilled his task for Custer and they went different ways, the officer left him with a standing offer. Custer invited Cody to scout for him the following summer and also said if he was ever out of work he could scout for him, and he looked forward to sharing more trail time together. "This was the beginning of my acquaintance with General Custer, whom I always admired as a man and an officer," Cody said.[7] Whether it was because Cody was never out of demand for his services, or the stars did not align, he never scouted for Custer again, although they were linked in other ways.

The book Cody's sister Helen Wetmore wrote was called *The Last of the Great Scouts*, and by all indications Cody was a great scout. Now in his twenties in the 1860s, he had experience and savvy, could ride a horse, and had a nose for sensing trouble and choosing the right direction. In 1866, and for most of 1867, business on the Plains was quiet compared to the coming storm of the ceaseless Indian wars as the American government began its shameful ethnic cleansing. Most often, Cody could operate without scrapes, delivering dispatches between cavalry outposts.

In the closing months of 1867, action on the frontier heated up, and Cody's job became significantly more dangerous. When he rode ahead of columns sniffing out the best travel routes, there was every chance he and other scouts would be discovered by hostile Indians defending their territory, or at the least taking umbrage at these trespassers. Conflicts were inevitable—and sought. Cody enhanced his reputation with his competence and instincts. People wanted to hire him to lead the way into the unknown.

In August of 1868, Cody took on the dual role of guide and hunter for the Tenth Cavalry, which interestingly was a segregated unit of black soldiers led by a white commanding officer. That man said it was easy to please Cody by giving him $60 a month and a good mule to ride. Some already knew what kind of work Cody could do with a mule under him. The next month, Cody signed on to chase livestock at Fort Larned. He did so well at that he was soon acting as a scout and being paid even more than he had been with the Tenth Cavalry.

Cody had truly found his calling. Whatever else he did in his varied life, it was clear to those who knew him and watched him, Cody was a superior scout. If he had never gone on to fame in any other endeavor, Cody would have maintained a reputation in history as a great scout. Only that's where those descriptions would have stayed. He would not have become well known or be remembered, simply someone whose name would be read by students and historians and swiftly forgotten.

By no means, of course, was the job of a scout to be confused with a Boy Scout. Cody earned his merit badges in other ways, as a route finder, as someone who read signs in the wilderness, as a dispenser of information, and as someone who fought when called upon. The job of a scout carried a romantic connotation. It was understood, among the citizenry and among the soldiers, that scouts led dangerous lives. They were the intelligence officers of their time, sent out on fact-finding missions that hopefully led the commanders to make wise field decisions and win battles and wars. Louis Warren, one of Cody's biographers, suggested the American public was conditioned to view a man like Cody as someone who had adopted and mastered Indian ways, being close to the land, and through those traits gained understanding that would make him successful.

Given that the ranks of the U.S. cavalry were peopled with men who grew up in the East, led by officers schooled at West Point in New York, there was a paucity of local experts in a thinly settled region of the country to share knowledge. Cody knew the landscape and bridged the unknown with the soldiers, whom he did understand, having spent considerable time with them during the Civil War and even on jobs like the one he performed for Custer.

The most intense and brutal phases of the Plains Indian Wars had not yet begun. The government in Washington was still at least pretend-

5. Cody and Custer

ing to negotiate treaties with the resident Indian tribes. There was an effort to keep the peace. Cody was attached to Major General William B. Hazen, superintendent of Indian Affairs for the Southwest Plains out of Fort Larned. Treaties had been made, but Indians were not moving to agreed-upon reservation sites. The tribes depended on buffalo, but were promised whatever food was necessary, and General Sheridan tried to deliver it. It seemed to be a lull period, with actual peace a possibility. But tensions rose from there, buffalo herds were decimated, force was applied to transfer Indians to reservations, and in some cases starvation set in. That was what was on the horizon.

During this period, when he was not scouting, Cody, who had by then acquired the Buffalo Bill name, rented himself out as a guide for hunting trips. This burnished his reputation and spread his name to other parts of the country. He was regarded as someone who could lead a hunter to game and make sure he did not go home empty-handed. This might have been easier to accomplish when there were still millions of buffalo on the Plains than in the coming years when the population crashed.

Comanche and Kiowa Indian tribes were situated near Fort Larned. Usually, there was no trouble. But then a small raid caused the post to refuse the demand for guns to hunt buffalo. At first that did not go over well, but following an investigation by General Alfred Sully, sent in to review the situation, a decision was made to provide the necessary armaments for the Indians to carry out their traditional hunt. Some chiefs convinced Sully that only a few young braves from one tribe were responsible for the event. He bought the argument.

While there may have been truth in what the chiefs said, the situation changed drastically while the Comanche and Kiowa camped in the shadow of the fort. Elsewhere in Kansas, some two hundred Cheyenne, supplemented by a handful of four Arapaho and about twenty visiting Sioux, ran rampant on the Saline and Solomon Rivers, killing settlers, raping women, and destroying homes. Fifteen white people, thirteen of them men, were killed before troops scuttled the Indian attackers. At about the same time, Bill Comstock, who had engaged in the contest with Cody for the right to use the name Buffalo Bill, was killed by Indians in another incident.

The Tenth Cavalry was sent from Fort Hays to track the killers. For two weeks following the raids, troops tried to find and apprehend the Indians without success. Still, the commanding officer wrote in his diary, "Bill Cody, one of our scouts and one of the best shots on the Plains, keeps us well-supplied with plenty of buffalo and deer."[8] While Cody returned to Fort Larned, Sheridan beefed up his scouting corps by advertising for fifty frontiersmen. In early September, when a column left Fort Hays, it was with James Butler "Wild Bill" Hickok as lead scout. Once again, Cody and Hickok were operating in the same sphere.

By then, Hickok had been scouting and guiding for a couple of years in Kansas. He was tasked with helping to enforce treaties, being paid $75 or sometimes $100 per month. On one mission he traveled with George Armstrong Custer and four companies of the Seventh Cavalry. Although there were skirmishes, there were no pitched battles, and Hickok mostly had to outrun pursuers to deliver messages.

Much has been made of Custer's devotion to his wife Elizabeth, or Libby. Unlike most other officers, even those of the highest rank, she traveled with him to obscure outposts. She outlived him by decades, not dying until she was ninety-one, and fiercely defended him against critics, in interviews, and in books. However, there were rumors that during this time period she had an affair with Hickok. No such thing was proven, though when Libby wrote a memoir in 1890, long after both Hickok and George were dead, she was flattering to the lawman-scout.

"Physically, he was a delight to look upon," she wrote. "Tall, lithe, and free in every motion, he rode and walked as if every muscle was perfection, and the careless swing of his body as he moved seemed perfectly in keeping with the man, the country, the time in which he lived. I do not recall anything finer in the way of physical perfection than Wild Bill when he swung himself lightly from his saddle, and with graceful, swaying step squarely set his shoulders and well-poised head, approached our head for orders."[9] Gushing with compliments, absolutely, but nothing damning in there and also something a man may well have written about a beauteous movie starlet who was well-shaped and universally regarded as sexy. The sharpness of Libby Custer's description really only confirms what others said about Hickok's build.

For a time in 1868, when both Cody and Hickok were between jobs, they joined up in Junction City. Hickok was more of a drinker and card player than Cody, but they socialized. Then Hickok, who had been approached to hunt down army deserters, invited Cody to become one of the pursuers. The Topeka newspaper reported the duo brought eleven prisoners to jail from this expedition.

Cody told one story of being waylaid and captured by Kiowa, but he fast-talked Chief Satana, telling him he was on assignment to bring cattle to the Kiowa. Wearing civilian garb helped Cody's credibility, but he had to hightail it back to the fort, chased all the while until he intersected a small group of soldiers. Earlier that day Satana's band had killed some woodchoppers, and the soldiers were out for vengeance. Cody had actually been on assignment as a messenger, galloping sixty-five miles from Larned to Fort Hays to inform General Sheridan local Indians were uprising.

While hardly faster than the telegraph to come, Cody earned lavish praise for being indefatigable in these circumstances. Grabbing a fresh horse after about five hours rest and riding back and forth between the forts, Generals Sheridan and Hazen updated themselves through Cody. An impressed and grateful Sheridan calculated Cody rode 360 miles in sixty hours (with another stretch of twelve hours rest), ironically shades of the Pony Express claims, though a recalculation indicated it was closer to three hundred miles in distance in fifty-eight hours. Perhaps arithmetic was more casually applied in the nineteenth century.

Running across Satana was perfectly plausible. As close as Cody rode to various Indian parties, it was a wonder he was not more often accosted. Maybe his scouting instincts saved him, though he admitted to close calls. Being a lone white man riding through country not controlled by soldiers was bound to bring risk. By mid–September 1868, Cody was scouting for Lt. L.W. Cooke of the Third Infantry and being paid $75 a month. Minus few exceptions, apparently some paychecks earned by Wild Bill Hickok, that was the top wage paid for such work by the army on the frontier at that time. Cody was only filling time, though, until Sheridan moved the operations of the Fifth Cavalry to Fort Hays. During a stopover there, Sheridan signed Cody again to lead the way on the prairie.

This is when Cody had his wagon conversation with Major Royall about hauling buffalo meat back to camp. Cody made a convert of a doubting Royall with his production. But that was buffalo hunting. The rest of the mission required Indian scouting. Experienced Plains fighter Brevet Major General Eugene Carr then took command. The cavalry was in pursuit of four to five hundred Cheyenne and Sioux braves. The soldiers caught up, but there were no stand-and-fight battles, only dashes on horseback with the fighting parties getting close enough to one another periodically to fire off shots.

Many of those were deadly, and by virtue of superior firepower, the cavalry's first accounting stated there were thirty Indian dead to one solider wounded. Cody later told a story about the first night in camp when a shot emanated from the darkness to shatter a plate held by a lieutenant seated near him at the campfire. After daylight, pursuit continued, but there was also a need for the troops to refuel with water. Cody said there was water a day's march away, but later that day, General Carr approached him and said other scouts felt he was wrong and they would not come upon water. Cody replied there was water within eight miles, but it was behind some beaver dams. When he was proved right, Carr labeled a little tributary Cody's Creek. The soldiers made camp beside the water.

On the move again, Cody went ahead. Being on his own this time nearly cost him his life. A shot ripped through the air and downed his horse. Cody was not hit and was fortunate the falling horse did not cripple him. He immediately used the dead animal's body as a shield as two warriors fired at him. His timing was lucky. Nearby Indians were breaking camp and simply trying to get away from the advancing soldiers, so these men did not focus on killing Cody. They threw down covering fire, but then disappeared. Carr and the troops were not far behind, and once Cody told him what he saw, he dispatched men to chase the Indians. A running battle lasted several hours, and Cody said many horses and lodges were captured by the whites.

These types of hazards were common for scouts, and Cody ran into such difficulties when he was hunting, as well, with only a few others accompanying him. One buffalo hunt was interrupted by warriors, and he reported that became another running battle lasting several hours. Four Indians were killed. Sometimes soldiers helped lead wagon trains through dangerous territory.

As the year ended, Carr assigned five hundred men to accompany a pack train to the Texas Panhandle and the Canadian River. Cody and Hickok were lead scouts. Going ahead, they ran into other scouts who were delivering beer to another expedition twelve miles away. After consultation, Cody and Hickok made an executive decision. They decided the beer was better off in their custody than in the hands of unknown buyers ahead. While both Cody and Hickok were avid drinkers, they did not hog the booty for themselves. There was so much it would have been impossible to imbibe it on their own. Instead, they provided a happy hour for the troops. "It was sold to our boys in pint cups," Cody said, "and as the weather was very cold we warmed the beer by putting the ends of our picket pins (horse stakes) heated red-hot into the cups. The result was one of the biggest beer jollifications I ever had the misfortune to attend."[10] It should be noted the beer was not donated to the soldiers in an act of generosity, but sold.

A series of commanding officers, lieutenants, majors, and otherwise, in addition to generals such as Sheridan and Carr, repeatedly praised Cody's work in the field as a scout, hunter, and wagon master when necessary, and kept recommending him for challenging jobs. On one winter occasion, in blowing snow and sub-zero temperatures, Cody played a key role in aiding Carr's command to relieve Brevet Brigadier General William H. Penrose, who was under pressure.

This was shortly after an infamous fight led by Custer on November 27, 1868, not his finest hour, at the Battle of the Washita River. Custer charged a camp of Southern Cheyenne under the leadership of Chief Black Kettle. This was a winter encampment, and these Indians came into Custer's crosshairs because his scouts had followed a trail of Indians who had killed some white settlers. This group was pursuing peace, but Custer's men massacred men, women, and children. Among those killed by the four groups of Custer's men were Black Kettle and his wife Medicine Woman, both shot in the back. Official military history states Custer suffered twenty-one soldiers killed and thirteen wounded, with about fifty killed and fifty wounded among the Indians. One group of Custer's men bore the brunt of the fight on the Washita. Major Joel Elliott, who was killed, and his troops were rushed by a combined band of Cheyenne, Kiowa, and Arapaho from other camps along the river.

Custer did not linger at the site and was accused by soldiers within the Seventh Cavalry of rashly departing without specifically determining the fate of Elliott's men. Captain Frederick Benteen, who was Elliott's friend and who later was an important character at the Battle of the Little Bighorn, was very resentful. A bit of nineteenth-century *National Enquirer*–style gossip also links Custer and Benteen in a completely different way. Benteen and chief of scouts Ben Clark claimed (through Cheyenne oral storytelling) Custer had unofficially taken a Native American bride in addition to his wife Libby. The woman was the daughter of Chief Little Rock, who was killed at Washita. Her name was Monahsetah, and it was alleged Custer was the father of the baby she gave birth to in January of 1869. Also according to Cheyenne lore, Monahsetah had a second baby later that year, also supposedly fathered by Custer.

In a 1996 book called *Custer: The Controversial Life of George Armstrong Custer* by Jeffry D. Wert, it was suggested some believed Custer had become sterile due to an attack of gonorrhea years earlier and the true father was his brother Tom. Further exploring this lesser-known aspect of Custer's always-controversial life, the woman described as the second child born from this union went by the name Gail Kelly-Custer. She wrote a book about the relationship between Custer and her mother called *Princess Monahsetah*. It was quite the tangle.

During this period in the late 1860s and into the early 1870s, Cody and Custer were both figures on the frontier associated with the U.S. Army clearing the Plains of Indian opposition, then the paramount domestic policy of the American government. Custer was better known at this time, with Cody's reputation still being established. Mustachioed with flowing blond hair, Custer was seen as a swashbuckler in uniform. Mustachioed with flowing blond hair, Cody was seen as a swashbuckler in buckskins. Custer, too, did sometimes wear a buckskin jacket, though mostly he was clad in uniform blue.

In 1869 and beyond, Custer, who was supposed to be tied up with military business, found time to make ventures onto the Plains as a buffalo hunting guide. He was probably doing this more often than Cody for the time being. Custer was very good at attracting attention from newspapers and magazines and was adroit (most of the time) in shaping his image. When he got into scrapes, including making an unauthorized trip back to the fort to visit his wife, public opinion was generally on his side, even when other generals were not.

That summer, Custer was at the forefront of a hunting trip for two wealthy and titled Englishmen. While one expects such a journey on the Plains to be conducted in quiet, this became quite the bash. More than 150 tourists (much like the curious that would join Cody on the Plains in the contest for the name Buffalo Bill) and two newspaper reporters (one from the *New York Times*) joined in. The group was serenaded by "The Garryowen," the tune the Seventh Cavalry played upon leaving for battle and which gained perpetual infamy for its playing at the Battle of the Little Bighorn. Apparently, a good time was had by all. As one observer noted, "Custer, ahead, was seen to rise in his saddle, with his long hair flying in the wind, his heavily fringed buckskin suit matching the color of his hair. He gave the Indian war-whoop—every horse and dog understood it meant a dash—a run at full gallop."[11] Heck, if he had been given the chance to write such a paragraph about the occasion, Custer probably would not have changed a word.

Near the end of 1869, no doubt still showing off, but with a clearer intent—to the right people who might be or become allies—Custer guided fifty people on a hunt. There were politicians, wealthy men, cavalry officers, and others led to hunt bison. The traveling party seemed as large as those settler wagon trains hurrying across the prairie to new lives. There were eight wagons, three ambulances, and many extra horses. It was a parade, with Custer as the grand marshal. He even took note of a comment made by a member of the group that indicated he was not so blind to see its incongruous magnitude. "One of the gentlemen remarked that the scene reminded him of events described as belonging to the feudal ages, when marshaling his retainers some ancient Baron marched forth to battle or to the chase."[12]

Sure enough, in 1872, Cody and Custer briefly merged forces for one of the most celebrated, if not the most famous, buffalo hunt of the age. "Buffalo Bill and the Boy General," a Broadway marquee might have read somewhere later. They were united to provide entertainment for Grand Duke Alexis of Russia under the auspices of General Philip Sheridan, the technical host of the expedition. The duke was on a grand tour of the United States in late 1871 and early 1872 and wanted to hunt buffalo. So exercising his power and persuasion, Sheridan organized this showy extravaganza, although he left many details to Cody.

At the time, Buffalo Bill was living in North Platte, Nebraska, in a

5. Cody and Custer

Buffalo Bill Cody (reclining in front) led many hunts on the Great Plains and in Wyoming (courtesy of Park County Archives).

Buffalo Bill Cody (left) on horseback with the prince of Monaco. Cody took the visiting monarch on a famous hunt (courtesy of the Library of Congress).

home he called "Scout's Rest Ranch," where he would base his operations for about a quarter century. That building is now a tourism show place and clearly must have been palatial in its times. It was to North Platte that the grand duke and his entourage sped by special train from the East. Officially, the man with the title was His Imperial Highness, Grand Duke Alexsai (or Alexei, depending on who was translating) Alexandrovich of the House of Romanov. His father was Czar Alexander II. At the time, during his tour of the States, Alexis, for short, had just turned twenty-one. He had spent time in New York City and Washington accompanied by officials, including a meeting with President Ulysses S. Grant, but was fascinated by the nation's open spaces and wanted to check out this buffalo hunting business. His train pulled into North Platte on January 13, 1872. The same train brought Sheridan, who had his own cars affixed to the duke's in Omaha. Custer was on board with Sheridan.

In Nebraska, Buffalo Bill was local host and partial on-the-ground organizer, with the approval of General Joel Palmer and with Sheridan giving the final sign-off. A contingent of U.S. Cavalry stood at the ready because this was not a guaranteed safe excursion. In New York, famed artist of the West Albert Bierstadt got involved in some of the planning, too. Bierstadt had numerous Russian contacts and had visited the country. In July of 1871, before Alexis's arrival, he suggested the idea of a buffalo hunt in a letter. "I have learned he is quite desirous of witnessing a buffalo hunt," Bierstadt wrote. "As his visit partakes of a somewhat national character, would it not be well to give him one on a grand scale, with Indians included, as a rare piece of American hospitality?"[13]

Indians were included, the duke's up-close-and-personal visit with them somewhat riskier, but somehow, sweet-talking Cody had convinced some local Indians to participate in camp activities to provide authenticity for the duke. This was some time before Buffalo Bill's Wild West exhibition took flight, but in some subtle ways this outing had some of the trappings of the future show. Cody approached Chief Spotted Tail of the Brule Lakota and explained that the visitor was a great chief himself from across the ocean. Cody built up Spotted Tail's ego by telling him Alexis had made the trip primarily to meet him. Spotted Tail rounded up other leaders and about six hundred warriors for the show and tell. He was also paid off big time. The Indians received ten thousand rations of coffee, flour, and sugar, and one thousand pounds of tobacco.

The location for the base camp was along Red Willow Creek, which a year later would be opened to homesteading. The three-day hunt from January 13 to 16 persevered unmolested, although the world developed at a sprint around it. It was dubbed Camp Alexis in honor of the esteemed visitor. It took eight hours to reach the camp for the

5. Cody and Custer

well-equipped hunters. Among the supplies Cody arranged for were three wagon loads of champagne and other spirits. The duke and Sheridan rode together in an open carriage.

The Indians, as they would in somewhat modified form during the thirty years of the touring Wild West exhibition, put on quite a show. They danced and provided displays of horsemanship, lance-throwing, and a bow-and-arrow exhibition for the duke's benefit. Some mock war exercises were included, but a real Indian intramural fight broke out. Alexis stopped it by handing out fresh gifts, colored blankets, ivory-handled knives, and silver dollars. Spotted Tail wore a suit (not a well-tailored one) and greeted the duke by saying, "How." Spotted Tail, Sheridan, and Alexis shared a peace pipe. Revealing what was really on his mind, Spotted Tail introduced politics to the gathering—for Sheridan—pushing for a government agreement allowing his people to hunt south of the Platte River and requesting expansion to more than one trading post. No deals were cut.

Sheridan planned well ahead for the hunt. The preceding fall he ordered Cody to scout locations of wintering herds, and that figured into this set-up. It was necessary to have buffalo nearby because the duke was not well-prepared for a horseback search. The hunt came to be termed "The Royal Buffalo Hunt." Buffalo Bill Cody, General George Armstrong Custer, General Philip Sheridan, General William Sherman, artist Albert Bierstadt, and a representative of the Russian monarchy, plus a cast of thousands with Indians and cavalry soldiers all around: it sounded like a Hollywood epic long before there was a Hollywood.

Not all Indians with Spotted Tail were happy to see Buffalo Bill. They realized he had been a Plains scout with several run-ins with different tribes. When they recognized him, there was a little bit of grumbling. "Yes, we know him well," said one member of Spotted Tail's party. "That is Pahaska [Cody's often-used Indian name translated as Long Hair]. That is our old enemy." Spotted Tail said yes, that was Cody, but he advised them to be nice, saying, "That is he. I want all my people to be kind and treat him as my friend."[14]

The Indians' camp was on Frenchman Fork of the Republican River, about one hundred miles farther away. When Cody visited recruiting, he was wary of the attitudes of some braves despite Spotted Tail's assurances. The hunting camp for the Duke filled four acres and was heavily populated with soldiers as well as the luminaries. The hunt began on January 14, with Buffalo Bill scouting for buffalo starting at 10 a.m. and reporting back there was a herd a mere fifteen miles away. Time to go.

It was decided that the guest of honor, the grand duke, would take the first shots. On the trip between camp and hunting ground, Custer gave him a tutorial. When they reached the buffalo, Custer steered his mount into the crowd to split off a bull for the Russian visitor. Alexis rode up to the beast and fired with a pistol, wounding it. It was finished off by rifle, and the duke sliced off the tail as a trophy. The accounts of how many buffalo were killed on the first day varied widely, from as low as four to as high as twenty or thirty. The likelihood of a true number is closer to the lower figure.

A larger group sought buffalo the next day, with Cody again ferreting out the animals. Alexis killed two buffalo and Sheridan two. Spotted Tail and his hundreds of warriors arrived the night before, and the chief and about eight of his braves joined the hunt and killed several more. One report claims fifty-six buffalo were killed on the second day. As souvenirs, Alexis saved the head of one adult buffalo and one calf to be returned to Russia with his luggage. It was a good haul and likely one of the highlights of Alexis's excellent American vacation.

Custer accrued another incident of fame for his work with the cavalry in 1874 when gold was discovered in the Black Hills. Until then, the U.S. government pretty much thought of that land, which would become part of the state of South Dakota, as worthless. The Native Americans viewed it as a sacred homeland. Custer led an expedition to find out more about the territory and when he reported back it ignited another gold craze. Newspapers went wild with the story. "The El Dorado of America," one reported. A valley was named after Custer. From then on it was impossible for the government, the cavalry, or anyone else with the slightest good intention of holding to Native American treaties to keep white men from invading the area. This provoked fresh violence and led to repeated treaty violations. The gold rush could not be contained.

After Custer's discovery, the Plains Indians Wars only intensified and escalated to the point where Custer woke up one day in late June of 1876 with his few hundred men surrounded by thousands of Indians bent on destruction. There was no escape at the Battle of the Little Bighorn, and the man who dreamed of one day becoming president of the United States was struck down by superior manpower with all of his men, including two brothers, at the hillock that came to be known as Last Stand Hill. Custer was thirty-six when he died.

When Buffalo Bill Cody, Custer's sometime partner and friend, received word of Custer's death, he was outraged and saddened. It was soon after, when Buffalo Bill was scouting and involved in a small battle, that he killed an Indian in one-on-one combat and then scalped the man, something he was not wont to do. It was a symbol of his anger at the loss of the young officer. Cody shouted, "The first scalp for Custer!" The phrase followed him for a lifetime. Later, when Cody was in charge of his touring Wild West exhibition, one of the staple programs was a reenactment of

5. Cody and Custer

Custer's Last Stand. It was one way Custer's name remained in the forefront of American minds for decades.

A few days after Custer and his men were killed, cavalry troops reached the location and buried everyone in shallow graves. It was said General Custer was buried about eighteen inches deep, wrapped in blankets and a canvas tarp on top of a stretcher. A year later, another cavalry group was sent to Last Stand Hill to retrieve Custer's body for return to West Point. Ironically, given the dispute over the location of where Buffalo Bill is buried, in 1991, anthropologists and other scientists questioned whether George Custer is really buried at West Point, despite the ostensible removal of his bones from the Little Bighorn burial ground in 1877.

When they found the site it was said animals had dug up and scattered bones, and they did not see the blankets, tarp, or stretcher. They scooped up a skull, a leg bone, and rib cage and called it good. One skeptic, author Bruce Liddie, said, it was unlikely the soldiers got Custer's bones, "that out of pure, dumb luck, they got the right body, but I doubt it."[15]

The forensic anthropologist Clyde Snow said, "It would be ironic if some buck private were buried up there at West Point. The thought that it might not be Custer is too delicious to put to rest." Doug McChristian, historian for Custer Battlefield National Monument, said "I've often thought in my warped way that Libby was sure surprised if there was some corporal lying beside her." Evan McConnell, who wrote the well-known book *Son of the Morning Star* about Custer, said he believes the men got the proper bones, partially because they brought back a lock of Custer's hair for his widow, and she said it was from him.[16]

Decades after Custer died, family members refused to have his remains exhumed to determine if they were really his. If they are not, then Custer's bones are still where he perished in Montana, along with those of the others from the Seventh Cavalry.

6

The Mrs.

Meanwhile, back at the ranch. Whether he was blinded by first love or just what, William F. Cody fell for Louisa Frederici and married her after they met and courted for a bit in late 1864 and early 1865 in St. Louis. One never can truly know what goes on between two people, as lovers and intimates, as friends or enemies, as they age together or fall apart. Clearly, the alliance between Cody and Mrs. Cody was not one of the great romances of the ages, not described in breathless tones like Romeo and Juliet. Certainly, as all couples do, they had their moments. But they also had their years apart. And years it was as Cody gallivanted around the globe while Louisa stayed at home, wherever home was at the time.

A famous and recognizable man, dashing in all regards as a daredevil of the Plains or as the head of his own business that played to millions of fans in states throughout the country and overseas, the handsome Cody was the object of desire for many ladies, and there is no real belief he stayed true to his marriage. At one point, after so many lengthy separations, Cody sought a divorce, yet a court failed to issue a decree, and the husband and wife were stuck with one another. Near the very end of Cody's life, they reconciled, to some degree. However, for the most part, this was a rocky marriage rather than a thriving marriage in the Rocky Mountains.

In Cody's memoir, he said he met Frederici before the end of the Civil War, a woman "whom I greatly admired and in whose charming society I spent many a pleasant hour."[1] Those were not exactly fiery words of passion, but it was the beginning of something. When Cody concluded his war service, he returned to Leavenworth, Kansas, for a short while before heading back to St. Louis to woo Frederici, by then admitting he "adored [her] above any other lady I had ever seen." By the time Cody left town on a frontier job, he said he had won her over. "Her lovely face, her gentle disposition, and her graceful manners won my admiration and love."[2] He secured a pledge of marriage and then went to work, as always, not in an office job or stationary position, but out on trails, driving wagons or riding his horse.

Cody found he could not bear to be away from his true love and not only abandoned the job, but decided he would settle down. In retrospect, that brief commitment is almost too funny for words. Thousands upon thousands of miles stretched out in front of Cody over the next several decades. He scurried back to St. Louis and married Louisa on March 6, 1866. He had just turned twenty. She was just shy of twenty-two. In his 1879 autobiography, Cody wrote, "from that time to this, I have always thought that I made a most fortunate choice for a life partner."[3] By then there had already been fissures in the marriage, and it would have been something to watch Cody struggle for the appropriate words in his phrasing. But a man's got to write what a man's got to write.

Louisa Frederici Cody (left) and William F. Cody persevered in marriage for decades despite considerable strains and a near divorce (courtesy of Park County Archives).

While Cody eventually became the most photographed man in the world during his lifetime, Louisa was not the most photographed woman in the world. There seem to be few photographs extant where she would be mistaken for a great beauty. She is usually seen wearing the most cumbersome of clothing, sometimes with awkward hats on her head and hair severely pulled back around a roundish face. There seem to be a shortage of pictures of her smiling, but that may be because she was almost always exasperated with Cody. Standards of beauty do change with the times, but it would not be far-fetched for an independent observer to wonder what Cody really saw in Louisa physically. They may well have sizzled together in the beginning when he was young, but most assuredly grievances did pile up with the passing years.

Cody may have had first crack on marriage commentary and was gentle. Louisa had last at-bats, hitting in the bottom of the ninth inning in 1919, two years after Cody's death. In her volume *Memories of Buffalo Bill*, Louisa wrote of spending time in a convent, but begins her tale living back at home in St. Louis and noting she seemed to have two suitors at once. One she had seen several times before, and he had expressed his feelings for her. The second, a friend of a male cousin, was Cody, and her cousin brought him for a visit, a meeting, in her parlor.

Even though there were some awkward moments because her cousin and Cody walked in and surprised her, Louisa's first impression was rather gushing, calling him "handsome, about the most handsome man I ever had seen! Clean shaven, the ruddiness of health glowing in his cheeks; graceful, lithe, smooth in his movements, and in the modulations of his speech, he was quite the most wonderful man I had ever known, and I almost bit my tongue to keep from telling him so."[4] They began chatting, and Cody told Louisa his mother called him Willie (the only one) and other men called him Bill. This was pre–Buffalo Bill coronation. Even during their first session together, they teased another man with stories of how long they had known one another, and even straight-facedly told him they were going to be married. Indeed, they seemed to quickly establish a tight rapport.

Their first-impression emotions did run high, and Cody endeavored to make a second visit the next night. Louisa's sister told her to rebuff him, to quell such impetuousness for her own good, so she would not find herself so willingly ensnared. That was a minor speed bump, and they began seeing one another more often and confiding in each other. Louisa did not believe Cody at first when he said he had engaged in shooting matches with Indians and killed a man when he was just eleven. His environment growing up differed so dramatically from hers. Her upbringing was sheltered, his involved having adulthood thrust on him while still a boy. She

6. The Mrs.

knew little of the wide world. He may have experienced too much of it too soon.

Cody was a bit rough around the edges, and maybe she was attracted by the wild side a bit. Louisa was already calling him Will after a few meetings. She attempted to be discreet about their blossoming relationship. He did not care who knew about it. Louisa said Will wrote poetry to her, but she either did not understand it or did not admire its quality. She was astute enough to recognize Cody was an adventurer, with that sort of blood coursing through his veins, but she also admitted being lonely and in love. Louisa gave Cody a picture of her for the road, but when he cut short his wagon driving and returned to her, he told him his younger brother Charley had died holding her picture because he had asked to see it. The little boy perished from an illness in 1865, so apocryphal or not, the timing fits.

In their courtship, and in the aftermath of their marriage, Louisa and Will seemed to have a playful relationship—the way she describes it. She makes reference to him calling her Lou, for short, though also often over the years he called her Lulu. Cody took her to Kansas, a much wilder West than St. Louis at the time, and said he belonged there in the open spaces. Louisa was frightened about the change and removal from her safe environment. They had to scrap for money, Cody needing those wagon-driving jobs and to hire on with Wild Bill Hickok to earn money.

Mrs. Cody minded the hearth as Bill Cody roamed around taking short-term jobs while trying to hook onto something permanent. One time he turned up at home in Leavenworth and said he would become a millionaire because he was helping to found a town, called Rome. That did not last long. They moved to Fort Hays, residing in the Perry Hotel. From the vantage point of fifty-four years, Louisa said there were happy days and stressful times with hardships, and she suffered health ailments. The best and the worst of society stayed in the hotel, and there were gunfights in the streets at times. It could be rugged living.

When Cody was away on jobs he arranged for a bodyguard for Louisa if she went out. There was somewhat more lawlessness in Fort Hays than they bargained for initially. Louisa had mostly spent time in a convent or in the home of a fairly well-off family. If she knew much of anything about the West, she probably read it in a newspaper and never imagined a life on the frontier for herself. It was Cody's lifeblood, but she was an alien transplanted to another planet. Cody tried to teach her how to shoot as a way to protect herself if necessary. But Louisa struck out. She said she probably missed the target a hundred times in a row. Before Will gave up on the tutorial, she commenced a second round of attempts and began occasionally to improve her accuracy. But it was a tough go.

Cody came and went. Eventually, even as Cody stayed out West most of the time, Louisa returned to her parents' house in St. Louis. There were no telephones, and letters, as the Pony Express showed, could only reach a destination so quickly. Periodically, Cody would come off the trail and surprise his wife. He would arrive with a clamor, yelling for her and his offspring from the front door. Once he returned not quite resembling the man who left. It was then he had grown his shorter hair long and added a mustache. She asked him what the heck he did that for, and he replied it was the fashion and a scout of any reputation had to look the part. "You're not a regular scout unless you've got this sort of rigout," he said.[5] Louisa apparently got used to the look, and later, after Cody had become Buffalo Bill and created the Wild West exhibition, she said the hair, mustache, and goatee helped make him Buffalo Bill. "At least he would not have been the unusual appearing character that he was," she said, "nor would he have been as handsome."[6]

The Codys had their first child, daughter Arta, in December of 1866. They gave her a brother and two sisters. The only boy was named Kit Carson after the scout, a man Cody admired and seemingly, like everyone else of note on the frontier, someone he knew. The other girls were Orra and Irma. One of Louisa's habits, hobbies, and useful skills was making clothes for herself, Cody, and the children. While Louisa gave birth to their first child without Cody at her side, he did rush back to be with her soon after and participated in the naming of Arta. By everyone's account, when Cody was home from his various endeavors, he was a doting father. He just was not there that much during the kids' upbringing.

The great early tragedy of the Will–Louisa marriage was the death of young Kit. Kit Carson Cody was born on November 26, 1870. Cody was attached to Fort McPherson, and Louisa and Arta were living there with him. He was in the field, on a long mission, when she gave birth to Kit. While Will had settled on a completely different name as Louisa waited on him, when he returned to the fort he said the officers urged him to name the boy after Kit Carson, and he liked the sound of it.

While most believe Louisa despised just about every minute she spent on the Plains, when she wrote her memoirs, in many ways she was generous in hindsight, making comments about moods that may not have been true at the time. She brushed away much of the hardship and consistently wrote glowingly about her husband. Louisa could have written a bitter memoir that tarnished Cody's memory without fear of retaliation, but she really did not delve much into what some might call his flaws. She talks of being glad when he came home and of his handsome bearing. Louisa even quoted humorous poetry about Will who became Buffalo Bill. It went, "Buffalo Bill, Buffalo Bill; Never Missed and never will; Always aims and shoots to kill; And the comp'ny pays his buffalo bill!"[7]

6. The Mrs.

When they were still living together in the West, Louisa said she got cabin fever from so often being stuck in a hotel or walking around with armed guards. She cajoled Will into accompanying her on a buggy ride to inhale the great outdoors and see the sunset, only the outing was cut short by an Indian threat. She was at first oblivious to any danger, chatting away and laughing, even as Cody became more somber and worried. She initially dismissed his fears, even as he tried to impress upon her that he was a scout and knew what he was talking about in these situations. She realized how serious the situation became when Cody told her if the worst occurred, imminent capture, he would try to save her from a fate worse than death by shooting her in the head with his pistol. "It's better for a woman to be dead, Lou, than be in their hands," Cody said.[8] Then added, "Remember Lou, if the worst comes, it was because I loved you."[9] This is by no means a widely circulated story in Cody lore, but Louisa included it in her memoirs. It could show how much her husband really loved her. The tale was fraught with adventure, danger, and romance. She reports they made a run for it, and when they were approached by some men from the fort as rescuers, she fainted.

On the Buffalo Bill front, Louisa writes of being present at the buffalo shoot showdown with Bill Comstock, an eyewitness to his great victory, along with Arta. Cody also reported they made the trip. Louisa repeated Will's story of his showoff finale, from the opposite vantage point, where the people were standing as he drove the last buffalo their way. She said the fans were getting edgy when Cody delayed shooting it as the big animal ran toward them. In Mrs. Cody's version of how the day concluded a little later, she placed husband, wife, and little Arta in a hotel room, Will playing with his daughter and then asking Louisa, "Mama [one pet name for his wife], how do you like being Mrs. Buffalo Bill?" Her reply sounds too obsequious and teenaged-girl-like. "Land sakes, Will," she quoted herself years later, "whatever made you ask that question? You know I'm as happy as a bug in a rug."[10]

After a time, the family relocated to West Chester, Pennsylvania, where there were cousins. By the early 1870s, Cody had started his Wild West show and thought being closer to the hub of the theater world might be advantageous. The place, and the relatives, were not particularly to Louisa's liking. She and the kids traveled some with dad on the show circuit, and they alighted in Rochester, New York, in a new dwelling. In 1876, before his sixth birthday, Kit Cody contracted scarlet fever and died. His father was acting on the stage in Boston when he got word of the boy's illness. He rushed to Rochester, but arrived too late for his son's last breaths. Cody was emotionally devastated by Kit's death.

When Kit was born, Cody acted in near-delirious fashion, according to his wife. "A boy!" were Will's first words about this family development, Louisa said. "A boy! I want him to grow up to be a real man, mama. A boy! He'll carry on the work when his daddy leaves off. He'll be the one to see the West that his daddy wants to build." Cody carried those kinds of dreams for his son that never came to fruition. Louisa said she truly believed "it was the greatest moment in Will Cody's life. He was to meet kings, he was to be entertained by royalty all over the world, he was to become the idol of every child who could read the name of Buffalo Bill, but never shone there the light in my husband's eyes as shone that day in the little log cabin as he gently kissed our baby's cheek and repeated over and over again, 'A boy! Daddy's boy.'"[11] The joy was subsequently counterbalanced by crushing loss.

Louisa said Orra and Arta were also sick with the same ailment, but Kit was so weakened by scarlet fever she understood the threat. Cody was appearing in the theater when she sent him that telegram to hurry home. He did, but not soon enough. "I knew that death was coming," she said. "I could tell it from the fear that clutched at my heart, the fear that tore its ragged claws into my very vitals. A mother knows. A mother can see in the eyes of the child she loves when the light is dimming; her own heart echoes the failing beats of the heart that is hers also."[12]

After little Kit passed away, Cody wrote an anguished letter from Rochester to his sister Julia, who was married with the last name of Goodman. The communication was dated April 22, 1876.

> To My Oldest Sister Julia,
>
> You are the first to write to after our sad, sad loss. Julia, God has taken from us our only little boy. He was too good for this world. We loved him too dearly he could not stay. God wanted him where he could live in a better world. So he sent the Angel of death to take the treasure that he had given us five years and five months ago. And how dear he had grown to us in that time. But when he sent that hasty, cruel messenger scarlet fever, there was no hope from the start….
>
> Goodbye from Brother Will[13]

While the boy was buried in Rochester, the family uprooted again, partially because of the pain of bad memories. In 1878, Cody was able to purchase 160 acres in North Platte, Nebraska, and the surviving members of the family moved here. The cost of the property was $750. This became known as Scout's Rest Ranch, and Cody said he wanted to retire there, not predicting future events in his life and not realizing he might never really retire. Eventually, the Cody land grew to four thousand acres. In 1911, it was sold, but in 1964 came under the purview of the Nebraska Game and Parks Commission. It is now known as Buffalo Bill Ranch State Historical Park, open to tourists. But various Codys spent many years in residence at, or at least coming and going from, the place.

6. The Mrs.

By then, Bill Cody was involved in show business. He acted on the stage, a prelude to the Wild West exhibition of a kind. The tension that descended on the family from the death of little Kit did not bring Will and Louisa closer than ever, but seemed to drive a bigger wedge between them. She also very much hated his flirtation with the theater. She disliked his heavy proximity to attractive actresses. She disliked everything about that world. This was not the Bill Cody she thought she married. They were operating in separate spheres, except for his visits back to North Platte.

Once, before Louisa took the kids and removed herself to North Platte, she was in a theater building at the end of a run. Cody went to a room where the four ladies of the cast and two other men were waiting to be paid off for their work. They mingled, drinking beer. They recounted stories of the season, and then Cody kissed the women goodbye. He thought the entire scenario quite innocent. Louisa did not. Louisa heard much of the merriment from the room next door and became furious. "And we were a little jolly, laughing and talking," Cody said many years later. "When I went to leave the party, the ladies all jumped up and they said, 'Papa, we want to kiss you goodbye.' They called me papa. And I kissed them goodbye and we were all laughing and joking."[14] Louisa found nothing amusing about the circumstances and was not among those laughing and joking. She resented the affection shown. Cody could not understand that, essentially saying they were showing him respect and thanking him for being a good boss who paid them on time, knowing they were not going to see him again any time soon.

For that matter, given Cody's habits and inclinations, his travels and the tug of the West, it was not clear when the next time his wife would see him either.

7

The Persuasive Mr. Buntline

Fast-talking, creative, brimming with money-making schemes that could spring from his pen, one of the most influential figures in Buffalo Bill Cody's life was an easterner with a gleam in his eye who had a real name and a pen name. He was both Edward Zane Carroll Judson, Sr. (on his birth certificate) and Ned Buntline on his byline. Cody was sufficiently impressed by Judson/Buntline, close enough to him, and intrigued by his actions that so remarkably boosted his fame that he was planning to name his son Elmo Judson Cody until the soldiers at Fort McPherson talked him into the Kit Carson Cody alternative.

The dime novel (which sometimes cost five cents, sometimes fifteen, and often ten cents) burst upon the American scene in 1860, pretty much the first paperback books, though their size, shape, and printing also had a kinship with the modern comic book. It was cheap and easy reading to appeal to those who enjoyed fictional tales of excitement. The popular diversions sold millions of copies, riveting audiences with swashbuckling tales. Publishing companies such as Erastus and Irwin Beadle's press churned them out. The very first one produced by that company was on a western topic called *Indian Wife and White Hunter*, dated June 9, 1860. This was a wildly successful new genre.

Initially, the 100-page books, printed weekly, came in salmon-colored paper. However, after twenty-eight publications, the firm began adding striking illustrated covers that drew the eye. The Beadles' idea caught on, and they faced many competitors. The West was a very popular topic among readers, although the subject matter diversified over the years to include detective books and more.

Judson/Buntline was born in 1821 in Harpersfield, New York, and spent his childhood in Pennsylvania. When he was thirteen, he ran away to sea, became an official member of the navy, and served on several ships.

7. The Persuasive Mr. Buntline

He was a sergeant in the Union Army during the Civil War but received a dishonorable discharge for drunkenness. Always a writer, Judson/Buntline had his first story published in 1838. He founded newspapers and what were called story papers, but they went out of business. It was in 1844 when Judson became Buntline as he became more accomplished and better known in his field. The failure of his start-ups ran down his bank account, and selling off his wife's jewelry did little for matrimonial harmony.

Rather bizarrely, Buntline was an active campaigner for temperance, even though he drank liberally. He was a sought-after speaker on the topic and traveled widely to give such anti-drinking lectures. During the 1860s, James Butler Hickok, or Wild Bill, was becoming prominent in the East. It was Buntline's goal to track down Hickok and enlist his cooperation in writing a book about his exploits. When Buntline showed up in Nebraska in 1869, he was seeking Hickok.

Hickok had been embroiled in the famous gunfight with David Tutt and his people in 1865. *Harper's New Monthly Magazine* sent a correspondent named George Ward Nichols West to interview Hickok about that event after he was acquitted by the legal system, and a story appeared in print in 1867. It was the publication of this article that established Hickok's fame outside of the circles he traveled in and made him sound like an invulnerable gunfighter. Hickok gave little thought to what might be written about him based on his meetings with Nichols, but the story goes that when the men parted, Hickok pleaded with Nichols not to write anything that would embarrass his mother. "I'd like her to know what'll make her proud," he said.[1] It was never clear whether or not that was the result of Nichols's piece, but what he wrote impressed many others on the topic of Hickok's prowess with a pistol.

Buntline was on the prowl for Hickok to write a book about him, a dime novel. Instead, he hooked up with Cody. Initially, Buntline wanted Cody to tell him stories about Hickok, but after hanging out with Cody for a while, he decided Cody would make the better subject. After his experience of gaining too much unwanted fame, Hickok pretty much frowned on such a detailed telling of his life anyway. Buntline made the stop in North Platte because he heard tell of a significant cavalry fight with Indians at Summit Springs and desired to learn more about that, too, as a potential novel. At least one source indicated Buntline was the highest paid writer in America at the time, making $20,000 a year. While Buntline was well known and his work widespread, that also sounds like a "fact" he would spread about himself to both stroke his ego and enhance his reputation. He was that kind of guy. The author heard the main hero of the Summit Springs encounter was Major Frank North. He was looking for him, as a supplement to Hickok, before he crossed Hickok off his list.

When at last Buntline caught up to North, the man wanted nothing to do with him. He had no truck with writers and was not about to reveal his innermost thoughts, or his version of colorful stories to this stranger. Instead, North steered Buntline to Cody. In Cody's version of their first meeting, it was another officer who rather routinely introduced them. In Buntline's telling, North pointed him out. "If you want a man to fill that bill," North said of a paperback hero, "he's over there under the wagon."[2] Cody was trying to take a nap. Shielded from the sun, he lay under a wagon.

Cody was stationed at Fort McPherson as a scout when Buntline showed up on the frontier. In Cody's version, a major introduced the writer as a famous novelist, but also known as Colonel Judson, and in his autobiography Cody gave his first impression. Buntline "was rather stoutly built. He walked a little lame as he approached me."[3] Instead of presenting a temperance lecture that night, Buntline said, he preferred going on a scout that might lead to a fight. Buntline rode a borrowed horse and during the short excursion peppered Cody with questions. He then stayed with Cody at the fort. The visiting writer also witnessed a horse race. This incidental meeting had great consequences for Cody.

Buntline wore a blue uniform-type coat with honors and medals of some vagueness attached. At the time he happened to be married—to two different women who had taken the last name of Judson in two New York counties. When he departed the frontier to return to the metropolis, Buntline wrote stories featuring Buffalo Bill Cody. He later claimed it was his idea to label Cody Buffalo Bill. The exaggerated stories did not truly depict Cody's actions in the West, but they did promote his name. *Buffalo Bill: King of the Border Men* appeared and was a sensation, partially because it inspired other dime novels about Cody and partially because it inspired a play based on the contents. Buntline's book began as a 23-part serial in *New York Weekly*, which was owned by the famous editor James Gordon Bennett. Bennett founded the *New York Herald* and was the boss who sent reporter Henry Morton Stanley into the jungles of Africa to locate explorer David Livingstone, who had not been seen for six years. When Stanley found him, he greeted Livingstone with the sentence, "Dr. Livingstone, I presume," which became part of American lexicon.

One day, between jobs in Kansas in 1872, General Philip Sheridan approached Cody and informed him Bennett had wired $500 to the post to cover costs of a trip to New York. By then, Fred Meador's stage play based on Buntline's serial novel and Cody's exploits was being performed. Cody discovered Buntline's writing had turned him into a New York celebrity. This was quite a thing. It was akin to Edgar Rice Burroughs's Tarzan arriving in the big city from the jungle. Cody did have the foresight to make a shopping trip for more civilized clothing than buckskins when his train

7. The Persuasive Mr. Buntline

paused in Chicago. Cody, too, was more sophisticated than when he graduated from the army and had evolved into a more mature scout. Still, his comfort zone was really the frontier.

One reason why future students of Cody's life in the West had difficulty separating fact from fiction were the dime novel tales of Cody's exploits, which basically almost all sprung from imagination. Buntline and Cody both were tall tale tellers who dealt in fiction as much as fact, especially if it better suited their purposes. They were ultimate purveyors of stories that set a tone and image, though some of these matters were closer to the mark than others.

Still, this was quite an occasion. Buntline's writing had swiftly turned Cody into a mythic figure. He did not slink into New York as an unknown, but someone the wealthy and famous wanted to meet. Alerted to his coming, reporters from competing newspapers clamored for opportunities to chronicle Cody's moves. A presentation of a specially made rifle was staged with Buntline, a newspaperman himself, being in the center of the action by handing it to Cody. Others took Buffalo Bill to dinner. Bennett, who financed the whole outing, made sure his newspaper kept up with fresh stories on the scout. Cody was a highlight visitor to a ball at the Academy of Music. Cody was far from the accomplished showman he would become, but he found himself enjoying the limelight.

A turning point on the six-week trip occurred when Cody attended the theater, sitting in Buntline's box. The show was the adaptation of Buntline's book, and the story line followed Buffalo Bill's life. How peculiar it must have been for Cody, more at home on horseback than in a cushy seat, to sit quietly and observe a production that alleged to explore many highlights of his life, even though he had never lived them, and beyond that to watch an audience react to these story lines with appreciation. More startling was when audience members recognized him and spontaneously began clapping for the real-life man of the stage version, providing him "with an ovation such as actors at the more aristocratic theatres never received," the *New York Herald* said.[4] The crowd demanded he make a speech, and Cody was coerced into taking the stage. At this point in his life, Cody was like a junior high student being forced to give an oral talk in front of the class, but too nervous to deliver with authority. He said a few words and got out of there. Taking in the three-act play, and the wildly positive response from the paying customers, made Cody think the acting business was an easy one.

So Cody was susceptible to the notion advanced by Buntline that he write a play featuring Cody called *The Scouts of the Plains*. Cody figured if a fake Bill Cody could wow a crowd, the real one was bound to do better. Buntline wrote a letter outlining the idea of putting on a fresh show and told Cody to meet him in Chicago and, by the way, to bring a bunch of Indians who could play themselves in the play. Buntline promised the theater manager Jim Nixon that he had two genuine scouts and nearly two dozen Indians on the way. Buntline was a bit disappointed when Cody showed up without the supporting Indian cast and only his good friend "Texas Jack" Omohundro in tow. Nixon was more upset than Buntline. Theater goers wanted to see real Indians, he declared. He was more perturbed when he asked to see Buntline's script, and the writer informed him it had not yet been written. The scheduled opening was four days away. So Nixon canceled the deal with Buntline to put on his show. Buntline responded by asking how much it would cost to rent the theater on his own for a week. Given a price tag of $600, Buntline accepted the offer.

This left the cocky Buntline with the same issues Nixon faced—no real Indians available and no story to tell. Buntline solved the script problem by basically taking Meador's play and massaging it slightly, adding one new character. He pretended it was new stuff and bragged that he wrote this play in four hours. That was probably how long it took to more or less copy it. Then he scoured the local acting fraternity to add twenty fellows to the cast to pass as Indians if appropriately attired. Content he had conquered these obstacles, Buntline turned over scripts to Buffalo Bill and Texas Jack with orders to memorize their lines. This was wistful, optimistic thinking. The men were daunted by the number of pages set in front of them. Texas Jack asked Buffalo Bill, "How long will it take you to commit your part?" Bill replied, "About seven years, if I have good luck."[5]

Or maybe longer given what occurred when the show made its debut on December 16, 1872. The good news was the theater sold out, and that put $2,800 into the coffers. At least the rent was covered. The bad news was Cody either could not remember his opening line that kicked off the show or was too nervous to do so. After the curtain went up, he was supposed to start talking, but instead, Cody, Omohundro, and Buntline—also dressed as a buckskin-wearing frontier character, the figure added to the script—stood in silence.

It was Buntline who jump-started things with an off-the-cuff cue about a buffalo hunt Cody took with a friend named Milligan. Milligan, it so happened, was a real-life person in the audience. The jolt got Cody going, and while following no script, he told a lively story about this buffalo hunt. His stage presence carried the day rather than any words. The audience was transported to the frontier, as planned, albeit by a route that was not planned.

The show meandered along in this manner, Buntline, apparently the only one of the trio not too frightened to speak without prompting, following up his first nudge of Cody with repeated one-liners that got the scouts talking. The nature of the performance shifted to action when Buntline warned there were Indians sneaking up on them. The hired Indians attacked, and Buffalo Bill and Texas Jack fought them off. The spectators were so enthusiastic they could practically be classified as rowdy. Things went off the rails for a bit, though, when all of a sudden, apropos of nothing, Buntline launched into one of his temperance speeches.

This offbeat interjection did not enhance theatrical reviews of the play. It was more along the lines of provoking a reaction of "Huh?" It was an odd time-out from the point of the story line. With great difficulty and gymnastic ability, Buntline also introduced a love interest into the scouts' conflict with Indians. Although no one claimed the scouts could act in the slightest, the crowds were good and applauded strongly, more responding to Buffalo Bill's and Texas Jack's real-life exploits than their performances. The show concluded its run in Chicago and moved on to St. Louis.

But there was a glitch upon arrival in that city. Buntline had long before been a resident and was living there when a riot began. He was wanted on an old warrant, charged with inciting the riot. He denied doing so, but said all the witnesses who could support him were deceased. He went to court, was bailed out on $1,000 bond, and made it to the theater on time for that night's show. Some believed Buntline had trumped up the entire incident to draw publicity. But he jumped bail and fled the town. The tour reconvened in Cincinnati, Boston, and Albany, New York, in preparation for opening in New York City, the mecca of the theater world.

Scouts did not receive rave reviews from critics for the slickness of its performances, or the substance of its plot. But a writer for one paper, the *New York World*, liked what he saw from Buffalo Bill. "The Hon. William F. Cody enters into the spectacle with a curious grace and a certain characteristic charm that pleases the beholders," an astute comment for someone who had seen so little of Cody. "He is a remarkably handsome fellow on the stage, and the lithe, springy steps, the round, uncultured voice, and the utter absence of anything like stage art, won for him the goodwill of an audience which was disposed to laugh at all that was intended to be pathetic and serious."[6]

That New York stop was not the finale. The play continued for a run in Philadelphia before disbanding. Cody made $6,000 from his stage experience, which was a sight more than he made in other endeavors. Buntline claimed a profit of $200,000, but that sounded far-fetched. Business was good, though, and he planned for a renewal the next year in expanded form. Buntline had it in his head to go beyond the confining walls of standard theaters and return in outdoor venues with live horses as part of the cast. Buntline was taken aback, though, when he was informed by Buffalo Bill and Texas Jack, the genuine article scouts, if not actors, that they were cutting him out of the show and replacing him onstage with Wild Bill Hickok. Hickok had attempted one stage venture that had failed and did not want to act again. But he needed money, and Cody offered him $100 a week, so he signed up.

Undeterred, Buntline resumed touring with an altered show where he added two real-live Indians to the mix. This division did not prove out for any of the principals. Buntline ran into a series of problems, including a divorce case with one of his wives and issues with his new show on the road. There was a new love interest in the Buffalo Bill show, and Giuseppina Morlacchi, of Italian descent, and Texas Jack fell in love. Above all, Hickok learned quickly he gained not the slightest bit of enjoyment from acting. The show featuring Bill and Jack did not last. Hickok departed fairly quickly. Jack and his paramour got married.

As always, Buffalo Bill had the frontier to fall back on. Being a stage actor was an off-and-on, but flashy episode in Cody's life. When he was not acting in the 1870s, though, there was a demand for his services on the Plains.

8

Medal of Honor

What a dashing figure he was, flamboyant in his buckskin jacket, soft-cloth, malleable cowboy hat, thick mustache, signature goatee, galloping aboard a strong horse into the unknown. Buffalo Bill Cody slashed his way to glory across the barren Plains, courting and avoiding danger from fired arrows and hostile combatants who sought his scalp.

Buffalo Bill the scout was in his element, in and out of official military service, but seemingly always on call if one of the generals he knew and had impressed needed some assistance leading their men through the sage brush, rocky, dry terrain, or mountains. The threat of being killed by an Indian tribe desperate to defend its homeland against the encroachment of white civilization in the form of blue-clad cavalry troops was ever present.

Cody knew his way around. Either he had been to seldom-visited areas before on previous assignments, or he possessed a sixth sense in his ability to lead the way, but he had a talent that was nearly always in demand by the country's high command. Cody was a man who led a remarkable and diverse life, and the stories of that life are both readable and unbelievable, but at the same time many are true. From the Pony Express rides to the Wild West grand tours, there were several exploits that boosted Cody's name and fame. If the most notorious and most vividly documented of those episodes are what Cody is best remembered for, it is his scouting that laid the predicate.

There were many witnesses to Cody's achievements in the wilderness, in battles, and of the manner in which he performed his duties, though it is also likely some exaggeration attended even the most prominent among them. But when it came to guiding and scouting, Cody really was first-rate. In the words of twenty-first century Cody scholar Dr. Jeremy Johnston, who is the curator of the Buffalo Bill Museum at the Buffalo Bill Center of the West in Cody, Wyoming, "He was the real deal. He really did stand out as a scout." Though maybe not in the beginning of his Plains adventures when he was so young, such as in 1864 when he was attached to his Kansas regiment at eighteen. "He claimed he was a scout, but that might have been pushing it."[1]

There is much to support the fact that Cody was a good shot and a good rider, Johnston said, whether it be outrunning pursuers who sought his scalp or hunting buffalo. If only half the scrapes Cody got himself into where he had to slip away from those chasing him and dodge bullets and arrows while fighting back, are true, his résumé was pretty fancy. And there is the matter of the generals who kept coming back to Cody when they needed someone to feed the troops and lead them on risky errands.

The Medal of Honor is the highest military honor the United States can bestow on its soldiers and representatives in war. The individual who receives such recognition has done something very special to distinguish himself in battle and usually something unselfish. Many of the recipients died in the performance of the act that gained them a nomination for the award. In the course of the average person's life, receiving the Medal of Honor would be viewed as the greatest honor and accomplishment of his life. Not so in Cody's case where he was known for many other things; for him, being presented the Medal of Honor was just one of a list of superlatives attached to his name.

The Medal of Honor was created in 1861 to acknowledge heroism and gallantry afield. While mere mention of the Medal of Honor in the context of someone's career now earns automatic respect and admiration, in Cody's era, the medal was new and may not have carried the same cache to others right away. Physically, the medal is only a couple of inches long, distinguished by a red, white, and blue ribbon in the form of a flag attached to golden pieces above and below. The bottom portion features an eagle and a star.

It was a scouting mission, which was actually more than that, that led to Cody's nomination for a Medal of Honor. On April 26, 1872, Cody was part of a patrol out of Fort McPherson. The lead-up to the situation was an Indian attack on McPherson Station, which was about five miles from the fort. A few men were killed and horses stolen. The goal was to punish the Indians and reacquire the horses.

Cody was the lead scout seeking the Indians' trail. His friend "Texas Jack" Omohundro was with him. Cody said while he was able to pick up the trail, it was tricky to follow because the Indians put great effort into covering their tracks. This pursuit went on for two days. At that point, the commanding officer detached six men to follow Cody and continue the search. After this split, Cody and the others found the Indians camped just a mile away. This was no great raiding party, but a small number of Indians.

8. Medal of Honor

Buffalo Bill picked up the narrative in his autobiography: "I determined to charge upon them with my six men rather than return to the command because I feared they would see us as we went back and then they would get away from us entirely. I asked the men if they were willing to attempt and they replied that they would follow me wherever I would lead them. That was the kind of spirit that pleased me."[2]

From there the approach was a quiet stalk with the aim of taking the camped Indians by surprise. "I finally gave the signal to charge and we dashed into the little camp with a yell. Five Indians sprang out of a willow teepee and greeted us with a volley, and we returned the fire. We nearly ran over the Indians who were endeavoring to reach their horses on the opposite side of the creek. Just as one was jumping the narrow stream a bullet from my old 'Lucretia' [Lucretia Borgia, his favorite hunting rifle] overtook him. He never reached the other bank, but dropped dead in the water."[3]

The attack roused the Indians guarding the horses, and Cody said the count of warriors was thirteen, down to eleven after the initial charge. Still seeking to press the advantage, Cody said he urged his strong horse, Buckskin Joe, onward. This horse had a good vertical leap so he jumped the obstacle of the stream. Cody thought he was leading a group charge, but the others could not convince their horses across the water, so he was alone facing the incoming Indians.

Cody was in a precarious position. He yelled to a sergeant for the men to dismount and follow him on foot. However, he was in a pincer, two Indians coming at him, exchanging gunfire at short range. Cody shot one of them, but also realized he was wounded. "I felt blood trickling down my forehead," he said, "and hastily running my hand through my hair I discovered that I had received a scalp wound."[4] The Indian who shot him, though, turned aside when he saw his companion fall.

Now backed by the men on foot, Cody galloped his horse after the Indian who wounded him, chased him down, and shot him. The rest of the cavalry company was near enough to hear the shooting and ultimately rode in as reinforcements, Cody saying the Indians scattered after losing six braves. The official report, though, says there were three Indians killed. The troops lost one man, and Cody was the only other one wounded. He said he later noticed Buckskin Joe had also suffered a wound.

For Cody's actions, patrol leader Captain Charles Meinhold recommended Cody for the Medal of Honor. He wrote, "Mr. Cody had guided Sgt. Foley's party with such skill that he approached the Indian camp within fifty yards before he was noticed. Mr. William Cody's reputation for bravery and skill as a guide is so well-established that I need not say anything else but that he acted in his usual manner."[5]

Cody was widely praised by the generals he served, even though he was not officially a solider during any of this period. He was a soldier during the Civil War, but never again, only attached to various commands as a scout. Scouts took orders, but they were not like enlisted men. Beyond the agreements he signed to lead at different times, Cody could come and go as he pleased, go visit his family, and travel to New York to see a show and be feted. The on-the-scene cavalry commander submitted the names of Cody and three other men as nominees for the Medal of Honor. General Philip Sheridan and the War Department received the paperwork and approved it. Cody, who never bragged about receiving it, was awarded the Medal of Honor in May of 1872, about a month after the battle where he distinguished himself. In the context of the times he might as well have been a soldier when in the field, eating the same food, facing the same hardships, experiencing the same dangers. But there was no such true rank as scout and eventually, many years later, that came back to haunt Cody's family.

The saga of winning a Medal of Honor generally peaks on the battlefield with the driving drama and pathos of the moment paramount. Then the nomination process begins, devolving into Washington paperwork. The recommendation may be rejected, or it may be accepted. Cody's nomination was swiftly accepted and the medal awarded. But that was not the end of the story. As with most things Cody, a simple conclusion to an event proved more elusive as time went by.

In 1917, very soon after Buffalo Bill died, there was a review of all past Medal of Honor awards. As the cases were revisited, a panel revoked 911 of the medals, including Cody's. He was one of five scouts who had been deemed worthy and celebrated with this most prestigious honor. The basic reasoning for the withdrawal of the medal was that it was designed for those serving in the military, and as a scout Cody, despite his duties, was not an official member of the military. Cody relatives were outraged, protested, and appealed. That began a quest to reinstate the medal that lasted more than seventy years.

Meanwhile, it was not very easy for the military to actually confiscate or take back the medals themselves. The recipients of the revoked medals were simply asked not to display them. The whereabouts of Cody's medal was an issue for some time. At one point, Cody, apparently in a fit of spontaneity while visiting his relatives in West Chester, Pennsylvania, gave the medal to them as a gift. This may seem shocking to many given the revered nature of this award, but it dovetailed precisely with his character as someone who routinely gave family members belongings that they seemed to appreciate more than he did. Cody did not save memorabilia. Likewise, it comes as a surprise when the championship rings

8. Medal of Honor

and trophies earned by modern-day sports figures turn up in auctions, or for sale on eBay. Such dispatching of valuable personal possessions being exchanged for money did not exist in Cody's day. In an era long before Babe Ruth's uniform jersey, Ty Cobb's dentures, or some other superstar athlete's belt sold for significant money, it is also unlikely that for a second Cody thought his prizes would have great monetary value. "He gave away things left and right," said Lynn Houze, a former assistant curator at the Cody Buffalo Bill Museum.[6]

For a long time Cody's Medal of Honor apparently was in the hands of the Pennsylvania branch of the family. It was only by accident the Buffalo Bill Center of the West discovered it and acquired it. Paul Fees, the Buffalo Bill Museum curator at the time, stumbled upon an advertisement listing Buffalo Bill's Medal of Honor being for sale. Fees brokered a deal to obtain it, and the medal has been in the museum's hands since 1983. Fees said museum policy prevents revealing how much it pays for any object added to the collection. At times the medal has been displayed in a glass case at the museum.

That accounts for the original medal. Possibly. But on a rare occasion, at least a rare known occasion, Cody came to regret his casual parting with the medal. Between 1895 and 1903, Nelson Miles, one of Cody's old

As curator of the Buffalo Bill Museum in Cody, Wyoming, Paul Fees obtained the Medal of Honor that once belonged to William F. Cody but was given to family members (photograph by the author).

friends from his scouting days, was the general of the army. Cody wrote a letter to Miles explaining what he had done and asked for a duplicate Medal of Honor. This request was obliged.

That explains why the Buffalo Bill Museum and Grave in Golden, Colorado, can also display the genuine Buffalo Bill Medal of Honor in its own glass case. In other words, that made for two real Buffalo Bill Medals of Honor. The one in Golden was donated by Johnny Baker, a long-time sharpshooting star in the Wild West exhibitions. Although not officially adopted, Cody and Baker had a father–son relationship. They were extraordinarily close, and Baker was the surrogate grown son Cody never had because Kit Carson Cody died in childhood. Baker had a vast Cody memorabilia collection, and his materials were the foundation of the Golden museum's operation. Officials at the Colorado museum prefer to believe the one in their collection, given over by Baker, is the true medal originally presented to Cody, not a substitute. As for Fees's contention the medal bounced from Cody to the Pennsylvania relatives, former Golden museum director Steve Friesen said, "That's his theory. I find that's a little dubious."[7]

The much larger Cody museum in Wyoming dwarfs the Cody museum in Colorado in size. While there is generally a good working relationship between the two institutions, at times dialogue can get a bit frosty over claims. Friesen, as is to be expected, was a staunch defender of the underdog operation. Houze, the former curator in the Cody museum, did not give much credence to his protests. "Steve is like the little brother who keeps pestering you, because this is the more well-known museum."[8]

There's more. Cody descendants never gave up in their attempts to get recognition of his Medal of Honor status restored. A new attempt was ramped up in the 1980s after the physical Medal of Honor came into the collection of the Buffalo Bill Center of the West from Pennsylvania. Adopting a new tactic, Fees wrote the appeal and directed it to Wyoming's representatives in the U.S. Senate, Malcolm Wallop and Alan Simpson. Simpson is a member of a distinguished multigenerational Wyoming family with tentacles that include former stays in the governor's mansion, U.S. Senate, state legislature, and courthouses. In 1989, those efforts paid off. William F. Cody's stature on the Medal of Honor list was restored by the Army Board for Correction of Military Records. That board reversed the 1917 ruling and reinstated the honor for not only Cody, but the other four scouts. Speaking for the family, Cody's grandson Fred Garlow Cody, then 76 years old, expressed gratification and said family members always had faith the medal would one day be restored.

True West magazine, the most thorough and creative periodical of the current day when it comes to analyzing stories of the Old West, wrote a piece in 2014 discussing Cody and the Medal of Honor. This included the restoration adventure, and the story said the Cody family was given a replica of the original. That would have made for three medals. That is unclear, though. Neither Cody businessman Bill Garlow, Fred's son, who inherited his father's family memorabilia, nor Senator Al Simpson recall that being the case. "I would doubt it," Bill Garlow said. "I have some of my dad's stuff and it would be there."[9] Simpson recalled the reinstated medal was only a declaration on paper and was not physically reproduced.

However, the announcement of Cody regaining recognition for his medal seventy-two years after it was revoked made things sound quite different. The following was spelled out on U.S. Army letterhead, dated July 6, 1989: "The Army Board for Correction of Military Records, after extensive review of the circumstances which caused the forfeit of the award of the Medal of Honor in the case of William F. Cody, has directed that the award be restored."[10] The letter, addressed to Senator Simpson and signed by Charles E. Dominy, Major General, U.S. Army, goes on to say, "All Department of the Army records will be corrected. Additionally, the Department of the Army will issue to Mr. William G. Cody, his grandson, the Medal of Honor on behalf of his late grandfather."[11] This was Bill Garlow Cody, but he had passed away by the time of the restoration of the medal. No third medal has surfaced yet.

While the Medal of Honor was the most notable battlefield recognition Cody received from his time in the field by the U.S. Army, it was not necessarily the most celebrated of his actions in Indian fighting lore to the public. The Fort McPherson campaign of 1869 that included Fifth Cavalry battles against a group of Cheyenne called Dog Soldiers under Chief Tall Bull was much more famous. Tall Bull's band had been killing settlers along the Solomon River and also kidnapped two women. General Eugene Carr organized the attempt to rescue them.

Conflict began on June 15 when the troops were resting and watering mules. The Indians made a run at stealing them. One guard stumbled into camp with an arrow in him. Cody, who was on a horse instead of a mule, began the chase, though he was slower getting started than a group of Pawnee Indians working with the cavalry. The mules were spread out all over the landscape and a roundup commenced covering fifteen miles. Cody took note of one of the Pawnees' horses and made a trade for him. It was Buckskin Joe, and the beginning of a beautiful relationship. There were a series of skirmishes between the troops and the Indians spread over a few weeks. On July 8, an abandoned Cheyenne camp led the military to follow a trail north. Carr pushed the men hard, and there were indications they were closing in as they passed two more used camps.

At the head of about 450 men, including Pawnee allies and scouts, Carr drove his outfit, and on July 11, the first sighting of a couple of horsemen put them within striking distance of a village where the body of Tall Bull's warriors were located. There was a three-way split in the trail between the parties approaching the South Platte River, but it was Cody, according to Carr and another of his key officers, who provided the intelligence allowing the men to choose the proper route to initiate an attack. This was Cody's account: "Acting on my suggestion, the general made a circuit to the north, believing that if the Indians had their scouts out they would naturally be watching in the direction whence they had come." Carr said, "Cody's idea was to get around, beyond, and between them and the river." Captain George F. Price, the troop's historian, said, Cody "guided the Fifth Cavalry to a position whence the regiment was enabled to charge the enemy and win a brilliant victory."[12]

That victory began with a bugle sounding a charge and the troops pulling out pistols as they rampaged at the surprised Indians who had mere seconds of warning that the enemy was upon them. The cavalry easily overpowered the unsuspecting group, killing fifty-two men, capturing seventeen women and children and eighty-five lodges, and commandeering 274 horses and 144 mules. One of the two women who had been held hostage was rescued. The other was killed in the battle, it was said by an Indian woman who smashed in her head with a tomahawk, possibly one of Tall Bull's wives. Tall Bull was killed on the scene, and this ended the threat of the Dog Soldiers. While not specifically recorded in official documents, the participating soldiers said it was Cody who shot Tall Bull. Although most of this battle is precisely recorded by military authorities, there was a lone dissenter from official versions. Luther North, a scout who was less renowned than his brother Frank, kept writing accounts of the battle diminishing Cody's role and exalting his brother's, alleging Frank is the one who killed Tall Bull. Although it seemed Cody and Frank North had no grudges against one another, and Frank rode for the Wild West exhibitions, Luther North kept up this harassment over decades, making it very clear he despised Cody.

In the cavalry version of what happened to Tall Bull, he was observed holding a baby daughter, handing it off to his wife, and then telling her to flee with one of the prisoner women so she might be able to trade her to save her own life. It was said Tall Bull sent his wife away and killed his own horse. His wife said she saw him killed. Cody offered a slightly more elaborate version. He said the battle was nearing an end and he noticed a horse he might fancy once things were decided. Then he noticed the Indian atop it was giving orders and this last band was retreating and fighting. "I noticed that the Indian, as he rode along the skirmish line, passed the head of a ravine not far distant, and it occurred to me that if I could dismount and creep into the ravine, I could, as he passed there, easily drop him from his horse without hitting his horse."[13]

Cody said he acted out his thought, achieved a good angle, and shot at the rider from thirty yards, killing him. The horse, he said, ran toward the army lines and was secured by another soldier. A lieutenant ran to the downed Indian and grabbed his war bonnet while another soldier turned the horse over to Cody. After climbing aboard, Cody rode the horse to the spot where the surviving Indian women and children were encircled. One woman began to cry at the sight of him on the horse, saying it was her husband Tall Bull's favorite. Cody let her know her husband was dead and no longer had a need for a horse. Later, in a book that Cody's name appeared on, whether he wrote it or simply advised, an account appeared that had him saying he shot Tall Bull at a range of four hundred yards. However, General Carr's version of his adversary's defeat and demise tracks Cody's as to who was the shooter of Tall Blue, the prize of the horse, and the encounter with Tall Bull's wife.

These clarifications and claims were of some value because in later years, after he started his Wild West exhibition, one perennial skit enacted was the Battle of Summit Springs. In that reenactment, both the kidnapped women survived, and it can best be described as historical fiction. Also repeated constantly in the Wild West exhibitions is a role of Cody as conqueror in taking a step to avenge the death of General George Armstrong Custer at the Battle of the Little Bighorn.

The Seventh Cavalry, led by Custer, was overwhelmed by Sioux Indians in Montana during the summer of 1876. Viewed as virtually invincible, Custer's death stunned the nation. With two brothers by his side and more than two hundred men, Custer and those who followed him were massacred, even as other columns of the group were elsewhere, either in the midst of their own sieges or too far away to save the day and prevent the definitive cavalry defeat of the Plains Indian Wars.

Buffalo Bill was in as much disbelief as anyone that such a debacle had unfolded and that Custer was finished. Given that the men had known one another fairly well, had shared hunting adventures, and respected one another's abilities, Cody took the news personally. There was no bringing back Custer and his men, but there would be chances to avenge them in battles to come.

General George Crook was in command of the cavalry in Wyoming as fighting grew fiercer in the Indian Wars and the government in Washington, DC, revved up to once and for all eliminate the threat that Native Americans posed to its own idea of civilization and to the flood of men, women, and children moving West to settle the land. Cody was on a theatrical tour when he received a telegram that the same troops which he had traveled with against Tall Bull could use him again. "Your old position open to you," the message read. "Join us here."[14] "Here" was Cheyenne, Wyoming. Crook and other soldiers were in the field, and Cody, who accepted the offer, could not quite parachute in to join them directly. Cody took a train to Cheyenne to meet up with General Carr. It was then-Lieutenant Charles King, who would be an eyewitness on Cody's behalf about what was to come, who met him.

A private in the cavalry took notes about Cody's arrival back on the frontier. "At noon on the 9th, W.F. (Buffalo Bill) Cody joined the command as scout and guide," he wrote. "There is very little change in his appearance since I last saw him in '69, except that he looks a little worn, probably caused by his vocation in the East not agreeing with him."[15]

Cody signed up on June 11 and joined a contingent sent to Fort Laramie the next day where there was a rendezvous with General Sheridan. The riders moved out to Red Cloud Agency next. Cody investigated ahead and was joined by a small group of men, of whom King was one, though not in command. A long pursuit followed to the Cheyenne River before Indians were seen. Although only a few shots were fired, the Cheyenne were pressured into racing off and leaving behind critical supplies. It was in the field, twelve days after the battle occurred, where these soldiers learned Custer had been wiped out.

It was on the morning of July 7, King said, as a group was saddling up "came the dread and dire news: Custer—'The Long Haired'—the daring and dashing leader, with five of his favorite companies, had been swept from the face of the earth. Perhaps no man felt it more than Cody, who had ridden with Custer on many a run for buffalo. Perhaps no man more eagerly welcomed the news that now the regiment would be recalled to Fort Laramie to fit out with supplies."[16]

While most of the soldiers were likely still unaware thousands of Indians had participated at the Battle of the Little Bighorn, the immediate concern was that a thousand Cheyenne appeared on the verge of fleeing from Red Cloud Agency. They were supposed to prevent that from happening. When the Indians moved out, the plan was to get ahead of them, prevent them from dispersing on the Plains, and head them back to Red Cloud.

By now it was July 17, and the Cheyenne had advanced twenty-eight miles away from Red Cloud. The cavalry planned this expedition as if it was heading off and turning a buffalo herd. Cody brought word that the Indians were breaking from this camp and planning to move on, farther away. There was considerable activity in the vicinity. The major encampment of cavalry was in one spot. The large group of Indians was only a few

8. *Medal of Honor*

miles distant. A wagon train guarded by soldiers inside and out of sight was approaching, led by three soldiers who were supposed to connect to the larger body first. There were thirty to forty Indians, first seen by Cody, separating from the main group of Cheyenne, who seemed to be eyeing the three couriers. Finally, about seven Indians were on the move not far away, either. It was an explosive situation.

Cody, two scouts, and a half-dozen other riders set out on reconnaissance. Lt. King was watching through binoculars from a ridge. "As the stars began to pale in the eastern sky and a faint, gray light to steal over the landscape, the outlying sentries began peering over the banks and ridges behind which they were crouching." The southeast—the direction from which the hostiles should come—was the important front.[17]

The area where conflict would be centered was called either Hat Creek or War Bonnet Creek, the latter being a more colorful choice. One of Cody's biographers said the official count of his battles with Indians numbered fourteen with the Fifth Cavalry, and this was probably the most memorable, again because it received more publicity than almost any other of his scouting field actions. It was King and a corporal who first saw the approach of distant Indians and notified the higher ranking officers and Cody, who was with them. The main body of cavalry was shielded from the Indians' view, secreted in some rocks, but ready to ride. Cody and his group set out to intercept the band of Indians apparently hoping to prey on the trio of wagon train couriers.

Cody's group and the Indian group charged full blast at one another. "They met by accident and fired the moment they faced each other," said Chris Madsen, another soldier on the scene.[18] Buffalo Bill fired and shot the leading Indian through the leg, a bullet that also penetrated his horse. "The Indian's bullet went wild. Cody's horse stepped into a prairie dog hole and stumbled, but was up in a moment. Cody jumped clear of his mount."[19]

The Indian tumbled to the ground as Cody approached. Madsen said each man shot at one another once more. He said Cody's second blast went through the Indian's head and killed him. A more dramatic version says the Indian had lost his gun in the fall and whipped out a tomahawk and that briefly, he and Cody fought hand-to-hand in close proximity, as if their wrestling match was winner-take-all for both sides. Not even Cody tells such a wild story, going with the explanation that has the two men shooting back and forth at each other. Cody killed the man and then scalped him; of that, Madsen said, "there is no doubt about it."[20] Nor has there ever been any denial.

Throughout this combat, the identity of the Indian was unknown to Cody, although King said he was sure at least some of the Cheyenne braves recognized Buffalo Bill. Initially, this Indian was referred to as Yellow Hand, but later translations indicated his name was Yellow Hair. Early on, Cody sent a letter to his wife Louisa summarizing the confrontation like this: "We have had a fight. I killed Yellow Hand, a Cheyenne chief in a single-handed fight. You will no doubt hear of it through the papers." Cody said that the scalp he took was going to be sent to a friend who owned a store in Rochester, New York. "I have only one scalp I can call my own, that fellow I fought single-handed in sight of our command and the cheers that went up when he fell was deafening."[21]

Louisa Cody had her own take on the scalp business, including where it was sent:

> There was a knock on the door, and I answered it, my heart pounding strangely. But it was only the expressman, with a small, square box. I looked at the label. All that it told me was that one of its shipping points was Fort McPherson and that the consignor was William Frederick Cody. But that was enough. It told me that Will was still alive and apparently safe. Hurriedly, I sought the hatchet and pried open the lid of the box. A terrific odor caught my nostrils. I reeled slightly, then reached for the contents. Then I fainted. For I had brought from the box the raw, red scalp of an Indian![22]

What a romantic gift! Weeks passed before Louisa saw Will again. She was, of course, glad to see him freshly safe from warfare, but then refocused her anger over the scalp box. "Will Cody! What on earth did you send me that scalp for? Aren't you ashamed of yourself? It nearly scared me to death."[23]

Hubby told her he thought she would like it. Cody engaged in many conflicts with Indians, and sometimes he took lives. To take a scalp was very uncharacteristic, and it is the only known time he did so. This can be attributed to his fury over the death of Custer. But even when he calmed down he did not act ashamed of this behavior in the heat of battle either.

Cody may or may not have yelled, "First scalp for Custer!" after he took Yellow Hair's hair, though he said that he did. Also, in later years, when he included this incident as a skit in his Wild West exhibition, it was definitely portrayed as revenge for the Little Bighorn result. When he wrote his autobiography there was an excellent chance that Cody's relaying of his confrontation with Yellow Hair-Yellow Hand was spruced up a bit.

"One of the Indians, who was handsomely decorated with all the ornaments usually worn by a war chief when engaged in a fight, sang out to me in his own tongue, 'I know you, Pahaska. If you want to fight, come ahead and fight me.'" Cody said, "I decided to accept the challenge." Then their shootout commenced. In this telling by Cody, his shot did not strike Yellow Hair in the head when the chief missed, "while mine struck him in

8. Medal of Honor

the breast. He reeled and fell, but before he had fairly touched the ground, I was upon him knife in hand, and had driven the keen-edged weapon to its hilt in his heart. Jerking his war bonnet off, I scientifically scalped him in about five seconds." Both Yellow Hair's men and Cody's realized that he was vulnerable in the middle of a sort of no-man's land and both sides rushed toward him. The cavalry got there first, and Cody said he "swung the Indian chieftain's top-knot in the air and shouted, 'The first scalp for Custer.'"[24]

Cody said he did not learn the name of the Indian he battled until the troop returned to Red Cloud Agency. While there, he said, he was also told Yellow Hair was a son of Cut Nose, a prominent Cheyenne chief. Word got around it was Buffalo Bill, or Pahaska, who had finished off Yellow Hair, and one day Cody said he received a message from Cut Nose offering a deal. He promised Buffalo Bill four mules if he returned Yellow Hair's guns, war bonnet, and other items he took from the body. The scalp did not seem to be mentioned. At least Cody did not say so. Cody double-talked the chief, saying "it would give me great pleasure to accommodate him, but I could not do it at this time."[25]

It was unclear exactly what Buffalo Bill may have meant by that. He could if he had wanted to, but was probably not in such a generous mood. His state of mind was probably somewhat euphoric following this one-on-one showdown. It was reported widely by newspapers at the time. Also, Cody's mindset was his action reflected a bit of vengeance on Custer's behalf. It is unlikely Buffalo Bill ever returned any of Yellow Hair's possessions to his father, and he most assuredly never returned the scalp.

Buffalo Bill Cody's fame kept spreading. The nickname alone won him attention. Stories with quotes from generals praising his scouting talents popped up. The dime novels ran amok, even if they spread untruths. And spectacular battlefield reports, like this meet-up with Yellow Hair, all added to Cody's luster and to his growing stature as an American icon, a man's man who stood up to danger and stared it down. Name recognition alone would have made William F. Cody a formidable candidate for office—somewhere, at some level. Indeed, he was approached in some clandestine discussions apparently, to give politics a try. In her viewpoint, as explained in her book years later, Cody's sister Helen Wetmore said there indeed was some talk about the topic, but her brother had no interest. In a comment she attributes to him, which could stand on its own today just as well for someone with the same opinion, she wrote, "No. Politics are too deep for me. I think I can hold my own in any fair and no foul fight. But politics seems to me all foul and no fair. I thank you, my friends, but I must decline to set out on this trail, which I know has more cactus burrs to the square inch than any I ever followed on the Plains."[26]

The last of the great scouts, as Wetmore called Buffalo Bill, could not imagine that the level of his fame was at a low ebb compared to what awaited in the near future. He dabbled in show business as an actor in plays, the character he always played being himself. Soon, Buffalo Bill Cody's horizons would expand so grandly that his life no longer knew any borders and his name was on the lips of the young and old all over the world. In a way, he was about to invent a new kind of show business.

9

Rodeo and Wild West Beginnings

The little pins tell a phenomenal story. Maps of the United States and Europe hang on a wall in the Buffalo Bill Center of the West, the Cody, Wyoming, museum founded to honor Buffalo Bill Cody a century ago. In one corner of the Buffalo Bill Museum, the section of the center devoted to Cody himself, a visitor can view a testimonial to the wide reach of the Wild West extravaganza that Buffalo Bill created. The sharp pins stick in the wall, pinpointing every community where Buffalo Bill and his traveling exhibition—he refused to call it a show—paused to entertain, in this country and overseas, for thirty years. The comprehensive look at the miles traveled, the places visited, courtesy of railroads and ships since there was no air travel yet, is staggering.

While spreading the word of the West as it was fading out, Cody was reenacting its realities and reinventing its myths. He established for all time through his troupe's performances what people who came along too late would come to believe about the Old West, not only in his own country, but across the world. There was a reason it was said William F. Cody was the most famous man in the world in his own lifetime. It was because, as Johnny Cash once melodically stated, "I've been everywhere, man." He was. He did. If Cody had a sticker attached to his suitcase for every community he visited, he would not have been able to lift his suitcase. Its original color would have been completely obscured.

Starting with the United States, the Wild West exhibition went on to perform in Canada, Austria, Belgium, Croatia, England, France, Germany, Hungary, Italy, Luxembourg, Scotland, Spain, and Wales. Notwithstanding his fine relationship with the House of Romanov through Grand Duke Alexis, the exhibition did not make it to Russia. The Wild West exhibition stayed around long enough to perform in forty-eight states, missing out only on Alaska and Hawaii, which did not gain statehood until decades after Buffalo Bill's and his Wild West exhibition's demise.

The Buffalo Bill Museum and Grave in Golden, Colorado, compiled a list of every city and town where the Wild West exhibition showed itself with the dates, too. Wyoming, where Cody helped found Cody, did not become a state until 1890, but the Wild West exhibition appeared in Cheyenne and Laramie years earlier. Over the ensuing years, the Wild West exhibition also came to Evanston, Rawlins, Rock Springs, and Sheridan, as well as making return engagements in Cheyenne and Laramie. Some might find it ironic that the Wild West exhibition never played in Cody, Wyoming, which was founded in 1896. However, Cody spent plenty of time in the town and even conducted auditions for the Wild West exhibition in what would today be considered the middle of town. Perhaps he felt the locals were too familiar with him, seeing him all the time, and would not pay out for a show he headlined.

Buffalo Bill prepped for the Wild West exhibition with his work in the theater and his touring with stage productions. The positive reaction of crowds planted the seed of the idea that blossomed into the Wild West exhibition. He spun the idea in his head over and over and discussed it frequently with his friend John Burke, who was a natural promoter. Cody thought big, not only with the scope of the show, but also in its presentation. He did not want to be confined by walls, but rather to use horses, animals, and wagons in large dirt arenas, stadiums compared to theaters.

To Cody's surprise, the play *Scouts of the Plains* could not alone sate a public thirst for adventures of the Old West. Everywhere he looked, producers were staging the show (without him or any financial reward accruing to him) and creating other melodramas with similar subject matter. In the universe of supply and demand, Cody could not fulfill the demand the way he was operating. Burke, Cody, Ned Buntline, Wild Bill Hickok, and even circus impresario P.T. Barnum each harbored vague visions of ways to harness this latent, near-bursting enthusiasm for the Old West in broad fashion and make big bucks. By 1876, when the Seventh Cavalry was massacred, ending the meteoric rise of General George Armstrong Custer, and Buffalo exacted his revenge, he had another play circulating named *Life on the Border*. In the lead-up to the release of his autobiography in 1879, other works, with Cody's name adorning the cover, edged their way onto bookshelves. Between dime novels and Cody's casual reporting of exaggerated facts, the stuff of fiction and fact became forever blurred. To one publisher, Cody even commented, "I am sorry to have to lie so outrageously in this yarn. My hero has killed more Indians on one war trail than I have killed in all my life. But I understand this is what is expected of border tales."[1]

9. Rodeo and Wild West Beginnings

As his idea was still forming, Buffalo Bill made the most of his stage appearances. For a time he hooked up with Captain Jack Crawford, who was not as famous as friend Wild Bill Hickock, but who was a colorful and accomplished scout himself. Crawford also wrote successful plays and short stories when he was not riding on the frontier. Cody named his theater enterprise the Buffalo Bill Combination. In 1876, Crawford became one of the leading men in the cast—aside from Cody, of course. Just as Cody was, Crawford was the genuine article in the West, a noteworthy scout who had the same kind of hair-raising adventures as Buffalo Bill. He is not as well remembered today because he did not have the same longevity in the show business limelight. Once a hard drinker, Crawford gave up booze and signed a temperance pledge. He cajoled Cody into signing it, as well, but Cody was off the wagon after about four months.

During one performance, in which Crawford was playing Yellow Hair in the show, Cody accidentally shot him in the groin area. Crawford needed bed rest for two weeks and required crutches afterward to get around. This was the end of the season, and the show disbanded. Cody planned to resume with a new tour a few months later, but when he offered Crawford a part, he declined. Cody returned to Nebraska, where he established a ranch about sixty-five miles from North Platte. Later, Crawford teased Cody. He wrote to say Cody never would have been able

Fort Cody is a gift shop in North Platte, Nebraska, with a Buffalo Bill Cody theme (photograph by the author).

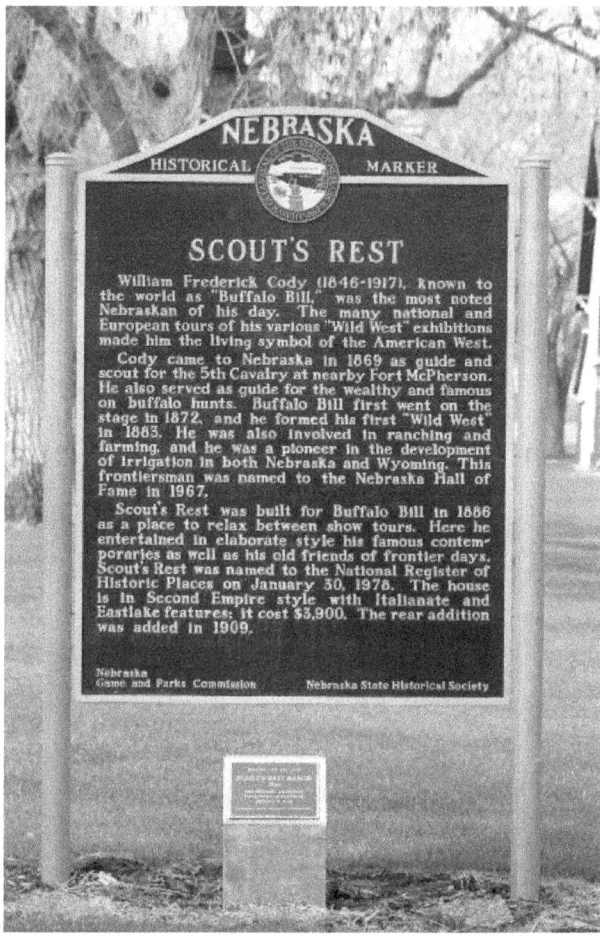

A plaque stands at Scout's Rest Ranch in North Platte, Nebraska, where Buffalo Bill Cody lived for years and where he started his Wild West exhibition (photograph by the author).

to afford the set-up cost of $22,000 if Crawford had not kept him from drinking those four months. Crawford said he served the intervener role "as a she bear would watch her first cub."[2]

It was several years between the germination of the Wild West idea and it coming to fruition. Buffalo Bill did not love performing on the stage, especially since none of these plays would have been future Tony Award nominees, but were rather mundane, inexpensive productions for entertainment of the masses who gobbled up anything to do with Buffalo Bill, cowboys, and Indians. At one point, when Cody's sister Helen caught up to him and saw a show in Leavenworth, Kansas, he did not invite her cri-

9. Rodeo and Wild West Beginnings

A sign welcomes visitors to Buffalo Bill Cody's old ranch in Nebraska (photograph by the author).

tique, but sealed her lips before she could say anything. "Oh, Nellie, don't say anything about it," Will told her. "If heaven will forgive me this foolishness, I promise to quit it forever as soon as this season is over."[3] Actually, the seasons dragged on into the early 1880s with performances of *White Beaver* and *Prairie Waif*. Cody might have found his roles stultifying, but audiences showered him with applause and did not mind that the plots were simple and the writing quality minimal.

Meanwhile, he did pine for the time when he could burst beyond those confining walls and really give the Old West its due with a bang. "Take the prairies and the Injuns' and everything else right to 'em," Cody told Burke. "That's the idea. There ain't room on a stage to do anything worthwhile. But there would be on a big lot where we could have horses and buffalo and the old Deadwood coach and everything! That'd be something they'd never seen before. That'd be showing them the West!"[4]

John Burke went by Arizona John Burke or Major John M. Burke, each of them being a curious choice since he was not from Arizona and was never a military officer. He and Cody first met in 1866 in Montana where Cody was a scout. Burke worked as his personal assistant. In 1877, Burke joined up with Texas Jack Omohundro on a stage venture, but he was Cody's sounding board as the born publicist kicked around Wild West ideas with him. When Cody was ready to take a flyer on the plan, Burke was by his side. Burke was ahead of his time as a pitch man, hanging out with newspaper reporters, developing press kits for their use, employing billboard-type advertising for the Wild West exhibition, and promoting the events and Buffalo Bill in new towns around the clock. While performing the job of a public relations man, Burke used the title of general manager of the Wild West exhibition.

Just as the Wild West exhibition was about to take off, Cody and Louisa had a major falling out over the Nebraska property. Cody made huge money for the time, estimated at $100,000 over a five-year period. But he was profligate, drinking much of it away when he was not refraining, and giving money to his sisters, their families, and others. He also raised money for his shows by mortgaging property. The Codys had testy relations. There was Scout's Rest Ranch and another house in town. Cody discovered Louisa took money he sent her for living expenses and invested it in other property—in her name. Besides the shakiness of their relationship, she had to worry if Cody might squander all they had. Cody wanted her to mortgage property and give the money to him for his fundraising, but Louisa said no. They had serious arguments over this. In September of 1883, Cody wrote a letter to his sister Julia which read, "Well, I have got out my petition for a divorce with that woman. She has tried to ruin me financially this summer. I could tell you lots of funny

Now a historical site, this was Buffalo Bill Cody's ranch home in North Platte, Nebraska (photograph by the author).

9. Rodeo and Wild West Beginnings

things how she has tried to put up the horse ranch and buy more property and get the deeds in her name."[5] There was no divorce at that time, but the glow had definitely worn off the marriage. Buffalo Bill and Louisa were almost constantly apart anyway due to his adventures, but the Wild West exhibition kept him away from home for longer periods from greater distances.

Burke was an essential member of the team with the Wild West exhibition from the very beginning. So was Nate Salsbury. Salsbury was a marketing man. He could look at an inanimate object and bring it to life and make people want to buy it. During the early part of 1882, Cody was doing his thing at the Grand Opera House in Brooklyn while Salsbury was not far away at Brooklyn's Park Theatre. Salsbury was well aware of Cody's fame by then and had been ruminating on how he could capitalize on putting together a live Wild West show. The men met at a restaurant near their theaters. Salsbury supported the whole concept, but there was no immediate plan set in motion.

From talk to action, the notion of a Wild West exhibition took a huge leap forward on July 4, 1882. The legendary exhibition was kick-started in North Platte as a holiday celebration of the country's birthday. While there is no disputing Buffalo Bill made it all happen, some of the beginnings of his connection are slightly murky, as in who asked him to take charge.

A barn on the Scout's Rest Ranch property in Nebraska (photograph by the author).

One story goes that the town leaders had in mind a rodeo-type competition that featured bronco busting, and they asked Cody to organize it. Cody delivered a somewhat more splashy origin story. In either case, the first modern American rodeo took place in North Platte on Independence Day in 1882, assuredly presided over by Cody. In Cody's telling, he asked around as to what the community had planned for the big holiday while visiting with a group of men in Foley's Store. The men more or less shrugged and said there was nothing special planned. "Oh, we've got to be more patriotic than that," Cody said.[6]

There happened to be a congregation of two hundred cowboys and two thousand horses (give or take; some say one thousand cowboys participated) on the outskirts of North Platte because of a roundup that had just concluded. Cody rounded them up to enter what was called "The Old Glory Blowout." Interestingly, although Buffalo Bill had little to do with rodeo ever again, the residents of North Platte, who acknowledge his memory in several ways, do boast of this July 4 competition as "America's First Rodeo." To this day, North Platte hosts an annual Buffalo Bill Rodeo.

The earliest American rodeos were basically intramural competitions between ranch hands who issued dares to coworkers in terms of who could ride faster, rope better, or last longer on bucking livestock. They were day-off types of challenges. Then came some between-ranch challenges. "Then someone came up with the idea of bringing cowboy games closer to the public, to the stage, as entertainment," a rodeo history book noted. "That someone was none other than William F. Cody—Buffalo Bill. His first public spectacle was presented on the Fourth of July, 1882, in his hometown of North Platte, Nebraska. The North Platte celebration in 1882 is considered the beginning of both the Wild West show and of rodeo."[7]

Other locations dispute the claim of North Platte holding the first rodeo, perhaps employing slightly different verbiage in a definition. The Pecos Rodeo in Texas, is one of those places, but its first rodeo was a year later, on July 4, 1883. The Frontier Rodeo in Prescott, Arizona, bills itself as the birthplace of professional rodeo dating to its July 4, 1888, event.

Once Cody had the cowboys and the horses, this is when the gleam came into Cody's eye as he pondered his long-held desire to stage a Wild West show. He hired some Indians, bought the old Deadwood stagecoach, and added a routine where cowboys held up the wagon. He threw in a small herd of buffalo, too, that could be chased through the grounds. Five years had passed since Cody and Burke first discussed a Wild West performance and five months since he had talked things over with Salsbury. "I tried it on my neighbors," Cody said, "and they lived through it and liked it, so I made up my mind right then I'd take the show East."[8]

The "I" was figurative. Burke was with him from the start and gushed

9. Rodeo and Wild West Beginnings 99

over the Nebraska translation of concept to reality. "Cody not only scored a howling success," Burke said, "if possible adding to his popularity, but the casualties were few and the result a revelation, even to those familiar with the possibilities of excitement, reckless daring, skill and devil-may-care fun, represented in a program where all were untrammeled and unconventional stars."[9] If you could follow the flowery words, you could find a combination of compliments to Cody and to the worthiness of the show.

This was basically a practice run. The Wild West exhibition did not emerge fully formed from one day of activity. Locally, Dr. A.W. Carver, a

A Buffalo Bill Cody caricature seems to be levitating next to an intricately carved reincarnation of the Wild West exhibition (photograph by the author).

dentist and a trick shooter, wanted in and became a Cody partner. Gordon Lillie helped sign up some Pawnee Indian tribe members for the show and worked as an interpreter. This is how Lillie earned his nickname "Pawnee Bill." Lillie eventually went out on his own and produced his own popular western shows. Late in Cody's career the two became full-fledged partners. The scout Frank North, who went way back with Cody, also signed on with the original Wild West exhibition. Salsbury was invited to join, but he did not want to work with Carver and originally declined, though he became a tremendously important part of the operation soon enough. Ranch hands and cowboys were given jobs.

By the 1880s, Americans were used to such entertainment barnstorming through town. It was called the circus, featuring animals, acrobats, and other acts. The modern circus originated in England in 1768 under the auspices of Philip Astley, a trick horseback rider who soon added jugglers, a clown, and tightrope walkers to his show. The first American circus took place in Philadelphia in 1792. Barnum's American Museum, founded by P.T. Barnum in New York City in 1841, was a stationary circus of sorts. Barnum exhibited people called "freaks," staged hoaxes, and liked to be called the Greatest Showman. Later, he introduced the traveling circus, which became legendary after an 1881 merger with James Bailey and

Some of the twenty thousand handmade pieces created by Ernie and Virginia Palmquist for a miniature replica of the Wild West exhibition (photograph by the author).

A sign advertises the Palmquists' work (photograph by the author).

James Hutchinson. The name of the circus became Barnum & Bailey and was seen by millions upon millions of families before it folded in 2017. Barnum did not foresee the wild success of the Wild West exhibition and sniffed at Buffalo Bill's early showings, sometimes hinting that he could do it all better.

The Wild West exhibition had a slightly different name when it opened on May 17, 1883, at the fairgrounds in Omaha: "The Wild West, Rocky Mountain and Prairie Exhibition." From the start,

A giant Buffalo Bill Cody overlooks the Fort Cody Gift Shop in North Platte, Nebraska (photograph by the author).

a skit that involved the long-dormant Pony Express was included in the script. Cody rode into the arena and from horseback fired at and broke glass balls thrown into the air to demonstrate his marksmanship. Indians competed in a bareback race on ponies. There were battle scenes with other Indians. There were rodeo-like demonstrations within the framework, such as roping, though of buffalo, not steers, and bucking bronco rides. As long as he already had it, Cody staged an attack on the Deadwood stagecoach, which would be a decades-long staple of the Wild West exhibition. Somewhat disorganized, the key elements were in place, but needed fine-tuning.

The Wild West departed Nebraska and toured the East, as Cody had long envisioned. Internally, there were numerous conflicts. Carver went into rages, and Cody could not stand being around him after a while. Cowboys fought among themselves. Salsbury saw a New York performance and emerged concerned about the future. By coincidence, he was in Chicago when the Wild West exhibition came there. Cody begged him to join as a partner. When Carver quit and said he would not be back, Salsbury agreed. It was the best move Buffalo Bill could make to salvage his dream. Cody and Salsbury together, with Burke pumping out the publicity, shaped the Wild West exhibition into the colossus that it became. Carver became like the fifth Beatle, forgotten by history.

The circus went on, and the Wild West exhibition came in. Although both offered the theme of fun for all ages, they competed in the sense that spectators had finite budgets and might choose one over the other if they both came to their communities.

10

The Wild West Goes Wild

The May 1883 opening of the Wild West exhibition in Omaha began the thirty-year odyssey of Buffalo Bill's revolutionary show that bumped along the first season, but demonstrated great enough potential that he was sure he had something special in the works if he could only smooth the road. Moving from town to town, trying to establish the new operation, dealing with the daily issues, and seeking to win over audiences, Buffalo Bill Cody had little time for personal correspondence. But he did sit down to write his sister Julia, from Coney Island, New York, on August 16 to basically provide a status report.

> Darling Sister,
>
> I am now located at this place, have went to big expense fitting up a place here—and as the watering season is about over it won't be worth much this year, but will be good for next. I am not much ahead on the summer on cash, but I have my show all clear, and a fine place built here. I have over a hundred head of stock here, have ten head of fine race horses, the finest six-mule coach train in the world, and seventy head of good saddle horses—the foundation laid for a fortune before long. The papers say I am the coming Barnum—I wish you could see this show.[1]

No wonder P.T. Barnum was a little miffed by Buffalo Bill's burgeoning success. Others were making comparisons. The tone of Cody's letter was upbeat, even if the show was having its troubles, especially with personnel. But he sensed he was poised for a breakthrough, or saw it that way because he was such a strong believer in his idea. "I am improving wonderfully in shooting," Cody continued. "Tell Al [her husband] I broke eighty-seven glass balls out of one hundred thrown from a trap twenty-one yard rise with a shotgun riding a horse at full speed. I have broken seventy-six out of a hundred with a rifle, horse running at full speed."[2] He signed the letter "Brother Will." These casual mentions of Cody's success rates at trick shooting do support the fact he was a good shot on the Plains.

Buffalo Bill Cody (center), astride his typical white horse, as he welcomes spectators to the Wild West exhibition. He was often flanked by Native American chiefs and braves (courtesy of Park County Archives).

Cody's sister Helen Wetmore said 1883 was a watershed year for her brother because of the Wild West exhibition's beginnings. "Will was able to put into execution his long-cherished plan," she wrote. Enumerating several of the acts, such as Indian war dances, the Pony Express, and the attack on the Deadwood stagecoach, Wetmore said, "These are the great, historic pictures of the Wild West, stirring, genuine, historic. It was a magnificent plan on a magnificent scale and it achieved instant success. The adventurous phases of western life never fail to quicken the pulse of the East."[3]

The 1883 season did not start out magnificently, but it proved to be a trial run. There were definitely kinks, and there were problems within the management structure. Cody was not unhappy to say goodbye to original partner, A.W. Carver. The Wild West exhibition took on a whole new life in 1884 following the shakedown and addition of Nate Salsbury to the operation. An orphan from Illinois who had been a Union Army drummer boy in the Civil War, Salsbury was also a showman at heart. Salsbury was an actor and a comedian and was taking those kinds of specialists on the road under the name of Salsbury's Troubadours when he joined the Wild West exhibition. He was a good logistics man with creative ideas, and he helped streamline operations. He had also performed in Australia, so he thought grandly.

10. The Wild West Goes Wild

This union paid great dividends in the future and skidded to a difficult ending, but the optimism and talents of Buffalo Bill, Salsbury, and John Burke overcame any obstacles to truly challenge the circus as the Greatest Show on Earth. Just not in 1884 when the trio was making the transition to the post–Carver days. They had limited experience working together, and they endured growing pains.

The Wild West exhibition played Coney Island for thirty days at the end of 1883, and then Buffalo Bill geared up for his revamped show with new partners. There was much feeling things out, but the theme was established by Burke as he churned out reams of publicity to herald the performances. Included in an early program was Burke's laudatory analysis of the stars of the show, "a part of the development of the great West," genuine, hard-bitten, experienced men of the trail and the frontier who were "keen of eye, sturdy in build, inured to hardship, experienced in the knowledge of Indian habits and language, familiar with the hunt, and trustworthy in the hour of extremest danger, they belong to a class that is rapidly disappearing from our country."[4]

There were real Indians in the show, real buffalo, both, it might be said, survivors of the slaughters on the Plains wrought by the U.S. government. From the start, the Wild West exhibition was advertised to communities by fantastically colorful poster art, still viewed today as fabulous representatives of the genre. They remain widely duplicated and distributed as copies for inexpensive purchase, sometimes $15 or less. The originals are another matter, if they can be found. Even some of the Rocky Mountain Prairie Expedition from 1883 were lavish in presentation, featuring the faces of Cody and Carver in their snazzy hats with a hint of their buckskins showing. The words "U.S. Scouts" figured prominently across a red, white, and blue shield, and there were two American flags crossed near the top of the message and a buffalo head smack in the middle. The poster was tasteful, but in no way subtle. You knew what this show was going to be about.

It would be foolish to declare the posters were merely decorative. The Wild West exhibition toured for three decades and attracted millions upon millions of spectators, and while it is impossible to calculate precisely how many of those people bought tickets because they were enticed by one of the colorful posters, there is little doubt they wooed the crowds into arenas. "Art in the form of Wild West posters perpetuated the art of the exhibition, cemented the celebrity of the progenitor, and elevated the stature of the signature performers," wrote one graduate student who focused on the genre. "It amplified the fame of a West that never really was, or was rapidly changing. It reinforced the contemporaneity of the exhibition and ensured that it kept pace with a changing world and changing definitions of what constituted 'the frontier.'"[5]

Informative and entertaining, brash and colorful, bright and enticing. That all described the posters, as well as the Wild West exhibition, and the advertising complemented the performances in the flesh well. They were so vivid, so well done, that the posters remain popular more than a century after the Wild West exhibition ceased and desisted. The content is just plain fun, featuring Buffalo Bill, stars of the performances, horses, buffalo, and splashy scenes of action. Buffalo Bill Cody truly gauged the appetite for stories of the Old West by those who had never been there and had only been teased by newspaper stories. He was here to tell them what it was all really like because he had lived it all in person.

Burke went wild in his program copy, noting that easterners, indeed, perhaps anyone living east of the Mississippi River, were in the dark about the lifestyles and skills of these western scouts and cowboys, saying they were "comparatively unknown." The Wild West, as presented by Cody and Carver, Burke said, "will illustrate life as it is witnessed on the Plains, the Indian encampment, the cowboys and vaqueros, the herds of buffalo and elk, the lassoing of animals, the manner of robbing mail coaches, feats of agility, horsemanship, marksmanship, archery, and the kindred scenes and events that are characteristic of the border."[6] Cody could say, "Been

A stagecoach plays a part in a 2017 Wild West exhibition reenactment in Denver, Colorado (photograph by the author).

there, done that," about almost all of those things. Burke's summation of the Wild West exhibition could pretty much have been applied forever. There were changes each year, but there were allegiances to the origin, and many parts of the exhibition never changed.

Any public space was fair game for displaying the posters. Graduate student Stephanie Fox Knappe could not pin down precisely how many were issued during the thirty-year run of the Wild West exhibition, but she advanced an estimate of between three hundred and four hundred different designs. An attempt to collect all of those would take an individual a lifetime. The posters were ubiquitous when Cody was headed to town. "It would not be unusual for the Wild West's indefatigable advance men to arrange for local bill posters to cover seemingly every available vertical surface with between 6,000 and 8,000 of 'Bill's bills' in the hard sell of a one-day-only appearance."[7]

Multiple printing companies were employed to produce the high volume of posters, and in turn they were very good customers of paper product suppliers. Knappe concluded that in a changing time there was much nostalgia attached to both the appeal of the posters and the Wild West. One of those printers was Calhoun in Connecticut, and the local *Hartford Daily Courant* extolled the quality and talents of those productions. "The-

Acrobatic riders dressed as Cossacks imitating the Congress of Rough Riders in the late 1800s from a Wild West exhibition reenactment in Denver, Colorado, in 2017 (photograph by the author).

atrical people say the Carver and Cody bills are the finest specimens of the show engraver's art they have ever seen," the newspaper stated.[8]

Cody, as he had bragged to his sister, was doing okay as a marksman in the Wild West exhibition. Carver was known for his slick shooting, and a major reason he wanted to be part of the exhibition was to show the world just how good he was with his guns. There was still another sharpshooter in the cast of note. Captain Adam H. Bogardus was a featured member of the group. Bogardus invented the launching mechanism to throw the glass balls in the air that Cody shot at and also massaged the development of the glass ball target itself. In addition, he was a key figure in inventing trap shooting. No one fires at glass balls today, but trap shooting, which originated with live pigeons as the targets but now employs hard, colored discs, remains popular. Bogardus had three trained shooting sons, Edward, Peter, and Henry, and it was the Bogardus clan that first season, dad included, who took center stage in shooting during the Wild West exhibition.

Bogardus called himself the best wing shooter in the world, and to back up his claim, on one long day in Gilmore Garden in New York—January 3, 1878—he shattered five thousand glass balls in five hundred minutes with some short rests along the way. That's a lot of ammo. Bogardus was timed as starting his repeated shooting of glass balls out of the air at 2:40 p.m. and concluding at 10:31 p.m. That made for a busy afternoon and evening. He may well have suffered from a repetitive strain injury from loading and firing nearly constantly. Every thousand or two thousand hits or so, Bogardus took a break for some food and drink and to rest. One rest period was as long as forty-seven minutes. As Bogardus's marathon shooting went on and on, his right arm began to swell, so much so that the affliction of weariness was noticeable to spectators. He began having rubdowns when he paused for his breaks. Assistants helped by applying brandy and arnica, a substance made from the yellow flower called mountain arnica. A report from the occasion said Bogardus reached his goal with 19 minutes, 35 seconds to spare.

This achievement gave Bogardus a showpiece item for his résumé, and there was no question the man was a brilliant shot. However, when he engaged in shooting contests against Carver in the Wild West exhibition, Carver prevailed nineteen times in twenty-five matches. Whether or not that was too much for Bogardus's ego, he departed the exhibition after just one season, missing out on its growing success.

Buffalo Bill did not make money in 1883, but he anticipated a sea change in 1884. There were glitches that were costly, however, keeping as much money as he had hoped from piling up in the coffers. At times, the Wild West exhibition ran across abysmal weather. That is a chief hazard for shows performed in the outdoors. Cody was also probably in a somewhat shaky mental state. He and Louisa were not living together, she did not offer support for his Wild West plot, and even worse, another of their children, Orra Maude, had passed away.

He had been talking divorce from Louisa, but Orra died suddenly from an illness at age eleven. As expected, this caused great distress in the family. Cody, per usual, was traveling with his embryonic show when he received word of that tragedy in late 1883. Orra was buried alongside her brother Kit in Rochester. Louisa was distraught, and Buffalo Bill was about as devastated. He was already under massive stress and could see Louisa was in no condition to discuss a permanent parting. That is why he gave up the divorce plan at the time. The anguished Louisa wrote, "If it was not for the hope of heaven and again meeting there, my affliction would be more than I could bear."[9] Psychologists have for years studied the reasons behind divorce. They are varied, with some more significant than others. But it has been said nothing puts more strain on a couple than the death of a child.

Buffalo Bill's personal life was pretty much a shambles, fraught with the type of huge ills it is difficult to recover from. The year 1884 was supposed to be a great one for Buffalo Bill as he set out to put a larger stamp on society than he had already made. Yet it is likely Cody never became more discouraged about the Wild West exhibition that year than on a journey to New Orleans. The Wild West exhibition was traveling to New Orleans by riverboat, but on the way to the Crescent City, it sank. No humans lost their lives, but livestock did, and the exhibition's equipment suffered grievous damage. Buffalo Bill, who liberally took advantage of spirits to boost his mood, was crushed. He wanted to go on a bender. Salsbury was still touring with his own gang, finishing his obligations, and was in Denver when he received an urgent telegram from Cody asking what to do.

The clear-thinking Salsbury formulated a reply: "Go to New Orleans, reorganize, and open on your regular date."[10] Cody followed the advice, and the show did go on, as every live show tries to stick with that outlook. Buffalo Bill did pull his act and the troupe's act together and resupply. That would have been a great comeback story. However, it rained and rained in New Orleans, drenching the arena and anyone who invested enough scratch for a ticket and refused to be a no-show. This double whammy seriously bummed Cody out. It was one of those times when everything that can go wrong does go wrong.

Cody was so frustrated by these developments that he raged in a tirade to Salsbury that he felt like giving it all up. "Fate, if there is such a thing," he despaired, "is against me. There is not one bit of use trying more. The longer we stick at this, the worse off we are. The sooner we give this outfit away, the better. I am thoroughly discouraged. I am a damned condemned Joner [Jonah, as in the whale guy in the Old Testament] and the sooner you get clear from me, the better for you." Cody added, "There is no heaven. If so it can stay there and be damned." Salsbury, who must have been familiar with Cody's moods by then (certainly he recognized when he had been drinking), took the rant casually, calling it "a charming diatribe."[11] The Wild West exhibition was not going anywhere—except on to the next stop.

The New Orleans debacle was not the only significant setback the Wild West exhibition faced in 1884. The loss of Frank North, an integral member of the cast, and a long-time scouting acquaintance of Cody's, was another blow. North, it should be remembered, was first approached by Ned Buntline wishing to catalogue his exploits. Major North had also been a prominent scout on the Plains, and he was the assigned leader of Pawnee scouts for years.

North was severely injured in a horse accident during a performance in Hartford, Connecticut, in 1884. He incurred several injuries, including seven broken ribs that sidelined him. Weakened, North contracted an illness and never recovered. Not only did he not ride in the Wild West exhibition again, he died in March of 1885 from the worsening of the injuries and sickness. It was North's brother Luther who blamed Buffalo Bill for Frank's early death at forty-five and spent decades denigrating Cody, although there was no particular blame to be placed except for Cody's leadership of the Wild West exhibition. Throughout the life of the Wild West exhibition, Cody always sought to publicize the performances as the way the West really was, even if in reality he definitely applied poetic license in his interpretation of events. In the earliest stages of the Wild West exhibition, Frank North told Cody to skip any suggestion of adhering to the whole truth and nothing but the truth. "Use some old hack horses and hack drivers," North said. "To make it go, you want a show of illusion, not realism."[12] It can be argued Cody's recipe was to rely on both as key ingredients, a blending.

The lineup gave John Burke much to work with. It was no exaggeration to say the Wild West exhibition was something new and special and provided a tremendous day of entertainment. Nowhere else could a spectator see the return of the Pony Express put to action, mock holdups by men on horseback, live Indians who were not shooting bow and arrows or rifles at them but performing on horseback, and a reenactment of the Battle of the Little Bighorn. To the ticket buyers this was history come to life, even if Buffalo Bill, the producer, took liberties with the plots.

"The Only Real Novelty of the Century," Burke exclaimed. "The Amusement Triumph of the Age," he stated. "The Romantic West Brought

East in Reality. Everything Genuine." And more: "A Year's Visit West in Three Hours." It all added up to this: "Actual Scenes in the Nation's Progress to Delight, Please, Gratify, Chain and Interest the Visitor."[13] Ta da! Oh yes, Buffalo Bill himself chimed in: "A true re-script of life on the frontier as I know it to be, and which no fictitious pen can describe."[14]

For all of the labor, for all of the fresh ideas, for all of the emotion that went into the first year of Buffalo Bill, Nate Salsbury, and John Burke combining their talents, when they quit for the season at the end of 1884, the Wild West exhibition had lost $60,000. Some $20,000 of that stemmed from the loss of so much gear in the riverboat sinking. Still, they had faith, and one thing Bill Cody and Salsbury never did during their partnership was stand pat. They were forever tinkering with the personnel, always looking to add winning acts. They knew this was all going to work out. In 1885, they managed to bring in one of the most infamous men in the country to the cast and another performer who would become one of the most famous women in American history. Sitting Bull, the Sioux leader who was reviled for planning the annihilation of General George Armstrong Custer, made for the unlikeliest member of a Buffalo Bill production. And while unknown, Annie Oakley was about to become America's sweetheart.

11

Sitting Bull

In 1885, the Lakota chief Sitting Bull was probably one of the most hated men in the United States. As the architect of the Native Americans' victory at the Battle of the Little Bighorn, the sweeping triumph that annihilated the Seventh Calvary and wiped out the famous General George Armstrong Custer, he was deeply unpopular among the millions of Americans who despised Indians anyway.

He could have benefited mightily from the pen of John Burke to do a little bit of image burnishing. Among many, nothing would have helped, but remarkably enough, less than ten years after the 1876 battle that remains one of the most famous in the country's history, he and Buffalo Bill Cody became the most unusual of bedfellows. And indeed, Burke's wizardry was applied to somewhat rehabilitating Sitting Bull's name.

At the least, the dignified Sitting Bull became an attraction for four months in the Wild West exhibition, setting stringent terms for his participation, an upset of colossal magnitude. Although they had been on opposite sides in the Plains Indians Wars, there was a respect between Buffalo Bill and Sitting Bull that was a bit difficult to pin down. But they did develop some type of rapport. For all of the anti–Native American sentiment, the racism, and genocide, there was an underlying fascination with Indian culture. As long as Americans did not feel threatened by tribes marauding on horseback and trying to drive them off their farms or mining claims, the culture with the upper hand seemed to view Indians as worth watching riding on ponies, dancing, or acting on stages.

Buffalo Bill had learned this early on in his own stage career when Ned Buntline and other producers demanded the inclusion of Indians in the shows. Except for his visible demonstration of anger when he proclaimed his "first scalp for Custer," Cody never really had grudges against the Native Americans he fought against. He was allied with other tribes, like the Pawnee, who were fellow scouts with the cavalry. He was paid to scout and sometimes ran across members of the other side that wished to

11. Sitting Bull

Buffalo Bill Cody (right) with Sitting Bull. The Sioux chief toured with the Wild West exhibition for four months in 1885 (courtesy of the Library of Congress).

do him harm, so he fought back. There must have been some entertaining conversations between Cody, Nate Salsbury, and Burke about the idea of trying to convince Sitting Bull to appear in the Wild West exhibition. One might imagine somebody gasping and saying, "That's ridiculous." Or, "That's impossible." Did everyone say, "Great idea," right away?

While Native Americans always found employment in the Wild West exhibition, it was hard to picture Sitting Bull joining up. Few other participants initially had starring roles. In a sense, they were extras providing riding talent and authentic color to battle scenes portrayed in the arenas. There was no chance Sitting Bull, who was in his fifties at the time, was going to prance around on a horse performing battle scenes as white audiences gaped at him, booed him, or applauded him.

Most Americans blamed Sitting Bull for Custer's death, even though he was nowhere near the site of Last Stand Hill. As a powerful leader, though, Sitting Bull played a large role in the planning. He also had a famous dream that encouraged other warriors. The vision that came to him in his sleep showed blue coated riders tumbling over and over as death came to them, the Indians riding away victorious. This was a sign from the Great Spirit that the huge gathering and union of Indians arrayed against the troops would win a great battle. Whether it was Sitting Bull's superior planning or other chiefs' precise execution in the field, the Native Americans overran the troops' resistance.

While satisfied for the moment, Sitting Bull almost immediately recognized that the reinforcements sent from the East would be so strong they might well hunt down and capture all of the Plains Indians and force them onto reservations. A great manhunt began for Sitting Bull, and over time, on the move, he led his people across the border into Canada to essentially seek asylum and live in peace and freedom away from the war-torn lands of his youth and away from any reservation. It was independence from the U.S. government he craved.

In May of 1877, Sitting Bull and his band entered Canada, which was ruled under British law. That was not a problem, and for the most part, those Sioux obtained the independence they sought. Over a period of time, however, it became apparent there were not enough buffalo to hunt. A frustrated U.S. government kept demanding the return of Sitting Bull and his people and ratcheted up pressure on the Canadian government. Sitting Bull and the Sioux remained in Canada for four years, but in 1881, tired and short on food, they capitulated and returned to the United States.

On July 18, 1877, Sitting Bull, leading 186 people, surrendered, and they were transferred to the Standing Rock Agency, which was located near the current North Dakota–South Dakota border. This containment on a reservation was apparently not good enough for the government. Sitting Bull and 172 others were transferred to another location in South Dakota and held as prisoners of war. They spent twenty months there before being transferred back to Standing Rock in the spring of 1883.

Sitting Bull believed he would be murdered by the troops as soon as he surrendered and was surprised he was not. From warrior, he was evolving into more of a statesman, an advocate for the Sioux more verbally rather than on the battlefield. Despite some basically calling him the most wanted man in America, the publicity attached to his name brought it to the lips of many citizens. Whether it was notoriety or fame, either way just about everyone knew who he was. His stature had actually increased to the point where it would have been a government embarrassment simply to kill Sitting Bull. The first person to promote Sitting Bull as a celebrity was not Buffalo Bill Cody, although he had tried. Cody approached Standing Rock Agency agent James McLaughlin, who intensely disliked Sitting Bull, but was turned down. McLaughlin said allowing such special privileges to Sitting Bull would send a mixed message to other Indians on the reservation.

Curiosity about Sitting Bull grew among Americans, and in 1884, a promoter named Colonel Alvaren Allen managed to obtain temporary freedom for the chief to appear in Canada and in some northern U.S. states in an event called the Sitting Bull Connection. Allen gained the assistance of others above McLaughlin's pay grade to make it happen.

When touring in Minnesota, Sitting Bull met Annie Oakley for the first time. Stunned by her shooting ability, impressed by her demeanor—and she of his—Sitting Bull bonded with the young lady. He felt Oakley was such a phenomenal shooter she had to possess supernatural powers. They developed a true fondness for one another before either was employed by Buffalo Bill. Sitting Bull went through a ceremony that basically adopted her as his daughter. He called her "Little Miss Sure Shot," a nickname that stuck for life.

Always working as a chief seeking to provide better living conditions for his people, Sitting Bull agreed to the Allen tour because he was promised he would be able to have a meeting with former President Ulysses S. Grant. Sitting Bull was in Bismarck, North Dakota, for the event commemorating the opening of the Northern Pacific Railroad. He carried a flag and signed autographs while sitting in the back of a wagon.

When Buffalo Bill learned what Allen pulled off, he was determined to get Sitting Bull into the Wild West exhibition. Cody renewed his lobbying of McLaughlin, who had strategically done his best to split allegiances between the Sioux leaders in his charge. He came around to letting Sitting Bull go off on another show business adventure. Once he secured McLaughlin's okay, Cody wrote a letter to Lucius Q.C. Lamar, then the secretary of the interior, asking for Sitting Bull to be released into his custody to perform in the Wild West exhibition. Buffalo Bill had some powerful allies in Washington, D.C., generals he had served with and befriended. He asked for their help and mustered support from generals such as Philip Sheridan, Nelson Miles, Alfred Terry, and George Crook.

Cody probably thought he was on his way, but Lamar refused to approve the idea of Sitting Bull joining the show. When he wrote back to Cody he underlined the word "no" three times. John D.C. Atkins, who was secretary of Indian affairs, sided with Lamar on the basis that Sitting Bull was a war criminal. Atkins said Indians should not be "roving through the country exhibiting themselves and visiting places where they would naturally come in contact with evil associates and degrading immoralities."[1] One might read between the lines and presume Atkins did not view the Wild West exhibition as wholesome family entertainment.

Cody kept lobbying and added the backing of Generals William Sherman and Eugene Carr, who had been his commanding officer as a scout. Cody wrote his own plea, explaining how he understood Native Americans and would ensure appropriate good care of Sitting Bull. Lamar backed off and gave his permission. Of course, after all this, Cody still had to persuade Sitting Bull to join him.

It fell to John Burke, as Buffalo Bill's emissary, to cut a deal. Cody, who had years of dealings with Indians in various ways, made sure to give Burke advice on his approach to the tribal members of the troupe. During Burke's first year with the Wild West exhibition, Buffalo Bill saw Burke give one of the Indians "a heap big cigar," as Burke called it, and told him he would return from town with an entire box as a gift. Cody informed Burke that he had better follow through. "Don't forget those cigars," Cody said. "Maybe you didn't mean it. But don't ever promise an Indian anything without giving it to him. If you break a promise to an Indian you'll be no good to me or the show. Get a box of cigars in town and charge it to me. Don't forget."[2] It was a matter of trust.

The Wild West exhibition was playing in Chicago when Burke began his journey west on June 6, 1885, to meet with Sitting Bull at the Standing Rock Agency reservation. It is not difficult to imagine Cody's orders to Burke as something on the order of, "Don't come back without him." Buffalo Bill had cleared the red tape with McLaughlin (who by then probably would not have minded if Sitting Bull never came back) and through Washington. One would think Sitting Bull would be an easy sell. He had to want to get away from the reservation and experience new environments.

Burke knew that from the moment he had returned to the United States and surrendered, Sitting Bull had been interested in learning as much as he could about the white man's culture, what these men were going to teach his children in a new kind of education, and had drunk in the trip with Allen as a learning experience. If he was going to be stuck in a different culture, he wanted all the background he could accumulate to adapt and to make sure his people could adapt and advance, too. Burke

11. Sitting Bull

understood that, above all, Sitting Bull had to be shown respect. If he was not treated with honor, he would not be an asset to the Wild West exhibition. Among the Sioux, Sitting Bull was seen as possessing strong medicine, and Burke, always the advance man for the Wild West performances, had to prove to Sitting Bull that he, Buffalo Bill, and the Wild West exhibition viewed him in that way.

One thing motivating Sitting Bull was his burning desire to visit Washington, DC, and obtain a meeting with the president, whom he, in Indian parlance, after years of cavalry officers using the term in a patronizing fashion, referred to as the "Grandfather." He viewed Buffalo Bill as a man who could get things done like arrange such a meeting. By that point in 1885, Grover Cleveland had replaced Chester Arthur as the chief executive of the United States. McLaughlin met Burke when he arrived, and joined by two interpreters, they rode in a wagon to meet up with Sitting Bull. It took until the end of the second day for the party to reach the area where Sitting Bull lived with two wives and ten children. They waited until well into the next day to visit with Sitting Bull.

Burke and Sitting Bull were formally introduced, both using flowery words about how glad they were to meet one another. It did not take long for Burke to put an offer on the table. The contract he was providing called for Sitting Bull, accompanied by some other Sioux warriors and their wives, to join the Wild West exhibition for a series of performances with the commitment they were going to be returned to this location when the tour concluded. Things proceeded at a leisurely pace. As Sitting Bull mulled the general terms of the proposal, Burke was invited to join the chief and his family for a meal. They then lit pipes and smoked. They adjourned for the night without discussing specifics. It was not until the next day that Sitting Bull said he wanted to hear more, to listen to more precise details of this potential business arrangement.

The writing of the contract took place at Fort Yates. Burke wrote out the proposal right in front of Sitting Bull with such provisions as paying him $50 a week. That was a large sum for the era, translating into well over $1,200 a week in present-day valuation. The salary would make Sitting Bull the highest paid performer in the Wild West exhibition. It also provided Sitting Bull with an interpreter of his own choosing. This was an important element in the deal because the chief did not much trust other white men. Other financial inducements included a direct advance payment to Sitting Bull of $125, plus the guarantee that Sitting Bull and whoever traveled with him, would have their expenses paid back and forth from the Dakotas. There was one more thing Sitting Bull requested in the contract. Burke may not have thought much about it, but from his experience on tour with Allen, Sitting Bull recognized a potentially valuable bonus would accrue to him if he retained the rights to his own autograph and photos that he could sell independently. That proved to be a lucrative addendum, and Sitting Bull profited handsomely from that arrangement. It is primarily due to the Allen tour and the Wild West swing that Sitting Bull autographs are available for collectors today. While Sitting Bull was not fluent in English and he likely learned more than he let on, his autograph was written in English and was a simple, legible, "Sitting Bull." Other accounts state Sitting Bull also asked to be able to sit regally on a good horse and make one lap of arenas.

One account of these meetings says Burke flashed some photographs of Annie Oakley as an example of the individuals who starred in the Wild West exhibition, and that when he recognized her from their previous encounter in Minnesota, Sitting Bull promptly signed on the dotted line. That seems like a fanciful description. Sitting Bull was too shrewd for that simplistic a response, even if he was aware she was going to be there as part of the exhibition.

Once this negotiation was finalized, Sitting Bull, several other prominent warriors, and several women from the tribe joined Burke on an eastward journey. When they hooked up with the Wild West exhibition, it was in Buffalo, New York, and that is where Sitting Bull made his debut. He did indeed sit astride a horse in the arena. There was no pretense he was playing a role. He was always himself. Some spectators booed him as the killer of Custer. Others lauded him, and many bought his photographs.

Sitting Bull was in his early fifties. He had a somewhat pockmarked face and a round head and stood about five-foot-eight. Sometimes he was photographed in a headdress and at other times wearing a single feather in his hair. He could appear austere and stern, but he always maintained his dignity. There are contradictory stories about how many watchers booed Sitting Bull and how he reacted. Visibly, he did not react. Others say he cursed the whites under his breath in Lakota.

Ernie LaPointe, Sitting Bull's great-grandson, wrote a book about Sitting Bull and also had a major role in a documentary called *Sitting Bull's Voice*. In 2017, LaPointe gave a talk in Cody, Wyoming, Buffalo Bill's old hometown. LaPointe said Sitting Bull put up with the verbal abuse. Since 1992, LaPointe has devoted himself to correcting the image of Native Americans in popular culture, created by everything from the Wild West exhibition to movies and books. "They made us the villains," LaPointe said. "They made us evil. They made us the bad guys. We're not evil people. We're not savages." LaPointe said it is his mission to alter ingrained notions of Native Americans and Sitting Bull. "To counter how they portray us as a people. They have it all wrong."[3]

After Buffalo, the Wild West exhibition moved on to Boston and to

11. Sitting Bull

Canada, through the eastern section of the country, far removed from the West where only a few years earlier Sitting Bull sought refuge. He did not have to speak, act, or do much besides sit on his horse and sign his name, but Sitting Bull's presence was electric. In an echo of what Buffalo Bill told Burke about being true to his promises with Indians, a newspaper story in Toronto addressed the topic. "In nine cases out of ten when there is trouble between white men and Indians it will be found it is the white man who is responsible. Indians expect a man to keep his word. They can't understand how a man can lie. Most of them would as soon cut off a leg as tell a lie."[4]

The most famous photograph of Sitting Bull and Buffalo Bill together was taken in Montreal. While neither man is smiling, they both appear almost regal. Sitting Bull is wearing full buckskin clothing and an extraordinarily long headdress. Buffalo Bill, facing away to the distance, is wearing a wide-brimmed cowboy hat, a dark shirt, and his trademark black boots. Although a black and white photograph, as all were in the 1880s, it was eventually colorized. A caption below the two figures reads, "Enemies in '76, Friends in '85."[5]

There were times when the Wild West exhibition crossed paths with some of the generals who led the cavalry on the Plains, had battled with Sitting Bull and other chiefs, and ended up capturing them, disarming them, and forcing them on to reservations. When such occasions arose and Sitting Bull was introduced to these men, he avoided shaking hands. He did not want to give those men respect when he felt he, the Sioux, and all Plains Indians, had been disrespected. Sitting Bull never got his meeting with the Grandfather, President Cleveland.

In one of the ultimate let-bygones-be-bygones commentaries of the era, Buffalo Bill was quoted extensively in another Canadian newspaper basically defending Sitting Bull against those who considered him a murderer for the defeat of Custer. "The Indians were being pursued by skilled fighters with orders to kill," Cody said. "For centuries they had been hounded from the Atlantic to the Pacific and back again. They had their wives and little ones to protect and they were fighting for their existence. With the end of Custer they considered that their greatest enemy had passed away. Sitting Bull was not the leader of the Sioux in that battle. He was a medicine man who played on their superstitions—their politician, their diplomat—who controlled their emotions through the power of his argument and his speech."[6]

This was the same man who shouted "First scalp for Custer" in a fight soon after the Battle of the Little Bighorn. He was not in such a forgiving mood then. Less than a decade later, Buffalo Bill had to admit Sitting Bull was good for business. And it is true that over the decades, following his scouting days on the Plains, Cody was one of the best friends Indians had anywhere in American society.

Several accounts of Sitting Bull's time with the Wild West exhibition indicate that for all the money he was raking in, he kept little for himself. He spread the wealth among family and friends, but tellingly, also distributed to needy people not of his tribe who he encountered on his travels. It was the Sioux way to share. He could not understand how this rich white man's culture did not take care of its own, especially poor children, and share its bounty with the less fortunate. So Sitting Bull gave money to beggars.

Participation in the Wild West exhibition by Sitting Bull helped make Buffalo Bill a fortune over the course of the 1885 season, which ended in St. Louis. The books read a gross take of $1 million, a profit of $100,000 on an estimated attendance of a million people. Sitting Bull, who called Cody Pahaska, the widely used Indian name applied to Buffalo Bill, and the boss, separated as friends. Cody gave Sitting Bull some special parting gifts. One was a white, trick pony that seemed allergic to the sound of gunfire. Another present was a cowboy hat, a Stetson. Back in South Dakota, at Standing Rock Agency, Sitting Bull entertained visitors with the horse and was very possessive of his new hat. He said, "My friend Long Hair (Pahaska) gave me this hat. I value it very highly, for the hand that placed it upon my head had a friendly feeling for me."[7]

This was true, and after such a successful run, Buffalo Bill wanted Sitting Bull to rejoin the Wild West exhibition in 1886. He sent John Burke back to Standing Rock to sign Sitting Bull to a new contract. However, obstructionist McLaughlin stood in the way. He said there was no way he was going to approve such an excursion again. McLaughlin invested a lot of time trying to diminish Sitting Bull's influence on the reservation, but when he returned, the chief used much of the money earned from the Wild West exhibition to keep some people loyal.

McLaughlin greeted Burke with a rant about how this money produced negative things on the reservation. He said of Sitting Bull, "is such a consummate liar and too vain and obstinate to be benefited by what he sees" and "made no good use of the money he thus earns, but on the contrary spends it extravagantly among the Indians in trying to perpetuate baneful influences which the ignorant and non-progressive element are too ready to listen to and to follow. I had a great deal of trouble with him, and through him with other Indians caused by his own bad behavior and arrogance."[8] More accurately, in McLaughlin's arrogance, he had failed to break Sitting Bull, bend him to his will, and convince him that becoming a farmer was a good idea. Sitting Bull stood for old school Sioux values. No, McLaughlin was not going to allow Sitting Bull to go back on the road.

11. Sitting Bull

Above all, Sitting Bull knew his greatest value was sticking with his people and helping them negotiate rough times as the government continued to consume traditional lands. From his uncertain perch at Standing Rock he continued to campaign for Indian rights and the return of homelands. As attitudes festered at Standing Rock, with McLaughlin more or less blaming Sitting Bull for all of his problems, a separate strong man rose up. A Paiute Indian named Wovoka led a fresh religious movement called the Ghost Dance Movement that was spreading eastward from Nevada. Wovoka encouraged special dancing and chanting that was supposed to bring relatives back from the dead—and the buffalo, as well. While Sitting Bull invited Wovoka in to his camp, he was not a believer. White officials, especially McLaughlin, and white settlers, grew fearful about what Wovoka was conjuring. If not actual spirits, he stirred strong emotions in his followers.

McLaughlin felt everything was Sitting Bull's fault, and he worried he was going to jump the reservation as part of the Ghost Dance Movement. There is no indication Sitting Bull felt that way. But tensions were high, and McLaughlin manipulated the situation to arrest and restrain Sitting Bull under the pretense he was behind the whole Ghost Dance Movement. Word reached Washington, and General Nelson Miles issued an urgent telegraph message calling upon Buffalo Bill to rush, on the double, to escort Sitting Bull to the nearest commanding officer of U.S. troops.

When Cody arrived in the Dakotas, he immediately sent a telegram to McLaughlin indicating he would reach the reservation the next day. At the same time, another telegram reached Cody, informing him his Scout's Rest Ranch in North Platte, Nebraska, was on fire. He continued on, but was waylaid by some of McLaughlin's men who insisted on buying the great Buffalo Bill some drinks. Stressed and torn by circumstances, Cody acquiesced and drank too heavily. It was a costly mistake. Delayed by a day, Cody left by wagon to try to reach Sitting Bull and convince him to come away with him. However, he was purposely misdirected on the route and lost even more time. Meanwhile, aware of Cody's progress, McLaughlin sent telegrams to Washington seeking to override Miles's directive to Buffalo Bill. Word reached Sitting Bull that Cody was on his way, hoping to intervene. "Is it true?" Sitting Bull said. He was assured it was true.[9] It was, but it was too late.

On December 15, 1890, in events orchestrated by McLaughlin, Indian police confronted Sitting Bull to arrest him. By then, McLaughlin had pledged there would be no bloodshed. However, things got messy as the men arrived at his cabin late at night. Sitting Bull's family members were present when the police showed up. Harsh words were spoken. Tempers grew testy. Sitting Bull bodyguards appeared to defend him. Sitting Bull told the police he was not going anywhere with them. Two different men assigned to arrest Sitting Bull shot him and he died in his own home.

Once Buffalo Bill learned Sitting Bull was dead, he turned back. A little while later, Cody overlapped with President Benjamin Harrison in Indianapolis. It was there Harrison informed him he personally rescinded Miles's order resulting in the deflection of Cody from the scene, and he was sorry he had done so. Harrison told Cody those who had his ear said if Buffalo Bill came, Sitting Bull would be killed, and then a new Indian war would start. He listened to the wrong people. "So, it was to spare the life of this man that I was stopped?" Cody said.[10] Instead, as a direct result of Cody being halted, Sitting Bull was killed. And there was no war.

12

Annie Oakley

Of all the renowned shooters, gunslingers, outlaws, Civil War combatants and participants in the Plains Indians Wars, Annie Oakley was probably the only one of the prominent western figures still remembered today who never fired a gun at another human being.

There is no true way of measuring—just as there is no way to compare baseball's all-time fastball hurlers like Walter Johnson, Smoky Joe Wood, and Bob Feller to modern-era pitchers whose every toss is noted on a radar gun—but Oakley was likely the greatest shooter ever. Yes, she was in show business, but someone who almost never misses, regardless of circumstances, regardless of the era, is something to behold.

If Buffalo Bill Cody was the most famous man in the world during his traveling tenure with the Wild West exhibition, it is likely Annie Oakley was the most famous woman. She was not the ringmaster, a la Cody, but her performances, stunts, and stunning accuracy gave her such a widespread reputation during her lifetime that it still endures. It should be recalled it was Sitting Bull, who saw a thing or two in his lifetime, who anointed her Little Miss Sure Shot even before she joined the Wild West exhibition.

Born Phoebe Ann Mosey on August 13, 1860, in a log cabin in Ohio, the girl destined to become the great sharpshooter endured a very difficult childhood. He father died when she was nine, and that triggered a chain of events costing her dearly. By the time she was seven, Annie was already prowling the woods shooting small game such as rabbits and quail to help feed the large family, and later brought some of the bounty to town to sell to hotels and restaurants. Most of her killing was done with an unwieldy muzzle loader, a big weapon for a little girl. These were challenging times, but Annie's life got worse.

As the family of nine children declined into poverty, her desperate mother sent Annie to work for another family. She was supposed to receive pay and continue her education. Instead, she was indentured into

Annie Oakley, later in life, poses with her gun years after retiring from the Wild West exhibition she performed in with her husband Frank Butler (courtesy of the Library of Congress).

near-slavery and abused mentally and physically by her keepers. Eventually, she ran away. Annie never identified her slave drivers by name, but for the rest of her life she referred to them as "the wolves." She then lived with a more acceptable family for a time before moving home again at fifteen.

At that age, Annie's reputation as a sure shot began to spread. Call it fate or serendipity, but one chance meeting changed her life. A touring showman who was an expert marksman was due to perform in Cincinnati. Frank Butler issued a challenge through a local hotel owner named Jack Frost that he would wager $100 he could defeat anyone who wanted to take a shot at him, so to speak. Frost knew what he was doing and lined up Annie to take on Butler. It was a riveting contest, coming down to the twenty-fifth shot. When Butler missed, Annie won.

Their attraction started with mutual respect at this showdown, but soon enough Frank and Annie were dating, and within a year, they were married. Butler was no longer a solo act. The shooting show now featured a duet. Initially, their base was Cincinnati, and Annie adopted the stage name of Oakley, presumably taken from a nearby neighborhood.

One of the Wild West exhibition's original headliners was sharpshooter Captain Bogardus and his family, but they left after one season. The Frank and Annie Show first approached John Burke about joining up after the New Orleans calamity. They had been working for the Sells Brothers Circus, but they wanted to make a move away to the environment it seemed Buffalo Bill was fostering. Burke wanted to see what Oakley and Butler could do, so they went to a target range. Yep, they were the real goods. At that moment, however, the Wild West exhibition did not have much money available. Also, Johnny Baker was already on the scene. Baker, who became known as the Cowboy Kid, was a blossoming shooter who morphed into a tremendous talent. Although never officially adopted by Cody, he became a son to him, and spent thirty years with the Wild West exhibition. Burke recognized the potential star power in the charming, petite, five-foot-tall Oakley, as well as the talent she and her husband showed. "Come see us in Louisville in the spring," he told them. "Then we can talk business."[1]

When the Wild West exhibition resumed in Kentucky in 1885, the Butlers followed up on Burke's encouragement and went through a rather fancy, boggling warm-up routine where Oakley impressed onlookers. As Butler threw glass balls into the air, Oakley, dressed demurely in a pleated dress, aimed her rifle backward. She rested it on her shoulder and sighted in by looking at a mirror. Then she pulled the trigger and shattered the glass. If that was not a show-stopper, what was? Nate Salsbury, who had already been informed of Oakley's talents by Burke, started to negotiate a deal, and Buffalo Bill made an appearance. He was dressed in his flashy buckskins and doffed his wide brimmed hat. "They told me about you, Missy," he said. "We're glad to have you."[2]

The connection to the Wild West exhibition began the same day. Oakley was twenty-five at the time, and she and Frank had been playing smaller venues for years. As marvelous a shot as Frank Butler was, over time he played more second banana in the act, fulfilling the role of Oakley's manager and representative. They were inseparable and spent sixteen of the next twenty-one years with Cody. Oakley became a sensation, the featured act in an exhibition jammed with eye-opening, colorful performances. For all of her hardships early in life, Oakley never lost her core personality, which was warm, friendly, and welcoming. Audiences saw that in her, and those traits aided her popularity. Her small physical stature, combined with remarkable gun-handling skill, also set her apart from the manly men identified with the West.

When the Wild West exhibition was still trying to establish itself, Buffalo Bill realized it was critical that the exhibition appeal not only to men, but also to families. He did not want to scare off mothers who made decisions on how the entertainment dollar was spent and could influence husbands to stay clear if they thought the performances would be too much for their children to stomach. For every Johnny Baker who fulfilled a dream by joining the Wild West exhibition from the time he was ten, there were audience members, especially from the East, who could be scared away by too much gunfire and too much wild in the West. Once Oakley joined the troupe, part of the strategy was to win over the fence sitters. If women saw Oakley do her thing and were wooed, that could pay off.

Burke addressed this very topic, saying that's why the organizers put Oakley's act first:

> It was our first thought when we planned the show that so much shooting would cause difficulty, that horses would be frightened and women and children terrified. It was when Annie Oakley joined us that Colonel Cody devised the idea of graduating the excitement. Miss Oakley comes on very early in the performance. She starts very gently, shooting with a pistol. Women and children see a harmless woman out there and do not get worried. Gradually, she increases the charge in her rifles until at last she shoots with a full charge. Thus, by the time the attack on the stagecoach comes in, the audience is accustomed to the sound of shooting. In all our history of the Wild West there has never been a horse frightened sufficiently to run away at any of our outdoor performances.[3]

In demeanor, Oakley could easily have been mistaken for a housewife content to be at home, modest, capable in sewing, in no way naturally flamboyant. But when she performed under the lights, showing off her talents, she was transformed. She was just like an actress playing a character, although the shooting Annie was as much a part of her as any other aspect of her being. Her shooting was so spectacular it could not be denied. While she often gave off the vibe being able to take it or leave it when it came to show business, that would be a misreading. The chance to show audiences what she could do was very much part of what made her tick. Also, when challenged to a match, she was a tiger in the competition. She was much like a professional athlete in that sense—the bigger the stakes, the more she dug down to prove she was the best.

The Wild West exhibition was the perfect vehicle for Oakley. It not only gave her the best opportunity to show her stuff to millions of adoring spectators, but to see the world, and do so with Frank, the man she loved. Although the Butlers never had children, for many years the company of the Wild West exhibition was family. In his book *The Colonel and Little Missie*, Pulitzer Prize–winning author Larry McMurtry, who created *Lonesome Dove*, proclaimed Buffalo Bill and Annie Oakley the United States' first superstars, the original celebrities, of sorts, of the entertainment world. It is a worthy argument. Together, under the Wild West umbrella, they became household names, cemented reputations and images in the American mind, and gave the world a primer on celebrityhood.

Not only was Oakley a brilliant shot standing still and firing at targets, she also conceived more daring ways to thrill audiences. As if it was not enough Oakley was blessed with an unerring aim and could blast many things to smithereens in short bursts of time, she added more complicated tricks to her repertoire. Even if Frank Butler and Nate Salsbury wondered if this was a great idea, both because she could fail or be injured, Annie added a routine where she fired her rifle or shotgun at targets while riding a bicycle. Then she moved on to firing from a moving horse. Soon enough she upped the ante, somehow figuring out how to lie down on the horse's back as it moved and still shoot with accuracy. Then she made the act harder by standing on top of horses and shooting. Always, she kept increasing the degree of difficulty. In other acts, Oakley hit a playing card held sideways from thirty steps away, shot cigarettes out of the mouth of husband Frank as they trailed from his lips, shot dimes out of the air, shot out a burning candle with one shot, and put several holes in playing cards before they hit the ground. Who would not pay to see such sharpshooting?

Upon his request, Oakley shot the ashes off the end of a cigarette being smoked by German Crown Prince Wilhelm II who was about to become kaiser, the head of the country. Enthralled by Oakley's shooting during one of the Wild West exhibition's European tours, he wiggled free of his bodyguards to jump into the arena—something she was neither expecting, nor welcomed, and insisted she shoot the ashes. No pressure. Oakley reluctantly agreed, raised her pistol and performed the trick. Some years later, when Germany was the enemy in World War I, some claim Oakley wrote him a letter offering to do the trick again. There was no answer. She also said she should have shot the kaiser the first time around, saving the world quite a bit of grief.[4]

When Johnny Baker was still quite young, he wished to graduate from errand boy of the Wild West exhibition to headliner. His goal was to become an accomplished trick shooter. The youngster, who would become a surrogate son to Buffalo Bill in lieu of the toddler Kit Carson Cody, had Annie Oakley as an instructor, and she helped all she could. Baker did eventually become the star shooter of the show with one of his specialties being an ability to shoot at targets while standing on his head.

Baker was once interviewed about just how serious, competitive, and good Oakley was when it came to matches, or even more casual shooting around the camps of the Wild West exhibition. He said he never saw Oakley ever let up, and she was always determined to do what it took to win. He offered insight into what made Oakley a special shooter:

> There was never a day when I didn't try to beat her. But it just couldn't be done. You know, the ordinary person has nerves. They'll bob up on him in spite of everything. He'll notice some little thing that distracts his attention, or get fussed by the way a ball travels through the air. Or a bit of light will get on the sights—or seem to get there, and throw him off. I wasn't any different from the average person, but Annie was. The minute she picked up a rifle or a shotgun, it seemed she made a machine of herself—every action went like clockwork. And how was a fellow to beat anyone like that? To tell the truth, it would have made a better show if I could have beat her every few performances. But it couldn't be done.[5]

Lillian Smith tried harder than anyone else. Smith was just fifteen when Buffalo Bill signed her for the Wild West exhibition in 1886 as another shooter. She came from California and had been shooting since age seven. In Annie Oakley's mind, the last thing the Wild West exhibition needed was another female shooting attraction. Oakley and Smith were opposites in terms of dress, demeanor, and flamboyance. Oakley was conservative, Smith flashy. There was not only a strong sense of rivalry between them, but apparently a dislike. Both Annie and Smith were part of the Wild West exhibition when Buffalo Bill took the troupe to England in 1887. They both met Queen Victoria, but also shook hands with a princess. This violated royal protocol. They were supposed to kiss the hand proffered, but while this gaffe was noticed, it was passed over without a big deal being made. Smith and Oakley performed a shooting exhibition for the queen, and each hit forty-eight of their fifty attempts.

No question Smith was a fresh star in the Wild West exhibition and a marvelous shooter, but she was not an enduring figure with the troupe. At the height of this rivalry, Annie Oakley left the group for two years, returning in 1889. While Oakley's legend lasted, Smith's popularity faded, and her name is virtually unknown except among scholars. In 2017, Julia Bricklin produced a book about Smith's life with the audacious title of *America's Best Female Sharpshooter*. Bricklin makes the case Smith was a better shot than Oakley, which is a reach. She may have been her equal in a given moment, but history sides with Oakley in debate.

As she departed her home as a fourteen year old, Smith billed herself as "The California Girl." Besides her uncanny marksmanship, part of her charm was her youth. Bricklin speculates Smith may have met Buffalo Bill in San Francisco in 1886. Cody was always on the lookout for Wild West talent, and he brought Smith on board in the spring of that year after she shot in some exhibitions near his home in North Platte, Nebraska. By then, Smith was fifteen, and those who witnessed her accuracy were won over. A newspaper report, perhaps forgetting about Oakley, labeled Smith "the best shot in the world."[6] This after she broke twenty glass balls in twenty-four seconds with a rifle and twenty balls with a single-shot rifle, reloading after each shot, in fifty-four seconds.

Smith received good notices with the Wild West exhibition. Oakley was frosty to her and, while it was not in her nature to voice animosity, clearly disliked this competitor to her status. One rumor circulated that Smith thought of Oakley as a has-been and herself as the heir apparent. Oakley began pretending to be younger, cutting six years off her real age. Even if there was some internal strife, the Wild West exhibition was becoming more popular. At venues large enough, a show might attract twenty thousand or more people. Fans oohed and ahhed over the shooting of both Smith and Oakley. From a public standpoint, the Wild West exhibition was big enough for the both of them. No grounds were large enough, though, it seemed, to put enough distance between Smith and Oakley away from the arena.

In somewhat of a surprise to many, Smith swiftly became enamored with a cowboy quite a bit older than she was, fourteen years, in fact, and after a brief fling, Smith and Jim Willoughby were married against her parents' wishes. Smith was no longer the innocent young teen. In England, Oakley was by far the bigger hit with the locals. Also, in a direct competition at Wimbledon (where the famous tennis tournament is played), Oakley bested Smith in a shootout. One way Buffalo Bill kept the duo from complete direct competition within the boundaries of the show was by keeping Smith focused on shooting rifles and Oakley specialized in shotgun shooting.

When Annie Oakley and Frank Butler split from the Wild West exhibition in 1887, no public reason was given. She had always retained the right to participate in exhibitions, which were quite lucrative to her, and that may have contributed to the couple's decision, in addition to the strong feelings against Smith. She may have decided she did not want to put up with discomfort daily.

However, this was just an interlude. It was Smith who did not linger with the Wild West exhibition. The Wild West exhibition and the Butler family operated in separate spheres for just two years, then they reunited. Smith went off on her own. As the calendar turned to 1890, Oakley's fame continued to grow and her association with Buffalo Bill Cody and the Wild West exhibition became indivisible. Cody and Oakley did not work together until death did them part, but were major players in a fantastic, worldwide phenomenon that thrilled and entertained the masses.

Buffalo Bill's star always shone brighter than any of the other stars he helped develop or featured, and that included Annie Oakley, Sitting Bull, or Johnny Baker. The show could always go on—and did—even if someone of the stature of Oakley went her way or retired, as long as Buffalo Bill's name was attached to the marquis.

Buffalo Bill was far from a financial genius, but he understood marketing, promotion, and the way he was viewed by the American public and the rest of the world, and he knew he had a good product people wanted to see. He was savvy about logistics, but not so much so that he did not need helpers like Salsbury and Major John Burke. Sitting on a horse, usually an impressive white one, Cody seemed majestic. He was handsome and distinguished looking with his trademark flowing hair, thick mustache, and goatee, and if he rode into your town there was no mistaking him. He was honest in his dealings and was generous to strangers, friends, and family. Certainly, he was not without flaws, his drinking often mentioned as a major one, but everyone wanted to know William F. Cody, and it seemed he did know everyone of consequence in American society.

Basically estranged from wife Louisa, Cody was footloose on the road, and a man whom women wanted to meet and get to know. He was rich, famous, somewhat powerful in presiding over his Wild West empire, and with Louisa often thousands of miles away, his marriage certificate must have seemed like a filed-away piece of paper. For those who viewed Cody as a rake, even if such meanderings were difficult to chronicle for most historians, or they did not much care to do so, it must seem as if Annie Oakley is the only woman who passed through his life with whom he never shared a moment's romance.

13

Love 'Em and Leave 'Em

When William F. Cody fell in love with Louisa Frederici, he was just nineteen years old, and while he may have been capable of drawing a map of the Plains on the back of his hand, he was not very worldly. The world awaited, though he did not know that in 1865. Louisa looked mighty good to him. They had a rapport. They were different kinds of people, but they somehow met in the middle—at first.

In retrospect, Cody's pledge to settle down and farm seems ludicrous. The couple had four children, and Cody was a good father to them when he was around, which was not very often, between first continuing his dangerous occupation of scouting for the cavalry and then finding his true calling as a showman in leading the Wild West exhibition all over the planet. He was generous to them when he could help them, and he always professed his love for them, but while their mother was a stay-at-home mom, he was a restless soul who was far removed from the concept of a stay-at-home or nine-to-five dad.

There is no question there was tenderness and love between Cody and Louisa in the beginning. But such feelings dissipated over time as Cody repeatedly left home for new adventures and Louisa came to realize how little she cared for the frontier, the West, and her husband's lifestyle, and how little she identified with it. When they got together, there were tensions. They became increasingly alienated from one another. Of course, Cody had come close to initiating divorce proceedings once and retreated after the loss of Orra, the second of their children to die. These early deaths had to take a toll on the couple, too. Louisa had her share of grudges, but the most interesting aspect of the book of memories she wrote about her decades spent with Buffalo Bill was that she overlooked almost all of the bad and wrote about only the good. Much of what she wrote glossed over facts with fictitious emotions.

It was her story, and she told it the way she wanted. Her Will was fixed in her mind. At one point in her memoir, Louisa recounted Cody's encounter with Yellow Hair and actually wrote, "...It was alluring because it called up to me all the fascination of the West that had gotten into my blood and would never leave."[1] Huh? Louisa would not have minded never seeing the West again. For a time she believed Cody would give up his successful stage career because he was weary of those types of performances. When he spoke of the creation of what became the Wild West exhibition, that did not bother Louisa at first either, because she thought it would be seasonal and he would be spending more time at home in the off-seasons. She never imagined how the Wild West exhibition would become such a grand spectacle and become so famous, keeping Buffalo Bill out there with his fans for months at a time, traveling great distances. Home was pretty much the only place he never visited.

When Louisa depicted those early days of the formulation of the Wild West exhibition, she portrayed herself as an equal partner in the planning, as if she was not only wildly enthusiastic about the venture, but that she also played a significant role in its origin. "And what a different thing it was from those foolish plays in which Will had been forced [by] public demand to appear," she wrote. "How clean, how bright, how sharp and bright, and how truly it depicted the West! Here was something that he could love and I could love—and we put into it everything our hearts possessed."[2]

Reality was far different. The Wild West exhibition expanded the chasm between them. It was the enemy. It was not the only issue between Buffalo Bill and Louisa, but the Wild West exhibition ensured that the distance between them, literally and figuratively, would never be bridged.

Cody once speculated the insecure Louisa even resented his close attachment to his sisters. He said sometimes when they were arguing and it seemed to be building, he definitely felt the urge to return to the Plains. "Our dispositions were not such as to get along well together," he said. "And I knew the longer I staid [sic] we were likely to grow into more trouble or something of that kind." On the issue of his devotion to his sisters, Cody was irked. "It kind o' grated on my nerves and I would pull out to the Plains, again," he said.[3]

After the scalp gift, the Codys engaged in some additional verbal scrapping, and Louisa informed Will she was leaving the frontier, taking the children, and returning to her parents' house in Missouri where they first courted. Cody reported dividing up the money and heading as far west as he ever had, to theater performances in California, while Louisa turned east. Then he received a letter from his sister May saying she and Louisa had a heart-to-heart talk, and Louisa changed her mind and wanted to get back together. Cody met her in Denver, and they went on to North Platte, Nebraska, where Cody built his fabulous home. Cody did say that for a time Louisa indicated an interest in the start-up of the Wild West exhibition. But once he aligned himself with more capable planners, she found no role for herself and no reason to travel with the performance. This all led to Louisa's resentment and Cody's letter to his sister Julia complaining about how she had tied up all of their money in land in North Platte and elsewhere.

These fissures kept forming, even as Cody's fame spread and he posed for photographs or sketches with anyone who asked. He seemed to get a charge out of it, especially if those requesting his side-by-side presence were attractive women. Cody had the gift of gab, and he seemed to be a bit of a flirt by nature. He enjoyed flattering women, whether or not he really believed his compliments. They loved to hear this famous symbol of western manhood glibly comment on their beauty. With Louisa so far away, Cody engaged in some dalliances, some of which resulted in evidence left behind. Chris Enss, who went in pursuit of documenting just who some of these women were for a 2010 book, took note of a Mollie Moses of Kentucky. Cody even wrote a letter to her that outlasted his own life, calling her "My Dear Little Favorite" and adding, "With love and kiss to my little girl—From her big boy Bill."[4] That hardly sounds like a harmless pen pal relationship.

Moses worshipped Cody from afar at first and chased after him. They met in November of 1885 after a Wild West exhibition in Illinois. A widow, she made sure to meet the star, and her intelligent conversation lured him. Cody was attracted to Moses. While such an infatuation from afar is often the sign of someone who may simply be beguiled by reputation only, in fact Moses was a mature woman and that part of her nature seemed to click with Cody's interest. They exchanged letters. Moses included the question of "What about Louisa?" Cody's response can be viewed as a stereotypical married man comment—he informed her they were separated. That may not have been true in a legal sense, but it was accurate in a practical sense.

Mollie did develop head-over-heels love for Cody, but being so involved in and out front with the Wild West exhibition everywhere he traveled, they did not rendezvous often enough for her liking. She might visit him on the road, but despite her constant invitations to her home, Buffalo Bill could not just up and leave the Wild West exhibition. He wrote Moses letters expressing his feelings—"With Fond Love," he closed one. She begged him for keepsakes to appreciate during his absences.[5]

To remedy this situation, Buffalo Bill hired Mollie Moses for the Wild West exhibition, starting at a stop in St. Louis, so she could be with him constantly. He also bought her a horse as a welcome present. Moses was not a natural horsewoman, and even being with Cody as the show went from place to place, she did not really feel she was with him. Cody really did work long hours. Finally, she gave up on Buffalo Bill as a romantic partner and returned to her home in Kentucky. Financial difficulties caused her downfall, and she died at forty-three.

It is unclear just how much Louisa may have known about Cody's affair with Mollie Moses, but she regularly chastised him for infidelities, real or imagined, and even became jealous when newspapers reported his meeting with female heads of state in Europe. Much later, it came out Cody was sick of Louisa telling him not to drink so much, and he said to her, "Oh, momma, hush. The only way a man can stand you is to get drunk."[6] This harshness of speech was not typical of Cody, but may have illustrated just how badly their relationship had deteriorated.

Cody said when he first journeyed to Europe, neither he nor Louisa wrote one another a letter for a year. And they certainly were not staying in touch via Skype. Actually, when the Wild West exhibition visited England in 1887, Cody's daughter Arta, then nineteen, accompanied him. Now that his surviving children, Arta and Irma, were older, they sometimes visited him at Wild West performances in different parts of the United States.

Things went haywire once, when Louisa showed up unannounced in Chicago in 1894. Buffalo Bill had a new paramour, someone he met in England: Katherine Clemmons, an American who wanted to be an actress and whom Cody agreed to help. He financed a play for her, entered into a business partnership, and lent her some Wild West exhibition horses. They were back in the United States, in the midst of their love affair, when Louisa popped in. Buffalo Bill and Katherine were listed at their hotel as husband and wife. Oops. Cody called Clemmons "the finest looking woman in the world."[7] If Louisa thought her appearance was going to repair her marriage, this was a serious blow.

Another time, Louisa got wind Clemmons was living with Cody in North Platte. Again, she showed up without warning. Even though she did not find evidence of Clemmons, she raged through the structure, tearing it up and said, "I cleaned out the house."[8]

Still another time, with Cody headquartered at the Hoffman House in New York, Louisa came to the city and registered at the Astoria. When she telephoned, a woman answered the phone in Buffalo Bill's room. It was press agent Bessie Isbell, but Louisa destroyed her own room in anger. Cody paid the damages.

Back and forth things went. One minute Cody and Louisa were not even speaking, and the next, at least periodically, they attempted a reconciliation, such as when they invested in property in Wyoming in the 1890s. Sometimes they were even witnessed being affectionate to one another in public. Mostly, though, they were at odds. Louisa had no interest in traveling with the Wild West exhibition, and Cody felt it too much of a distraction having her around because things were liable to blow up at any time.

Cody did have committed love affairs with Mollie Moses and Katherine Clemmons, and he might well have had one-night stands as well. Women regularly flirted with him and threw themselves at the big, strong, handsome man who single-handedly conquered the West, or so it may have seemed to them. As Cody said, he considered himself separated from Louisa, so felt he did not have much of a governor on his interactions with women.

While Cody possessed a rough appeal to women, especially when decked out in his western duds, he could clean up well, too. He brushed back his long hair when attending fancy functions, removed his cowboy hat, and even dressed in a suit at times. He could appear civilized on formal occasions, not riding his horse into the ballroom or anything like that.

As it turned out, Bessie Isbell did also share Cody's bed, as was discovered in a hotel by his valet, John Claire, a long-time employee of the Wild West exhibition in Texas. Claire walked in on them. Neither seemed particularly disturbed that he saw them in somewhat compromising, revealing attire. Isbell did not hurry to leave, but casually took her goodbye, Claire said. He heard her say, "Until later, my Pahaska" and saw her kiss Cody on the cheek.[9] Isbell may well have been paid as a publicity agent, but she also acquired other duties over time. While Claire said the two were lovers and Isbell had no function with the Wild West exhibition, Cody insisted she was a paid worker. Louisa hired a private detective this time to ferret out the truth. The detective reported back that "Buffalo Bill and Ms. Isbell have been on too friendly terms for some time."[10]

There was also an apparent affair Cody had earlier with Olive Logan Sikes, who worked for Beadle and Adams, the publishing firm that took the lead producing the dime novels that spread Cody's exploits (true and false, or false and true) over the decades. This was a less publicized affair, which became public fodder in the early 1900s when Cody at last sought a divorce and Louisa fought to prevent the legal dissolution of what had been a tempestuous union for so long.

For years, as the tug-of-war spanned the continent, Louisa lobbied her two remaining children, Irma and Arta, to stand by her, often bad-mouthing their father. Arta took the negative commentary to heart and even wrote Buffalo Bill a wide-ranging complaint letter once. Irma tended to side with her father in the disputes.

Louisa even burned with jealousy when news of Buffalo Bill's meetings with queens of foreign countries reached American shores. Once in a great while the rumor gets repeated that somehow, briefly, Buffalo Bill and

Queen Victoria had a liaison while the Wild West exhibition played in England in 1887. This is likely nonsense, but it was fueled by a gift of a fancy pendant Queen Victoria presented to Cody before returning to America.

Later, in 1902, when Cody built the Irma Hotel in Cody, Wyoming, named for his daughter, the cherrywood bar was reported to be a gift from the queen. While the ornate, magnificent bar stands in place today, one-time Buffalo Bill Museum curator Paul Fees believes he debunked the story of the bar originating with the queen. That story persists, and in such modern electronic communication vehicles such as websites, the Irma Hotel's in particular, it is stated that the bar came from Queen Victoria. Dr. Jeremy Johnston, curator of the Buffalo Bill Museum at the Buffalo Bill Center of the West, said the legend of the bar being a gift to Buffalo Bill from the queen "is not true. There is no archival information that the bar came from Queen Victoria. Also, Buffalo Bill never claimed the bar came from Queen Victoria, nor did John Burke. Believe me, if Buffalo Bill did receive the bar from Queen Victoria, he would have promoted the hell out of that fact."[11]

In addition, Lynn Houze, a one-time assistant to Paul Fees at the Buffalo Bill Center, said Fees, who was Buffalo Bill Museum curator for twenty years, "researched the heck out of this." She said Fees even con-

Buffalo Bill Cody (left) stands at the cherrywood bar inside the Irma Hotel. The bar was said to be a gift from England's Queen Victoria, but that is not true (courtesy of Park County Archives).

tacted Buckingham Palace, which keeps records of all monarchs' gifts, and the palace had no record of the bar being given to Buffalo Bill. "One part of the bar on the back has a French manufacturer's mark on it and the queen never would have given anything made in France to anyone, let alone Buffalo Bill. There are cherrywood bars all over this country, as they were quite popular in the late 1880s and early 1900s."[12] Houze believes there was no mention of the bar as a gift from Queen Victoria until the 1960s and thinks a former Irma Hotel owner started the story.

It is a reach to suggest such prominent personages as the queen and Buffalo Bill, whose every move was touted in the press during the Wild West visit, had time for clandestine meetings that basically would have gone unremarked upon for decades. Queen Victoria was sixty-seven at the time of the Wild West performances. Likewise, she died in 1901, the year before the Irma Hotel opened. Those who subscribe to the bar being from the queen say it was a token of the queen's esteem based on her long-ago pleasant memories of the Wild West exhibition and Buffalo Bill.

When the Wild West command performance concluded, the queen summoned Cody and other actors to her royal box. Perhaps with a wink, but also fuel for whatever low-key rumors surfaced, Cody said Queen Victoria told him she liked watching the exhibition. And she said more, but Cody said, "Modesty forbids me to repeat [it]."[13]

There is one tiny piece of correspondence in existence apparently sent to Buffalo Bill while he visited London, which raised a few eyebrows. Tucked away in the Buffalo Bill Center of the West's Harold McCracken Research Library is an item with a cover reading, "Diary, 1887." That is the year of the journey to England. Inside of this collection of correspondence is a sheet of paper that at top left is a drawing of a crown placed on a soft pillow-like item. To the right is the stationary's return address of "Windsor Castle, July 1, 1887." The content in its entirety reads, "Dear Bill—Come up at four and bring Red Shirt [a prominent Native American performer of the Wild West exhibition] with you. The beer is on ice. Don't fail. Ever yours, Vic R." Beneath that is the message, "Burn this" with those words underlined.[14] Paul Fees said some of the Garlows, Irma's marriage relations, always believed this paper proved Buffalo Bill spent time with the queen in her boudoir.[15]

Regardless of whatever words passed between the queen and the showman, there is no doubt Buffalo Bill charmed her. Although early in the exhibition's series of overseas tours, the England visit was one of Cody's and the Wild West's greatest triumphs. It was an important one, as well. It laid the foundation for future successes. Such glorious journeys were often a great respite for Cody, who had gone from fighting Plains Indians to fighting with his wife.

14

The Wild West Is the Toast of Europe and Everywhere Else

Queen Victoria was born in 1817 and ascended to the British throne in 1837. When she married in 1840, it was to her cousin Albert. Albert died in 1861, and the queen retreated into mourning, refraining from most public appearances for the next twenty-seven years. It was one of the Wild West exhibition's great achievements to draw the queen back into the public eye due to her curiosity about Buffalo Bill, the Old West, and Americans.

By 1887, the Wild West exhibition was an American hit. Buffalo Bill was famous, and his exhibition was in demand all over the United States. He played a dizzying number of venues. Nowhere was the Wild West exhibition better received than at Madison Square Garden where it played for weeks and attracted one million people. On Christmas Day of 1886, Buffalo invited ten thousand school children to attend his show.

It was after that notable New York stand that the boundaries of his own country became too fragile to contain Buffalo Bill. That year marked the fiftieth anniversary of Queen Victoria on the throne, and a consortium of American businessmen had made arrangements with British counterparts to participate in "An Exhibition of the Arts, Industries, Manufactures and Resources of the United States." They approached Buffalo Bill Cody and offered the opportunity to join them and spend six months in Europe with the Wild West exhibition. Cody and Nate Salsbury discussed the proposition and accepted.

Buffalo Bill gathered numerous endorsements for John Burke to use in promoting the operation. It was at this time Cody pondered his lack of a significant military rank. He was a scout, not an officer, and while

14. The Toast of Europe and Everywhere Else

Wanamaker's Department Store in Philadelphia, Pennsylvania. Buffalo Bill Cody is seated among those sitting cross legged in front (courtesy of Park County Archives).

Buffalo Bill Cody was always convivial with children. Here he cuts a birthday cake (courtesy of Park County Archives).

esteemed he was not sure what his British hosts would make of that. So he sought a way around the conundrum. His remarkable powers of persuasion worked overtime, along with the aid of Burke. The publicity majordomo approached Governor John. M. Thayer of Nebraska with an idea, and he bought it. Thayer commissioned Cody as a colonel in the Nebraska National Guard. Thayer blessed this knighthood of sorts, at least as far as Cody was concerned, by saying, "reposing special trust and confidence in the integrity, patriotism and ability of the Hon. William F. Cody, on behalf of, and in the name of the State, do hereby appoint and commission him Aide-de-Camp, on my staff, with the rank of Colonel."[1] It was not a pretend title, but not one his general friends would consider meaningful. Still, it would do when meeting high officials in other countries. They would not care what kind of colonel Cody was. Indeed, over time, some civilian friends got into the habit of calling Cody colonel as an honorific. Certainly, over the years, many have been labeled Kentucky colonels with few outsiders bothering to check for credentials. After all, one such famous personage to have that rank bestowed while not having earned it in the military was Colonel Harland Sanders, the Kentucky Fried Chicken founder.

Naturally, Burke went ahead to England to spread his publicity and warm up the audience. This is what the advance man excelled at, and he also helped oversee the construction of a massive arena that was estimated to hold twenty-five thousand, which even today is larger than many coliseums where professional National Hockey League teams and professional National Basketball Association teams play their home games in the United States and Canada.

It was quite the undertaking to move the Wild West exhibition across the Atlantic Ocean. That troupe included nearly a hundred Indians, some of whom were none too keen to sail so far offshore they could not see land, close to two hundred horses, and a Noah's ark worth of other species such as buffalo, elk, mules, wild steers, and deer. Besides such stars as himself and Annie Oakley, there where another eighty-five members of the cast and tons of equipment in the way of tents, wagons, guns and ammunition, and the Deadwood stagecoach. It was a two-week voyage and appropriately took place aboard the ship called the *State of Nebraska*. Presumably, the colonel did not outrank the captain of this vessel. The Native Americans feared the trip, and Buffalo Bill got seasick.

While welcomed heartily, it turned out many diplomatic and construction problems afflicted the start-up. But the arrival of the Wild West exhibition jump-started enthusiasm, Buffalo Bill Cody was hailed as a real hero, and Burke's genius in providing colorful material for the newspapermen once again did its job. Curiosity attracted famous Englishmen and

Englishwomen, royalty of other nations, and the average citizen, just to see how the troupe was going to set everything up.

A royal preview four days prior to the scheduled May 9 opening for Londoners, with guests such as the prince and princess of Wales and visiting royalty from France and Denmark, was a sensation. Albert Edward, who later became king, led the cheers, and that seemed to be a huge influence on the general reception of the Wild West exhibition. The royal guests even toured Cody's camp quarters and visited his tent. Everything, from horses to sharpshooters Annie Oakley and Lillian Smith, was popular. When the performance opened to the public, newspaper reviews were generous and flattering.

Hearing it not from the horse's mouth, but from her own son's, and seeing how her subjects reacted, Queen Victoria decided she must see the Wild West exhibition. She ordered up a command performance. The queen planned to bring the cast to Windsor Castle, animals and all, but when it was pointed out the venue was too small, she broke her quarantine and journeyed to the new arena. Traveling in a special carriage, the queen was accompanied by royal guardsmen, but she also brought friends and family, the prince and princess of Wales for a second go-around, assorted other royalty, and ladies-in-waiting. Burke seemed quite taken by that group, saying they resembled "a veritable pottiere of living flowers about the temporary throne."[2] Speaking of flowery.

Buffalo Bill started the doings by carrying a large American flag around the arena on horseback and stated it was a symbol of friendship and peace. The queen stood and bowed, and the others in the box also stood and the men waved their hats. There was some level of surprise from the Americans, who may have recalled the country's relationship resulting in the Revolutionary War, the Declaration of Independence, and the War of 1812 with the burning of the White House by the British. No tension this day, however. Cody said, "There arose such a genuine heart-stirring American yell from our company as to shake the sky."[3]

For whatever reason exactly, whether it was nervousness or a show of imperial authority, the queen said she intended to stick around for just an hour. But when that time elapsed and the performance was not over, she stayed, and stayed overtime, summoning the principals and cast members, as well as Buffalo Bill and Native American performers, to meet her at the royal box. She seemed quite taken with Annie Oakley's shooting, saying, "You are a very, very clever little girl."[4]

It is intriguing the queen made a journal entry about her experience and what a good time she had. In part, she wrote, "...we saw a very extraordinary and interesting sight, a performance of 'Buffalo Bill's Wild West.' All the different people, wild, painted Red Indians from America on their wild bare-backed horses, of different tribes—cowboys, Mexicans, all came tearing around at full speed. Col. Cody, 'Buffalo Bill,' as he is called ... is a splendid man, handsome & gentleman-like in manner."[5]

Apparently the queen did not keep her pleasure to herself. Some five weeks later, on June 20, she called for another command performance to include others of stature. This was attended by visiting kings, including those of Denmark, Greece, and other countries, and other royalty. Buffalo Bill himself as driver gave them all a spin around the arena in the Deadwood stagecoach. This led to a legendary quip by Cody; comparing this ride to poker, he said, "I've held four kings, but four kings and the Prince of Wales, such as no man ever held before."[6]

Recalcitrant Native Americans, who stayed behind in the United States because they disliked the idea of such a long trip or were scared of the ocean crossing, missed out. Those who came and participated loved the attention and experience. Red Shirt, one of the Sioux leaders, and some others, attended the London theater.

Black Elk fondly remembered Queen Victoria and the scene surrounding her appearance at the show. "She came to the show in a big, shining wagon," Black Elk said, "and there were soldiers on both sides of her. That day, the other people could not come to the show, just Grandmother England and some people who came with her."[7]

One published report, by the *Sporting Life*, relayed the stunning thoroughness of acceptance and enjoyment felt by those attending the Wild West exhibition. It read, "The opening of the Wild West Show was one of the signal successes of recent years. Such a vast concourse of the cream—or it may be as well to say, the crème de la crème—of society is seldom seen at any performance. The number of chariots waiting at the gates out-numbered those of Pharaoh, and the phalanx of footmen constituted quite a small army."[8]

Cody wrote a fascinating comment about his reaction when Queen Victoria requested the command performance, especially after learning she hardly ever appeared in public and never for entertainment. Not only did he and the cast members "feel highly complimented," he felt "the public would hardly believe it, and if bets had been made at the clubs, the odds on a rank outsider in the Derby would have been nothing to the amount that would have been bet that it was a Yankee hoax."[9]

When the queen showed respect to the American flag and the Americans gave forth with that mighty shout, Cody mentally rewound to the hostilities of the past. He felt as if he and the Wild West exhibition had definitely improved U.S.–British relations. "All present were constrained to feel that here was an outward and visible sign of the extinction of that mutual prejudice," Cody said, "sometimes almost amounting to race hatred, that has severed the two nations from the times of Washington and George the Third, to the present day. We felt that the hatchet was buried at last and the Wild West had been at the funeral."[10]

Did Cody read too much into the diplomatic value of the Wild West exhibition? Maybe, maybe not. After all, nearly a century later, President Richard Nixon opened the door to better relations with China through his vaunted ping-pong diplomacy. At the least, when Buffalo Bill's cowboys shot off pistols and rifles, they were not aiming them at the British.

The longer the Wild West exhibition remained in London, the more popular Buffalo Bill became. Various high officials of government and the business world sought his company at breakfasts, luncheons, and dinners, and he was invited so many places he had to work to keep up with the show schedule. He was also made an honorary member of several British social clubs. It was as if not to be outdone everyone invited him everywhere. In late June, after the second command performance when Cody played chauffer on the Deadwood stagecoach, the prince of Wales gave him a gift of a diamond pin.

Indeed, the prince and princess of Wales were repeat customers during the London run. One day, Buffalo Bill was surprised to receive a note from the princess saying she wanted to ride in the Deadwood stagecoach during the act. Her husband was not keen on it, but she superimposed her will and did so. Another time, Cody said, the princess sent a note indicating she "would that evening visit the show incognita."[11]

Even Cody recognized this as fairly brazen behavior. Even if the royals were not photographed any time they appeared in public, or written about any time someone moved outside Windsor Castle, the princess was one of the best-known personages in the country. This was going to be a tricky assignment. She did show up in her royal carriage, but then insisted on being seated among the people. The manager got the quick idea to seat her where newspapermen usually watched, but who were not scheduled to attend that day. The princess was accompanied by a single attendant, so there was plenty of room, until unexpectedly some newsmen wandered in. One remarked on the remarkable resemblance of the woman to the princess. Somehow, the manager talked around it, introducing the couple as his friends, "Mr. and Mrs. Jones from Texas."[12] The princess thought the entire episode hilarious.

After the performances concluded in London, the Wild West exhibition played in Manchester and Birmingham, England. Cody then took a vacation to Italy with his daughter Arta, who had joined him in London part-way through the engagement. The Wild West exhibition then sailed back to New York. It was a grand season and merely the prelude to numerous other trips overseas. Other countries constituted fresh markets.

Not that Buffalo neglected his base. He made sure his American fans got enough Wild West, too. An early Wild West exhibition supporter even pre–England was famed writer Mark Twain (a.k.a. Samuel Clemens). He was coming into his own as a respected man of letters following publication of novels such as *The Adventures of Tom Sawyer*, *The Adventures of Huckleberry Finn*, and *Innocents Abroad*. Twain was as mesmerized by the Wild West exhibition as other spectators and in 1885 wrote to Cody, "I have now seen your Wild West show two days in succession, enjoyed it thoroughly. It brought back to me the breezy, wild life of the Rocky Mountains, and stirred me like a war song. The show is genuine, the cowboys, vaqueros, Indians, stagecoach, costumes, the same as I saw on the frontier years ago."[13] Twain predicted a great reception in England. He was right.

After the marvelous run in England, Buffalo Bill predicted a great reception everywhere he traveled. In 1889, on a tour of Italy, Cody became fascinated with the idea of putting on the Wild West exhibition in the Roman Colosseum, but the Colosseum was actually too small to stage a full-fledged exhibition. Most Wild West cast members visited the Vatican and the Pope. John Burke was Catholic and was likely the most excited member of the Wild West exhibition over the invitation. Nate Salsbury wrote an account of the visit to the Holy See. "About ninety percent of the company was in its best bib and tucker when I arrived at the ground that morning," Salsbury said. "Arriving at the Vatican, we were escorted to the Courtyard that opens from the Sistine Chapel." It was the anniversary of the Pope's coronation, and when the troupe entered the chapel, there were hundreds of others present, including high-ranking members of the diplomatic corps. "It was one of the most impressive human ceremonies that I have ever witnessed," Salsbury continued, "as the Pope, borne on his Sedia, came down between the Wild West lines on his way to the Papal throne. It was a curious sight to watch the expressions on the faces of the people from the frontier of America as they gazed in awestruck wonder at the magnificence displayed on all sides, and marked the exhibition of respect shown His Holiness, as borne aloft, he waved his blessing to the worshipping throng."[14] Salsbury said the Pope paused in front of Cody, and Cody bowed his head.

Buffalo Bill first visited Canada before there was a Wild West exhibition, going to Ontario and Quebec in 1874, Ontario again in 1876, and Quebec again in 1880, and also in 1885 as the Wild West exhibition picked up steam. He first made a stop in France, playing a long engagement in Paris between May and November of 1889, but toured all over the country in 1905. Germany was a popular venue with shows in 1890, 1891, and 1906.

14. The Toast of Europe and Everywhere Else

Wherever Buffalo Bill traveled, he spread the gospel of the West, although over the decades—he was on the road for thirty years with one combination or another—he made some tweaks. Typically, a performance included the attack on the Deadwood stagecoach, Custer's Last Stand, the rescue of women who had been captured by Indians, the first scalp for Custer, fabulous shooting by Cody, Lillian Smith for a little while, and Annie Oakley and Johnny Baker for a long time, a buffalo hunt, and more.

It was a special occasion when Buffalo Bill came to town. Those splashy posters heralded his arrival. The performances were magnificently choreographed. Many towns preserved artifacts of the visits, keeping them in museums. Cody provoked the study of the American West in schools. He also influenced the German writer Karl May, who created his own version of a Wild West in novels. An extremely prolific author, May's series featuring an Apache chief named Winnetou and his white friend, and blood brother, Old Shatterhand were among his highly popular works, which in all sold two hundred million copies. *Winnetou*, written in 1892, was his most popular work and ignited his western series.

May's Old Shatterhand was a German tutor come to America in that role, but who stumbles into many adventures on the frontier, thus earning his nickname. "So there I was," his character said, "baptized again without my consent, with that fighting name, the name I have carried from that day to this. It is common in the West for men to have such names."[15]

The main fear when the Wild West exhibition returned to Europe each time, with the exception of stopovers in England, was a potential language barrier. John Burke proved his mettle paving the way, but most of the performances were visual, without much dialogue. Anyone from anywhere could appreciate Annie Oakley's marksmanship, Buffalo Bill's horsemanship, and the impressive horses and buffalo in the arena. Turned out Buffalo Bill transcended languages, even in person when invited out on the town and to parties in France. There is one poster of a pending Buffalo Bill visit that advertised the imminent arrival without even mentioning the name of the Wild West exhibition or Cody. In a dramatic statement of how famous Cody had become, this poster featured his visage, flowing hair, goatee under a cowboy hat, superimposed on a picture of a buffalo, and the simple words, "Je Vien." In English that means, "I Am Coming." Wow. That was confidence, and it was no mystery who was coming: Buffalo Bill and his buffalo.

Immortalized on so many posters and photographed more times than can be calculated as that technology advanced, and even recorded on film through the assistance of his friend Thomas Edison, who when not busy inventing the light bulb dabbled in movie-making (his three-minute features being the first movies made in the United States), the most significant painting of Cody ever done was done in France.

Rosa Bonheur was already well-established, and her reputation as the best female painter of the eighteenth century made for a natural match with Buffalo Bill. She was no expert on the West, but she wished to paint his portrait because of his fame. Bonheur attended the Wild West exhibition on a free pass from Cody and had enough fun watching that she invited him to her estate to pose for a portrait. What emerged was an epic view of Cody on a huge, imposing white stallion, the man in his full finery looking leftward from under a white brim hat. The original painting now resides in the collection of the Buffalo Bill Center of the West. Cody adored it, and once, when informed his house in North Platte, Nebraska, was burning, sent a telegram saying above all to save the painting and added he did not care very much about anything else. There were rumors, as seemed to follow Cody everywhere, that he and Bonheur were lovers. This was unlikely. Historical studies of her life suggest she was gay, and she lived most of her adult life with female partners. She was also much older than Cody, sixty-seven at the time of his visit, a contemporary of Queen Victoria.

One serious problem arose in France. Many horses came down with a serious disease, and most had to be euthanized. That was a blow to a show that relied so heavily on cowboy and Indian riders.

The Wild West exhibition received a fairly mediocre reception in Spain, only partially due to the weather, but it was a wild hit in Italy. The more regularly Buffalo Bill and his cast of characters toured Europe, the more welcome and familiar they became. Rather than tire of the spectacle that was unique in the beginning, dazzled spectators could not get enough and were further entertained when new acts showed up and old favorites reappeared.

It was said, as one way to make friends, Cody and his cowboys had a standing offer to respond to challenges set forth in England, France, Germany, and Italy to attempt to break and ride any horse people in those countries felt were unruly and could not be tamed. It was observed, "They were frequently given spoiled horses from the cavalry service in the different countries through which they passed, animals which the trained horse breakers of the European armies could do nothing, and yet in almost all cases the cow punchers and bronco busters, with Buffalo Bill mastered these beasts as readily as they did their own western horses."[16]

Before the turn of the century, Buffalo Bill added another partner, James Bailey of Barnum & Bailey Circus. Bailey was a logistics pro, and it was his idea to have the Wild West exhibition play one-night stands in certain places rather than setting up shop for months at a time in one

14. The Toast of Europe and Everywhere Else

locale. Given how much effort it took to transport people and animals and how long it took to erect camps, Cody was not initially receptive to this. But Bailey proved it could be done, and moving by train facilitated the whole operation. Bailey's arrival was fortuitous. In 1901, Nate Salsbury, worn down by the pressures of the job and weary from the travels, could no longer handle his Wild West duties and retired. It was quite the challenge to keep the Wild West exhibition growing, improving, and moving, especially after it grew to feature five hundred people at a time. He died a year later.

Following that splendid outing in England in 1887, the world really was Buffalo Bill Cody's stage. But he never overlooked his American audiences, particularly city crowds far from the frontier. New York was always big for him, whether at Madison Square Garden or on Staten Island. Whether it was in the United States or overseas, Buffalo Bill always promoted an image of the American West, and in the late nineteenth century and early twentieth century it was an image based on past reality—at least to him—that had faded from consciousness and dimmed in the minds of others who thought of it more in geographic terms than as a state of mind. There were not any cowboys riding horses or herding cattle anymore, were there? There were not any Indians taking scalps and driving off settlers anymore, were there?

Cody always sold the premise that the Wild West was "authentic."[17] He never wavered from that. The more years that passed, and as older people died who lived the western experience of the 1800s, the more Buffalo Bill's West became everyone's reality. Millions upon millions of people saw the West the way Cody presented it and that was all they knew, so that is what they believed. Cody was a master at shaping cultural perception, and his content was passed from generation to generation. John Burke, of course, was always on hand to give the concept a gentle nudge with his press releases.

The newspapermen who witnessed the Wild West exhibition were not so different from the average spectator. They were not men who rode the range, and they grew up where skyscrapers were beginning to sprout, not prairie grass. One review completely reinforced the Cody–Burke message. "The whole thing is real," it read. "There is not a bit of clap-trap about it. It is the picture of frontier life painted in intense realism, each scene standing forth in bold relief."[18]

Buffalo Bill demonstrated he could liven up and eclipse the excitement of a world trade fair in England in 1887. When Chicago was scheduled to host the World's Columbian Exhibition in 1893, he wanted in on it with the Wild West exhibition. But whether it was because the organizers did not recognize the potential Cody had for attracting crowds, or they were too snooty to see that a show about the past was as much of an attraction as predictions of the future, he was turned away. Big mistake. Buffalo Bill's revenge was sweet and grand.

By then, Buffalo Bill's Wild West exhibition had become "The Wild West and Congress of Rough Riders of the World." His company was a United Nations on horseback. This employment of the term "rough riders" predated by five years future President Theodore Roosevelt's usage to describe his men on their charge up San Juan Hill in Cuba. In perfect symmetry, once Roosevelt's military effort in the Spanish–American War leading that team of horseback attackers became legendary, Cody incorporated a San Juan Hill skit into his exhibition. Cody did keep up with the news.

After rejection from officials in Chicago, Salsbury went to work renting land that was basically across the street from the World's Fair to stage the cowboys' own World's Fair II. It was an extravaganza that became one of Buffalo Bill's greatest successes. He benefited wildly from location, location, location and even more so when the fair closed on Sundays and he went on. That was particularly valuable when patrons who did not realize the fair took the day off and arrived, only to be locked out.

The Chicago El, or elevated train, was new and ran directly to the Midway Plaisance, as the area of town was known. Cody was exiled to the parking lot at 63rd Street, and while he likely resented that at first, it did not make one bit of difference. Fans flocked to the Wild West. One advertisement read, "Every Day—Rain Or Shine—At 3 p.m. And 8 p.m. Voted A World Beater."[19] Translated into modern English that seemingly meant critics had bestowed five-star reviews. Another advertisement read, "450 People In The Saddle. Indians, Cowboys, Spanish Gauchos, Vaqueros, Detachments Of Cavalry, Cossacks Of The Caucasus, Arabs, Tartars, Syrians, English, French, Germans and Americans."[20] It is possible more nationalities were involved, but ad space probably ran out.

Further burnishing his image at the expense of fair officials, and consistent with his nature and what he had already done in New York, Buffalo Bill was right there after Mayor Carter Harris's request to allow poor children in for free one day was refused by fair officials. Cody trumped the stingy-appearing fair folks in every way by announcing not only would there be free admission for these children, he would supply transportation to make sure they could get to the Wild West exhibition and give them free candy and ice cream. It did not take a publicity genius like John Burke to see the benefit of that gesture.

As if he was not occupied by the doings in Chicago and he was not famous enough, Cody lent his name to an enterprise that began playing out hundreds of miles away and was supposed to coincide with great

14. The Toast of Europe and Everywhere Else

fanfare at the World's Fair and the Wild West exhibition. Nine riders signed up in Chadron, Nebraska, for "The Great Cowboy Race," the first rider reaching Chicago to receive a cash prize and a gold-plated pistol. Cody basically figured "What the heck" in lending his name and prestige to the race. Some years before he had competed in a long-distance horse race in Nebraska, so there was that tie. The finish line was him, and when he gave them their prizes, he would receive an abundance of attention and press where he was doing business for the summer. He barely had to work for this bonus publicity.

Actually, Buffalo Bill was so well known by 1893, he hardly needed any more publicity. It was valuable only if it sold more tickets to the show. While legions adored Buffalo Bill, bought into his vision of the West, and bought tickets to his performances, in some quarters he was almost viewed as an evil Svengali, one who could woo young boys away from their studies and responsibilities because of the depth of their fascination with Cody and his cowboys and Indians.

In 2017, at the Buffalo Bill Center of the West's 100th anniversary observation of Cody's death, a symposium brought together forty speakers to expound on his life over a three-day period. There has long been a metaphor for the reckless irresponsibility of circus life in that it enticed young

Dr. Jeremy Johnston, curator of the Buffalo Bill Museum in the Buffalo Bill Center of the West in Cody, Wyoming, speaking at a 2017 symposium honoring Buffalo Bill Cody on the 100th anniversary of his death (photograph by the author).

people to run away from home and join up. Well, the same was true of the Wild West exhibition. Johnny Baker was seven when he bonded with Buffalo Bill. Naoma Tate of Cody, Wyoming, a member of the center's Board of Trustees, told the story passed on through generations in her family that her grandfather, at age twelve, and some friends ran away from home merely to take in a Wild West performance in Philadelphia.[21] Humorous in retrospect, such doings were not considered very funny to authority figures. One scholar at the symposium, Martin Woodside, a professor at Rutgers University-Camden, in New Jersey, said some felt too much Buffalo Bill was bad medicine and boys' "minds might become deranged" by hero worship.[22] Who knows, they might go out and shoot buffalo or something.

In what seems like a bizarre theory, *True West Magazine*, citing others' initial comments, investigated the suggestion that famous French painter Vincent Van Gogh might have been murdered by someone inspired by attending a Buffalo Bill performance a year earlier. A teaser headline on the magazine's front cover read, "Did a Buffalo Bill Wannabe Shoot Vincent van Gogh?"[23] French authorities have not changed their verdict from suicide.

The horse race from Nebraska to Chicago proceeded apace, Buffalo Bill only barely paying attention to newspaper reports until coverage became alarming. Animal rights activists—yes, even then—protested the race was too difficult for the horses and tried to halt it. Riders and horses ran into constant challenges, and many contestants dropped out. On the morning of June 27, a lone rider staggered into the Wild West camp. It was John Berry, leader of the pack, looking for Buffalo Bill and his reward. Cody rushed from his tent to greet him with a hearty handshake, and the exhausted Berry tumbled to the ground while asking other cast members to care for his horse.

"I'm glad to see you," was Cody's welcome. "How do you feel?"[24] About ready to go unconscious was how Berry felt after an 885-mile ride. The Great Cowboy Race brought even more attention to the Wild West exhibition, which almost could not handle the crowds it attracted. Berry lay down in Cody's tent and struggled to his feet to check on his horse Poison, which was inhaling oats, even as the rider's breakfast was being cooked. Berry's private victory speech finally poured out of him to Cody and Burke. He said he had ridden the last 150 miles straight through in twenty-four hours and had not had much sleep at all for ten days. "Sore? Well, I should say I was. I don't feel much like sitting down, but am so sleepy that I can't talk."[25] Berry, whom officials seemed to disqualify at race start, arrived first, but was he the winner? Cody got Berry a hotel room to really sleep.

The drama was not over. Another rider, Emmett Albright, showed up

14. The Wild West Is the Toast of Europe and Everywhere Else

ninety minutes after Berry and said he thought he was the winner. Others thought Albright cheated by shipping some horses ahead by train. Burke did not believe he should be counted as first, saying, "Albright is the comedian of the outfit."[26] Albright's presence did produce a furor among reporters, though. A key element, both for the riders and the race, was the fitness of the horses that covered the route. They were checked over by veterinarians and humane society representatives and declared healthy. Just as a meeting was about to start to decide whether Berry or Albright should get the prizes, a third rider, John Gillespie, finished. More chaos. A newsman informed Cody and his committee he had seen Gillespie farther back on the trail riding in the back of a buggy and sleeping. There were stories about other riders shipping their second horses by rail and of some cowboys forming alliances to gang up on single riders.

That afternoon, inside the arena at Cody's matinee performance, the first six riders into Chicago sat on their horses and were introduced to the crowd as hardy cowboys. No announcement of the winner was forthcoming. That was reserved for the night show. Ultimately, Berry was given the title, $175, and a fancy new saddle. Others received a share of the purse. Gillespie was presented with the golden pistol. Despite the confusion, Cody did not panic and made the best of a complicated situation when he addressed people at the finish line. "It will show what the native American horse is worth," he said. "European nations are watching the result of this race with interest. It is a test of the hardiness of the bronco."[27] There was no telling what really happened out there on the Plains, but everyone came out of the Great Cowboy Race alive and basically escaped with no permanent tarring of reputation.

Chicago had been a staple stop for the Wild West exhibition over the years, though there was a gap between the 1886 visit and the World's Fair tie-in of April 26 and October 12, 1893. During the Wild West stay on the Midway, Buffalo Bill, Nate Salsbury, and John Burke reacted with glee as they sold three million tickets. It was an obvious rebuke to the fair stuff-shirts who did not believe cowboys and Indians were worthy of being included in the look to the future emphasized in the White City. The Wild West exhibition turned a $1 million profit from these performances. One Cody biographer termed it "a finger in the eye of fair officials, who came to regret their decision to include him. It is said that spectators sometimes mistook the Wild West show for the World's Fair and went home satisfied."[28]

Whether it was London or Paris, New York or Chicago, wherever Buffalo Bill's Wild West exhibition alighted it held audiences in thrall, sent adults and children home satisfied, and chronicled a period of the Old West and the frontier in dramatic fashion so that those in attendance felt

A Buffalo Bill Cody imitator in a 2017 Wild West Revival in Denver, Colorado (photograph by the author).

they were absorbing a history lesson. Even a century after his death, professors and other experts who dissected Cody's life speaking at the Buffalo Bill Center of the West symposium basically said to know and understand Buffalo Bill is essential to comprehending American character. "Studying Buffalo Bill is entirely necessary to American self-knowledge," said Patty Limerick, chair of the Board of the Center of the American West at the University of Colorado. "His life covers everything of significance in American western history. Cody's life is a parable of the highest order."[29] William F. "Buffalo Bill" Cody could have told you that. In fact, he may have been telling everyone that through the Wild West exhibition and other performances for thirty straight years.

15

Indians

From the time he first took the stage working with Ned Buntline, Buffalo Bill Cody had it impressed upon him the importance of including Indians in his theater shows if he wanted the public to view them. Once he learned that, Cody applied the same principle to the Wild West exhibition as soon as it started. No Indians, no Wild West.

When the Wild West exhibition began in the 1880s, Native Americans were basically a defeated people, persecuted by the U.S. government, forced to surrender their homelands, deprived of the opportunity to shoot buffalo when they wished to, stripped of most guns and ammunition because of fear of rebellion, consigned to reservations, and under pressure to abandon cultural traditions and turn to farming to make a living.

When Sitting Bull agreed to appear in the Wild West exhibition in 1885, he was basically a prisoner out on parole. While he was the most famous Native American in the country, Sitting Bull was a controversial figure, selling tickets by his mere presence. Most of the other Indians in Cody's employ had supporting roles, riding horses in races, shooting blanks at buffalo, and playing scenes where they imitated their relatives at the Battle of the Little Bighorn or in a rough imitation of the rescue of white women being held captive.

There were other Native American stars, or chiefs, who lent prestige to Buffalo Bill's performances over the years, though none stood out as much as his friend Iron Tail. Cody was the boss, but he and Iron Tail were genuine friends. During time off they sometimes hunted or otherwise shared time. Cody spoke Lakota to him. Iron Tail rose to prominence as the Wild West exhibition gained fame through its many travels. That included trips to Europe and shows in Paris, France, London, England, and Italy.

Iron Tail was an Oglala Lakota chief born in 1842 who died in 1916, spending decades alongside Cody in Wild West exhibitions. The date of his birth is unknown. The story he told about his unusual name was that as a baby his mother witnessed a group of warriors hunting buffalo, and she thought the animals' tails stuck out like steel. In his native language, Iron Tail was called Sinjte Maza, which he was told was new and novel as a name.

Iron Tail was a regal-appearing man, especially when adorned with a chief's headdress. As evidence of his growing fame, domestic and foreign, when the U.S. Mint chose to create what came to be known as the Buffalo nickel, or Indian Head nickel, Iron Tail was invited to pose for renowned sculptor James Earle Fraser. Fraser's father, Thomas, was a railroad engineer who helped developed the lines and track to the West. In 1876, the year James was born, Thomas was a member of a group of men sent to recover the remains of the Seventh Cavalry, Custer's regiment wiped out at the Little Bighorn. James was born less than six months after the battle in Minnesota. In his work, Fraser demonstrated sympathy to Native Americans. His most famous sculpture was "End of the Trail," a piece that shows a Native American slumped over his horse, a long spear pointing downward. It is one of the most recognizable of American sculptures.

The Indian Head nickel was minted in 1913 and reissued through 1938. Featured on one side is a full-bodied buffalo. On the other, a Native American in profile, facing right. Iron Tail was one of three models Fraser used, although those in the chief's circle preferred to call him the real model for the coin's portrait. Bee Ho Gray, another Wild West performer, accompanied Iron Tail to his sittings for Fraser in New York and Washington, DC, acting as an English interpreter. Buffalo Bill, who was showered with honors during his life, appreciated this recognition for Iron Tail and took the coin to be an homage to his friend and long-time fellow performer.

The content of the nickel was actually 75 percent copper and 25 percent nickel. While one of the most memorable of all American coins, there were problems with it from the start. Unlike most coins, there was a tendency for the date to wear off too easily, and the designs also faded. Complaints abounded. Under the law, the minimum time a coin could be altered without congressional action was twenty-five years. When that period ended, production ceased, and a replacement nickel featured President Thomas Jefferson.

Originally, Fraser submitted three sketches for review. The buffalo gained the strongest approval. Still, some changes were in the offing before manufacturing. Fraser had to fight to maintain what he believed to be the artistic integrity of his work. Finally, the coin was issued on February 22, 1913, at a ceremony dedicating the National American Indian Memorial in Fort Wadsworth on Staten Island, an event including President William Howard Taft shortly before his term expired. Not all reviews were

15. Indians

positive, some critics seeing the coin as a so-so addition to the nation's monetary system at best.

Some engraving changes were made over the following few years to fix problems. In comparison to other American coins of century-old vintage, the Indian Head nickel was not struck in the same volume. For its twenty-five years of existence, production problems plagued the coin. Fraser, who died in 1953, lived long enough to see his coin disappear from most Americans' pockets. In a 1947 radio interview he explained why he chose the design he did, noting, "Well, when I was asked to do a nickel, I felt I wanted to do something totally American—a coin that could not be mistaken for any other country's coin. It occurred to me that the buffalo, as part of our western background, was 100 percent American, and that our North American Indian fitted into the picture perfectly."[1] While a great professed fan of the buffalo, which during his lifetime had been wiped off the Plains, Fraser said the model for the animal was actually one in the Bronx Zoo.

The Indian Head nickel faded out of favor as time passed, but the Fraser design underwent a renaissance long after his and Iron Tail's deaths. In 2001, Colorado Senator Ben Nighthorse Campbell achieved the passage of legislation to mint 500,000 silver dollars featuring Fraser's work. The idea was so popular the run sold out swiftly, resulting in a $5 million donation to the building of the Smithsonian Museum of the American Indian. That was such a success that in 2006, the mint produced American Buffalo gold bullion using a modified version of Fraser's effort.

Meanwhile, coin collectors have discerningly picked out a selection of the nickels as valued due to rarity. A 1916 nickel has sold for $50,000. One 1926-S has sold for $3,650, though others from that year are valued at $19. Condition and scarcity govern prices, as they do in other collectible arenas. Many coins struck, those without a date and with wear, have seen no particular increase in value and are listed as worth 10 cents. Even one type of a 1913 uncirculated, first-year-of-issue Indian Head nickel may only be worth $24. One of those special edition silver dollars with the same design, with one ounce of silver in it, can be had for as low as $30.

Unlike Sitting Bull, Iron Tail was basically a peace chief. He never went to war. His claim to fame came through his association with Buffalo Bill and the Wild West exhibition. As one indication of how valued Iron Tail was, an exhibition paybook from a random month in the archives of the Buffalo Bill Center of the West lists the salaries of dozens, if not hundreds, of employees. Iron Tail was being paid $50 when others on the payroll made a fraction of that. For someone not fluent in English, Iron Tail did well in developing his public image through his actions. Photographer Gertrude Kasebier, who became prominent in her field in the early 1900s, was someone who had spent time in the West in her youth. Later, when she saw the Wild West parade toward Madison Square Garden right past her studio window on Fifth Avenue she sent Buffalo Bill a letter.

Kasebier wished to photograph Indians as she remembered the Lakota people she had known as a girl. She wanted to take these shots for her own edification and asked if she could take pictures of Sioux members of the cast. Buffalo Bill approved her request, and she visited the camp on April 14, 1898, looking for suitable subjects. The story goes that when she made her interest known several braves brought out the finery they wished to be photographed in. However, that is not what Kasebier was looking for—her vision was more of the everyday Indian. Eventually, she came to Iron Tail, and he was willing to be photographed in his regular garb. When she showed him her first pictures, Iron Tail tore them up, protesting they were too dark. When he posed for her next, he wore a chief's headdress and liked the way he looked in those pictures. A few years later, when she sold pictures to a magazine, Iron Tail's portrait was included.

In 1912, when Buffalo Bill and Pawnee Bill were working together, Iron Tail appeared in bright color on a Wild West picture, his intense face and headdress filling the entire poster. He appeared on some others, too, including in action when he joined the Miller Brothers 101 Ranch's Wild West Show after Buffalo Bill retired from running his Wild West exhibition. In the 101 poster, Iron Tail, in dramatic headdress, is riding a horse, and the two sides of the Indian Head-Buffalo nickel are superimposed on the left and right sides. Iron Tail had major billing on the poster by name. This is a colorful item, and an original from the period has sold for $10,000. It was Iron Tail's presence that gave the old poster extra value. "This 101 Ranch piece, featuring Chief Iron Tail, has historic value in that Iron Tail was arguably the most famous American Indian in the world during the early 20th century," a vintage poster expert wrote.[2] Still, the full-faced poster is the best overall view of how he looked in his later years.

Although Iron Tail did not speak English, he made friends easily by exhibiting a gentle and welcoming demeanor. U.S. Major Israel McCreight became a noted Native American authority in the nineteenth century, and he and Iron Tail bonded. Iron Tail and Chief Flying Hawk kept a home in DuBois, Pennsylvania, and called it "The Wigwam." McCreight visited often. In June of 1908, when the Wild West exhibition played to crowds of twelve thousand people there, Iron Tail adopted McCreight as an honorary Sioux chief and gave him a Sioux name, Chante Thanka, meaning Great Heart. The ceremony took place at Buffalo Bill's tent on the Wild West grounds and was witnessed by several other chiefs and another one hundred braves who were members of the Wild West cast at that time. As part of McCreight's initiation, Iron Tail placed a war bonnet on his head and adorned his feet in moccasins. McCreight and his wife Alice were also given a teepee. A banquet followed and during it Iron Tail was presented with a Winchester rifle. Deeply honored, McCreight, who had first visited with Sioux people in 1885, remained close to Iron Tail. He described him as "not a war chief, but a wise counselor and diplomat, always dignified, quiet, and never given to boasting."[3]

As a featured performer in the Wild West exhibition for years, as Buffalo Bill Cody's right-hand man, and his close friend, Iron Tail became internationally known and respected. While it was impossible to match Cody's fame, and since Iron Tail did not speak English to help promote himself, he still gained remarkable renown. Like Cody and Annie Oakley, he became one of the faces of the Wild West exhibition, closely identified with it and routinely associated with it. Over time, Iron Tail became more deeply established in American culture through the Indian Head nickel. As the view of Native Americans has changed with the maturing of the country, some scholars have focused on studying his life.

Dr. Emily Burns, an assistant professor of art history at Auburn University in Alabama, concluded Iron Tail lived his life as a cultural ambassador for the Sioux, both in the United States and perhaps especially so overseas. Echoing McCreight, in a speaking appearance in Cody, Wyoming, Burns repeated Iron Tail was not a war chief. "He was a performer," she said.[4]

Alive during the same time period was another chief called Iron Hail. This chief fought in some battles, not Iron Tail. When he was about eighteen, Iron Hail was with the Sioux warriors who defeated General Custer at the Battle of the Little Bighorn. Iron Hail is also one of the braves who followed Sitting Bull across the border to Canada and lived in exile. The similarity of the two names, Iron Hail and Iron Tail, created some written historical confusion in which Iron Hail's achievements in the field were sometimes attributed to Iron Tail.

Iron Hail was born in 1858 and lived a lengthy life. One aspect of Iron Hail's life confused with Iron Tail's was the loss of relatives at Wounded Knee in 1890. This was not true of Iron Tail. Like Iron Tail, Iron Hail had a lengthy career working with the Wild West exhibition. Iron Hail was actually an English translation of a Native American name, but this man used the English name of Dewey Beard later. He took the Beard name when he converted to Roman Catholicism. Iron Hail died in 1955 at either ninety-six or ninety-seven years old. He was the oldest Sioux survivor of the Little Bighorn, as well as the oldest survivor of the massacre at Wounded Knee.

Burns became a great admirer of Iron Tail the more she studied his life, describing him through his public persona as someone who "shaped and challenged" stereotypes of Native Americans and who demonstrated "fluidity and adaptability" to circumstances.[5] In addition to the posters that featured Iron Tail for the Wild West exhibition and the 101 show, Iron Tail's face could be found on postcards. McCreight had called Iron Tail a wise man, and Burns said his face veritably exuded wisdom. It was not only James Earle Fraser who sought Iron Tail to pose as a symbol of the American Indian, but another famed sculptor, Alexander Phimister Proctor.

Buffalo Bill pulled back from the Wild West exhibition in 1913, but Iron Tail did not wish to retire. He was famous enough to easily find work doing what he did best, playing himself. He joined the 101 Ranch Wild West Show, which Buffalo Bill also joined after becoming bored from sitting idle for a while and finding himself in need of money. In 1916, at age seventy-four, when Iron Tail was traveling with that troupe, he fell ill. The show was in Philadelphia when he was waylaid by pneumonia and hospitalized.

This was big enough news for newspapers, and McCreight read of this development. He sent a telegram to Buffalo Bill, urging the old scout to get Iron Tail transferred to the Wigwam by train. It is not clear what happened to the telegram, but Buffalo Bill said later he never got it. On whose authority and with what exactly in mind, Iron Tail was put on a train, but with a ticket to South Dakota. Iron Tail never made it to either the Wigwam or the Black Hills. A porter found him dead onboard in South Bend, Indiana. The date of Iron Tail's death was given with more precision than his birth as May 28, 1916.

Iron Tail's body was taken from the train in Nebraska and a few days later was buried on the Pine Ridge Indian Reservation. Cody was distraught to learn of his friend's death, and, still on the road, could not attend the services. As a tribute, he announced he would place a granite headstone on Iron Tail's grave featuring a carved image of the Indian Head nickel. However, Buffalo Bill himself passed away from illness the following January before he could follow through on this pledge.

There were always Indians. The Wild West exhibition needed them, and Buffalo Bill Cody certainly wanted no truck with actors made up to look like Indians. Given that the U.S. government was engaged in a policy of either annihilation or containment, Cody had to tread gently, recruit carefully, and treat those employees well. He was under no legal obligation to offer equal pay within the ranks to cowboys and Indians, but still he did so.

Some of the many hundreds of Native-Americans, if not thousands, who spent time with the Wild West exhibition over a thirty-year period were chiefs. Most were not. Besides Iron Tail, who was essentially the chief among chiefs except for the four-month period when Sitting Bull toured, and Iron Hail, other well-known figures who escaped reservation life, allowed the freedom to roam the country and the world, were Red Shirt, American Horse, Amos Little, Bad Bear, Charging Thunder, Flying Hawk, Joe Black Fox, Sammy Lone Bear, Takes Enemy, and Whirling Horse.

At the time, Buffalo Bill Cody, one-time Indian fighter, became Indian savior. If you worked for Buffalo Bill, you could travel far from your reservation, live in your own teepee on show grounds, be guaranteed a paycheck and your meals, demonstrate tribal dances daily, be provided with an English interpreter when needed, and often at the end of the season be given gifts of food, clothing, and bonus money. By comparison to reservation Indians, Wild West Indians were rich in both wealth and experience denied to most members of their tribes. Wives of performers made crafts and could sell them to spectators who visited the shows. Elders were paid by Cody as tribal police to keep order. That way, no Indian could complain he was bullied or mistreated because of white prejudice. Some touring Wild West Indians even made appearances in schools giving talks to white children about Native American culture. "Chief Flying Hawk, a Native teacher, often visited local white schools teaching Native philosophies and Lakota history," it was noted.[6]

For the first few years of the Wild West exhibition, most of the Native Americans were Pawnee. From 1885 on, Cody recruited members of the Sioux. Although most recently remembered for the roles they played in the skits of the Old West that included Custer's Last Stand and other events based on truth, thereby adding authenticity to the program, sometimes overlooked have been the demonstrations of Indian skills. Members of the cast rode their horses, showing off their handling talents, exhibited bow and arrow firing, and featured the tribal dances and music central to their beings. At the same time, those aspects of Native American culture were in many cases banned from the reservations. Some critics felt the roles of the Indians in the Wild West exhibition amounted to caricature and they should not be involved. That applied mostly to the sketches, apparently. But overlooked were the opportunities given to the cast denied to his fellow tribesmen back home. Not merely the secure employment and side benefits, but the psychic value of having the freedom to actually behave like an Indian.

As always in American life, people used their right to protest what they saw or to seek to undermine what they thought they understood. There was a body of opinion that the Indians should be left alone to meld into society and not regularly reenact what was considered to be a dead past. There were complaints the Indians were portrayed only as savages. Shrill protests resulted in the Office of Indian Affairs requiring Native

Americans wishing to work in Wild West shows to sign individual contracts under the agency's supervision. This could be interpreted as additional governmental paternalism, something the United States was long accused of doing in thinking of Native Americans as simple children.

In 1890, Indian Affairs representatives conducted a court-like proceeding where officials denounced show business in general as not being good for white people. Therefore, it could not be good for Indians. However, Wild West Indians testified and said they were engaged in good, solid work and were well treated. Especially, they observed, compared to the lousy conditions prevalent on the Pine Ridge Indian Reservation where the white man otherwise wanted them confined. Touché.

This was vividly demonstrated and contrasted with the tragedy at the very end of that year in the Massacre at Wounded Knee, the carnage at the same South Dakota reservation. On December 29, about 150 Native Americans were killed by the Seventh Cavalry after the escalation of what began as basically a police action. Some believe this regiment, Custer's old command, let loose as revenge for the results at the Battle of the Little Bighorn. It was also in 1890 that historian Frederick Turner wrote his famed essay, oft-cited by successors studying the nineteenth century, in which he declared that the frontier was closed. In other words, this epoch of the American West was over.

Following the incident at Wounded Knee, Buffalo Bill faced great difficulty recruiting Indians for his 1891 show season. Nate Salsbury was already exploring obtaining the services of as many foreign riders as possible when the government relented and permitted Cody to hire his usual complement of Indians.

Historians who came later reeled back and forth between noting Cody's frequent adherence to factual events, but also his fictionalizing of them. They marveled at the colorful, dramatic posters used for advertising and noted, as the process of reproducing photographs improved over time, how his programs better depicted Indians as they looked, individually and in action in the performances. "The copious illustrations reflect this brand of highly colored romance and solemnly invoked claims to factuality," one author observed. "But photographs in the program booklet also connect the Wild West spectacle with an emerging documentary tradition."[7]

In the United States, after decades of persecution, hijacking of their lands, and segregating them onto reservations, most of the rest of America viewed Indians as a subjugated people whose time had passed. Only rarely were they shown respect as individuals. For all of that, the Wild West exhibition made some individuals, such as Iron Tail, into stars, and opened doors for work to others. Cody was annually the largest employer of Native Americans in the United States through his Wild West

15. Indians

Steve Friesen, retired director of the Buffalo Bill Museum and Grave in Golden, Colorado, authored a book on the Native American experience in the Wild West exhibition (photograph by the author).

exhibition. As a man who once was an enemy on the other side of the battlefield, the better Cody got to know the men who joined him on his tours, the more he advocated for their rights. Beyond that, it was in Europe where Native Americans shone brightest. They were objects of curiosity, their customs little known, and they made strong first impressions in the company of the heralded Buffalo Bill Cody.

"Those American Indians who performed in Wild West shows were neither savages, nor naïve victims," stated authors who studied the Lakota traveling in Europe. "Faced with extinction or assimilation, they chose a third way. Buffalo Bill's Wild West was not a tool for exploitation of the Indians, as the politically correct, but historically confused argue today. The show represented not exploitation, but opportunity." The writers quoted Black Heart, one of the Wild West performers, who spoke with a clear head and a realistic assessment of the situation in 1890. "We were raised on horseback. That is the way we had to work. These men furnished us the same work we were raised to [do]. That is the reason we want to work for these kind of men."[8]

The visit to London and the command performance before Queen Victoria set in motion several other European tours for the Wild West exhibition. The Native Americans given this and other chances were thrilled because they truly enjoyed their visits to European countries so different from their homeland and also because they were treated with fanfare, respect, and earnest curiosity. David Bull Bear and Samuel Lone Bear even had business cards printed advertising their connection to the Wild West exhibition. Luther Standing Bear wrote he was reluctant to leave England to sail back to the United States. "I was sorry to leave this city," he said, "because I had been given a chance to see many wonderful sights and visit many interesting places."[9] Cody paid by the season, and in 1888, each performer earned $579. It should again be noted that except for stars who negotiated their own deals, the Indians and whites received equal wages.

For years, even decades, white reservation agents seemed not to be much different or more enlightened than James McLaughlin, who basically orchestrated Sitting Bull's death. Periodically, into the 1920s and 1930s, long after Cody's show runs concluded and others took the Wild West's place, some of those agents put their feelings in writing. They seemed bewildered the Indians preferred to be actors and showmen instead of stay-at-home semi-prisoners on reservations. One lamented he wished some of those shows demonstrated the type of progress (his word), Indians had made under white rule rather than performing in ways that related to their pasts. Luther Standing Bear had a ready reply for why he embarked on a life as a performer, and then a lecturer. "I determined that if I could only get the right sort of people interested, I might be able to do more for my own race off the reservation than to remain there under the iron rule of the white agent."[10]

One Sioux Indian, Lone Bear, not only spoke English, but through his multiple visits to Europe also learned French and German. Black Horn made five trips to Europe. White Buffalo Man took seven trips to Europe. The first time they traveled overseas was with the Wild West exhibition. Long after both Buffalo Bill and his Wild West show died, other companies continued to make western show trips to Europe. It was at a World's Fair exposition in Brussels, Belgium, in 1935 that an American newspaper reporter blundered into an attempted conversation with Chief Black Horn. The reporter asked, "Heap-big Injun likem Paris?" Black Horn said, "I think it might facilitate matters for you if I refer you to our interpreter, Sam Lone Bear."[11] That year, after Brussels, Wild West shows ceased to become an attraction in Europe. It was not long before tensions across the European continent erupted into World War II.

16

A Congress of Rough Riders

Bigger and bigger. Wilder and wilder. One thing Buffalo Bill Cody, Nate Salsbury, John Burke, and James Bailey did not do was stand still. They were forever thinking and plotting and marketing and expanding, always with an eye to lure in the customer with something fresh added to the Wild West exhibition's staple routines.

It was critical to think this way because once the Wild West established the western show as a touring genre, the list of competitors mushroomed. At various times over the years there were as many as twenty outfits willing to take on the Wild West in the show world. And that did not count the circus. Circuses, too, expanded and offered more entertainment. It was P.T. Barnum who proclaimed his circus was the greatest show on earth. Not everyone, Buffalo Bill included, agreed, because he figured the Wild West exhibition was No. 1.

The circus had exotic animals like lions and tigers and elephants. The Wild West exhibition had animals, too, like buffalo and sprinting horses. The circus had magicians and so-called freak shows. The Wild West had cowboys and Indians who could ride and shoot. Both were deluxe pageants of show business that could rivet the eyes for hours. The Wild West, however, had Buffalo Bill, Annie Oakley, Sitting Bull, Iron Tail, and other famous individuals. Neither the other western shows, nor the circus, could compete with that. But the Wild West organizers knew they had to keep hustling. They had to keep producing. They had to keep marketing. The core presentation had to be reliable, the complex travel arrangements had to be fulfilled, regardless of weather or other obstacles. There was no margin for slippage.

That kept the pressure on, but the Wild West exhibition not only met its obligations, it did so with flair. When the Wild West exhibition became more international, with tours of Europe, the heads of state and royalty in those countries viewed Buffalo Bill, the head man, the chief, the king of his operation, as fellow royalty. He was treated as such. He was praised as such. These kings and queens, princes and princesses, wanted to meet him. If the circus played your town it was fun for all ages, but the governor did not make it a point to stop by and request an audience with the top lion tamer. Buffalo Bill's celebrity trumped everyone else's in the show world. He had a cast of hundreds of people and animals, but he was the front man who was more visible than anyone else. Heads of countries could reach out and shake his hand, and they wanted to do so.

From the beginnings in Nebraska, the Wild West exhibition grew forever more renowned and in demand, and continued to spread its wings, astonishingly so in an era prior to airplane travel, though it would have been tough to transport the animals and the equipment by air. Still, the world had not yet shrunk, so it was a phenomenal logistical achievement for the Wild West exhibition to cross ocean barriers and countries' boundaries so readily. Who would ever have imagined in the 1870s that members of the Sioux nation would soon be hobnobbing with kings and queens in far-off lands?

The troupe's visit to England in 1887 laid the foundation for future European journeys. In 1892, Salsbury, vice president and general manager of the Wild West exhibition, invented the Congress of the Rough Riders of the World while in Europe. Initially, these riders performed military drills specific to different nations. The reception was positive. In 1893, the title of Buffalo Bill's Wild West changed to Buffalo Bill's Wild West and Congress of Rough Riders. This represented a change in the composition of the cast, adding more riders from foreign lands to the original membership of American cowboys and Native Americans. The timing coincided with the Chicago World's Fair stay. Besides Mexican vaqueros, riders joined up from Hawaii, Cuba, Japan, and the Philippines. This escalation was more in tune with what Salsbury had originally envisioned when he first joined forces with Buffalo Bill, a show "that would embody the whole subject of horsemanship."[1]

If only Sioux Indian interpreters had once been necessary for a smooth running camp and show, the Buffalo Bill group had now become so international it was a veritable United Nations. Across the United States, across the sea, the Wild West exhibition, its rough riders, and the like were everywhere and from everywhere. One official at the Buffalo Bill Center of the West in Cody, Wyoming, once calculated the travel of the exhibition for the year of 1899. Distance covered was 11,000-plus miles spread over 200 days for 341 shows in 132 cities and towns.[2] And that was just in-country that one year.

The choice of the words "Rough Riders" in the title was clever. They

16. A Congress of Rough Riders 165

were not used in everyday speech in the East, or anywhere except ranch country. Those who were rough riders were those who sought to break wild broncos. In modern-day rodeos, those who compete in the bareback and saddle bronc competitions are known as cowboys who ride rough stock. In 1898, of course, the words "Rough Riders" moved into common lexicon because of the name applied to Theodore Roosevelt's bunch in the storming of San Juan Hill. Opportunistic to the extreme, Buffalo Bill added a battle scene featuring rough riders in the show after the highly publicized war exploit. How could it miss being a hit?

When the Wild West exhibition headed to Europe after the Salsbury hiring binge, it had representative soldiers from Germany, England, the United States, and Argentina. And there were Cossacks. Cossacks? Cossacks were a subgroup within Russia's borders very active in warfare on horseback beginning in the eighteenth century and were considered a military class of people. They could ride like heck, which is pretty much what the Wild West exhibition was looking for, not a political background check. But Americans came to know Cossacks from a distance with negative connotations as they were employed as policemen to enforce czarist policies in the early twentieth century prior to the Russian revolution of 1917. From the eyes of different ethnic groups, they were viewed as murderous raiders. Though not those individuals riding for Buffalo Bill, who seemed to take on a special aura with their skills and were sometimes featured in the advertising posters promoting the Congress of Rough Riders.

Not only were there German soldiers linked up in the cast now, but the Buffalo Bill operation occasioned such great praise for its smoothness and efficiency, coming and going, loading and unloading, making camp and cooking for hundreds on a daily basis, that the kaiser (the one Annie Oakley said later she wished she had not "missed" by shooting the ashes off his cigarette) sent officials to observe how it was all done. Perhaps he was already preparing for war footing long before World War I began. "We never moved without at least forty officers of the Prussian Guard standing all about with notebooks, taking down every detail of the performance. They made minute notes on how we pitched camp the exact number of men needed, every man's position, how long it took, how we boarded the trains and packed the horses and broke camp. Every rope and bundle and kit was inspected and mapped."[3] There was probably only a slender chance the kaiser was investigating how best to start a moving company like a Mayflower or Allied Van Lines.

In Holland, when Queen Wilhelmina came to watch the show, she was a repeat customer, having seen the Wild West exhibition in England in 1887. Back in England, one review, from a Liverpool newspaper, virtually parroted Buffalo Bill—and John Burke's—message of what it was all about. The article called the Wild West exhibition "a piece of the Wild West bodily transported to our midst. It is not a show in the ordinary acceptance of the term because the actors are each and all real characters—men who have figured not on the stage, but in real life. The exhibition, moreover, is not merely entertaining, but most instructive."[4] For years, Buffalo Bill had been trumpeting that the Wild West was educational. He had to have smiled in satisfaction upon reading this newspaper story.

Just as in any big business or operation, members of the cast were constantly changing. While Buffalo Bill, Annie Oakley, and Iron Tail were around for years, and many of the American Indians chose to make participating in the Wild West exhibition a career, there were hundreds of others who came and went. Some stayed a single season. Others stayed for several years and then departed because they tired of the work, the grind, or the road, got into some kind of trouble, were homesick, or any number of reasons.

Charles Eldridge Griffin was one performer who stuck around for a while, spending four years with the Wild West exhibition and the rough riders starting in 1903, when it set off by ship for a most ambitious and adventurous tour of Europe. He wrote a book about his experiences, too. It began for Griffin on board the 540-foot long *Etruria*, of the Cunard Line, sailing from New York City on March 28, bound for England. Mimicking what occurred after a short time at sea (by the next morning) many members of the cast became seasick. The first dinner passed without incident, but overnight, it seemed, most of the travelers were stricken. It seemed only the veteran sailors resisted the rocking and rolling of the boat. "But the majority," Griffin noted, "seemed bent on feeding the fishes."[5] That was a polite way of saying many passengers leaned over the rails puking. So, there was that: to get to Europe you had to get there. The voyage took less than two weeks, though there was no guarantee of smooth sailing. Otherwise, whether watching seagulls or listening to live music performances, the time passed.

The group went directly to Manchester and opened the tour there on April 13. It was the kind of weather for which England gets its bad rap—bone-chilling dampness, rainy, sometimes even turning to snow. Griffin said Buffalo Bill was thrown from his horse during the show when the animal stumbled, and he sprained an ankle. For the next three weeks of the Manchester stay, Griffin said, Cody was grounded, unable to ride. It had to be a severe sprain to keep Buffalo Bill from riding. He was a director on horseback and made his crowd speeches from the saddle, so this was a disruption. Liverpool was the next stop, and the Bishop of Liverpool conducted church services on the grounds on a Sunday, Griffin reported. The bishop brought his own supporting cast along, and they sung up a storm, including, Griffin said, "Onward Christian Soldiers."⁶

Griffin singled out a special incident that occurred in Birmingham, something it is surprising did not happen more often during Buffalo Bill's travels. On June 7, he said, Chief Standing Bear and his wife Laura, of the Sioux nation, had a baby girl. It is not clear if his next assertion was true or not, but Griffin said it was the only Native American baby born in Great Britain. He may have meant during the Wild West exhibition's stays, or he may have meant ever.

The days seemed chock full of highlights outside the arena for Griffin. He proudly recorded being presented a gold medal taking note of his forty-fifth birthday. He also said "Ostrich Man," real name Alfonso and a member of the cast, was asked to demonstrate his swallowing prowess by an Englishman whom Griffin said "had more money than brains." So Alfonso downed a five-pound note fronted him. Griffin's comment: "Talk about being from Missouri. You certainly have to show them over there."⁷

With a show that included hundreds of people who traveled together for months, some unfortunate things were bound to happen. Griffin said on July 23, in Bristol, England, a Mexican rider named Isadore Gonzalez was thrown off his horse and killed on the spot. He was buried in that community. The Wild West exhibition generally did not ship bodies back to home locations if a participant died on the job. Griffin made it sound as if this casualty was just a hazard of a job since Gonzalez was making daring moves at fast speeds on horseback. "It is just as well, perhaps," Griffin wrote, "that the general public do not realize the danger that forever attends the participants of the Wild West performances. Every time they enter the arena, especially in the bucking horse act, they practically take their lives in their hands."⁸

Griffin enjoyed his first season with Buffalo Bill despite the abysmal weather that plagued the company. When the Wild West exhibition quit for the season, the Americans (though not Griffin among them) sailed back to the United States, and the gear and equipment was put into storage. When six months, or 194 days, were up, the tents were put up. Packed in were 333 performances with only one cancellation due to weather. It was too windy to go on that day. "The elements," Griffin said, "were against us most of the time. The weather conditions throughout the entire season were most depressing, and the fact is recorded by the English press that never in the history of the country has there been a summer where climate conditions were as bad as those of this year."⁹

Griffin chose to stay behind for the off-season, renting an apartment in London, a city he very much liked. He said there were numerous American stores in operation there. The subway system was pretty good, but not as good as the one in Boston, Massachusetts, he thought. He spent considerable time sightseeing, noting he enjoyed Piccadilly Circus. During these months it was he who was a tourist and the one soaking in unusual, unfamiliar sights, rather than those visitors to the Wild West exhibition.

Nor did Griffin confine himself to London. He made certain to explore. He wrote of spending a month in France, though he said he became weary of having to speak in sign language because he did not speak French, and he felt very much at home when returning to London. He was enamored enough, or curious enough, to desire seeing what it was like to be engulfed in a notorious London fog. This came under the heading of be careful what you wish for. Griffin seemed quite impressed with a big-time fog that descended on January 23, 1904. "The papers declared it to be the worst fog of the century," he wrote.[10] Evidently, Griffin kept up with the local news and believed everything he read in the newspapers. Joking aside, he said the members of the press he met during the show months were jolly good fellows.

By the beginning of the twentieth century, all of America and many in Europe thought they knew Buffalo Bill. At the least, they knew of him. He had been a for-real scout, and now he was an iconic showman, the transition aided by the time he spent on the stage. In the United States, people were turning to the automobile and away from the horse, but the spectators wanted to cling to the Old West they missed out on, and Buffalo Bill filled gaps in their knowledge, or at least in their impressions of what happened. He overwhelmed the crowds with the scope of the performances. When the Wild West exhibition was in the United States, it took fifty-two boxcars in a special train to get where it was going. The always-expanding cast reached 640 members. It was a commentary more on the state of the buffalo's precarious existence than anything else, but the Wild West exhibition's herd of just eighteen bison was the third largest remaining in the world. If anyone looks back from the vantage point of more than a hundred years to criticize the content of the shows, they should know negative commentary was not commonly applied in contemporary times. Not only newspapermen wrote glowing stories, but when interviewed, the surviving generals of the Plains endorsed what they saw from the man whom they had respected in the field earlier in life. Recalling there were competitors, it meant something when General George Crook, whom Cody rode with, called the Wild West exhibition "the most realistic performance of the kind I have ever seen."[11] That was one man who lived through the times, and sometimes alongside Cody.

Although the methodology might cry out for explanation, one magazine article estimated some twenty-five million words were written about

Buffalo Bill Cody during his heyday. Those dime novels, representing an explosion in the colorful truth-or-not tales about him, included 557 different stories. Cody may or may not have been "The King of the Border Men," as Ned Buntline wrote, but he was the king of publicity.

While some preposterously suggest Cody the buffalo hunter was single-handedly responsible for devastating the Plains herds, that would be a serious misreading of history. Nonetheless, he did earn his nickname from buffalo hunting, and he did hunt more than four thousand of them. Later, though, when he displayed his eighteen buffalo as part of the Wild West exhibition, he raised the consciousness of eastern and far-off spectators who believed they were all gone. His buffalo multiplied to a larger herd than was needed for the show, and Buffalo Bill donated some to zoos. He also encouraged ranchers to breed them. Cody would have been pleased at how the Yellowstone National Park herd of twenty-three (barely larger than his own herd) during his time period has flourished and expanded to about four thousand roaming the park's 2.2 million square miles. Rick Wallen, the bison expert for the National Park Service, calls the bounce-back of the bison the greatest conservation recovery of all time. Cody would have been equally happy to hear the bison, or the buffalo, as it were, is now the United States' national mammal. President Barack Obama anointed it such in May of 2016.

In 1963, a movie was released called *It's A Mad, Mad, Mad, Mad World*. A comedy, it featured just about every known film star in the universe at that time, including Spencer Tracy, Phil Silvers, Mickey Rooney, Milton Berle, Sid Caesar, Ethel Merman, and more. It is not much of a mental stretch to imagine life with the Wild West exhibition being equally madcap. Something was always happening or might even be caused by the exhibition.

Kings and queens and other heads of state were always dropping by. News reporters always wanted the inside scoop. Headline writers seemed to go mad themselves, expressing astonishment at various goings-on that were part of the Wild West script. The Buffalo Bill Center of the West research center, the Harold McCracken Research Library, contains all manner of scrapbooks relating to William F. Cody. Some of them include newspaper clippings from many of the places the Wild West exhibition toured. In the case of many snippets, the name of the paper itself does not appear, there are no accompanying photographs (boy, did they miss out), and in the 1880s and beyond, many stories did not even carry bylines identifying the writer. Some are written in other languages, and the only identifiable words are "Buffalo Bill's." One newspaper ad, apparently from 1893 when the Wild West exhibition was located just outside the front door of the World's Fair, noted admission was 50 cents, but for children under 10, just 25 cents. Part of the attraction, the billing suggested, was "A Monster Musical."

Other Chicago headlines noted "Buffalo Bill's Warriors Come From All Parts of the World," after the Congress of Rough Riders was added. And, living up to the pledge that the show must go on, there was this: "It is 'Rain Or Shine,' And Yesterday It was 'Rain.'" Some sort of spirit was shared at a breakfast just prior to the Chicago opening, and a paper noted "Loving Cup Quaffed." This was a gift awarded, and apparently some liquid refreshment was added and then passed around. It reached Cody, whom it was described as being somewhat hidden under a wide-brimmed sombrero. "Bill dropped his hat on the floor and shook his long locks defiantly. He raised an ovation as he raised the cup to his lips," his gulp equal to all but one of the participants. The room may have been crammed with Chicago politicians, but Cody showed them how it was done on the frontier.

Of course, the cowboy race from Nebraska rolled in and was reported on, as was the free day for children, headlined "Fun for the Waifs." Often, there were reminders that Buffalo Bill's Wild West was not an official fair exhibit—but that it might as well be. One clever headline read, "The Fair and the Affair! Just Opposite Each Other." Seemed like Buffalo Bill winking. Inside the event's program was a catchy claim reading, "Replete with Everything Wonderful! The Most Daring Acts of Man and Beast!" Including the overture and the conclusion, there were twenty-one listings under "Programme." One feature was a horse race between a cowboy, a Cossack, a Mexican, an Arab, and an Indian.

One day it was reported, rather breathlessly, that a visitor to the Wild West exhibition was an Indian named Rain-In-The-Face. He was heralded as, and credited with being, the killer of General George Armstrong Custer—or captain Tom Custer—the general's brother, at the Battle of the Little Bighorn. Maybe. At the time it was said to be true. Two newspapers described Rain-In-The-Face as "a crippled Indian," aging and needing crutches to get around. One derisively described him as someone who resembled the common beggars that congregated near Buffalo Bill's camp seeking handouts. Another account described him this way: "It was hard to picture this obese, unpoetical figure as the blood-thirsty chief of war paint and feathers. But so he was." Sitting Bull had come and gone as a Wild West exhibition attraction and inspired applause, boos, and some reverence for his stature. In America writ large, Rain-In-The-Face would have been viewed as famous for the wrong reason.

It was on one of Buffalo Bill's swings through New York that a big to-do was made in the *New York Sun* about him bringing Mexican food to the city. There were Mexican riders in the Wild West exhibition before it expanded to embrace most other foreign horseback experts, so it seems likely Mexican food was eaten in Wild West encampments. Steve Friesen, the former director of the Cody museum in Golden, Colorado, told an audience gathered for a banquet observing the 100th anniversary of Buffalo Bill's death, that Cody may have introduced Mexican cuisine east of the Mississippi River in the United States.[12]

Friesen based the notion on an 1886 old newspaper clip in which a *Sun* food critic took note of Mexican food brought to Madison Square Garden. A reading indicates the food was pretty spicy: "…it is the palate and the membranes of the stomach that are inflamed and excited by the hot chile peppers and the other condiments that burn like caustic." The paper attributed the food's arrival to Cody, saying he sat at the head of the table with his friends. It also made it sound as if the food was strong stuff for Buffalo Bill, too. "It was plain to see that the mysteries of the Mexican cuisine were as much a surprise to him as his guests."[13] Does this mean that Buffalo Bill, along with his other accomplishments, invented the burrito, too?

Leaving no avenue unexplored in his quest for providing an entertaining experience, the Wild West exhibition also showcased "Buffalo Bill's Cowboy Band." It may be little remembered today outside of Cody, Wyoming, where a recording of the "Star Spangled Banner" made by the band sometimes plays during a mock gunfight street show. The patriotic song was not yet the national anthem and did not become so until 1931, long after Buffalo Bill's death and the show's demise. But many credit the band for popularizing it and keeping it in the limelight for years. While Cody may have listened carefully and blessed the musical selections, the band was founded and directed by William Sweeney, essentially for the life of the Wild West exhibition, performing between 1883 and 1913. Sweeney was already on board in 1882 for the Old Glory Blowout in Nebraska. Buffalo Bill said the band boss's songs were "appropriate music from Mr. Sweeney's Cowboy Band" for the Wild West exhibition.[14]

As the calendar turned to 1904, Buffalo Bill Cody planned to continue touring Europe with the Wild West exhibition and the Congress of Rough Riders. But he decided after spending more time apart than together since they married, it was time to obtain a divorce from his wife Louisa. Bill Cody did not plan to tour with his Wild West exhibition forever. He certainly had made enough money from it by then, twenty-one years into building a deep fan base all over the country and throughout much of the world. One of the biggest problems was his ability to hold onto his money. He earned big paydays, but he did not save intelligently. He had hoped, perhaps a disillusionment he foisted on himself, that one day he would retire and live a tamer existence with his wife.

However, in January of that year, Cody gave up on that notion. It appeared to him he would never be happy with Louisa again. These days the term applied to the situation might be "irreconcilable differences." The couple certainly had those. In January, the middle of winter, before it was time to rev up the Wild West exhibition again, William F. Cody filed divorce papers in Cheyenne, Wyoming. What Cody did not foresee was being in for a rougher ride than the Congress of Rough Riders.

17

Divorce Trials

So it finally came to a legal showdown—one of the Codys filed for divorce. It was William F. and not Louisa, though through the lens of history it would seem either could have taken the step. However, based on what transpired, the world learned then, and from the vantage of point of more than a century passed, the world knows now, that Louisa would never have done so. This was her line in the sand. Even if she did not enjoy the marriage, she must have felt some pride or seen value in being Mrs. Cody, or Mrs. Buffalo Bill.

Whether it was the Civil War or the Plains Indians Wars, Buffalo Bill had never encountered war like this one. If for a moment he entertained the idea this proceeding would be a mere filing of paperwork, he grossly miscalculated. Even with Cody offering big money and substantial property rights, Louisa was not interested in a legal split. Maybe she viewed this as a humiliation attempt by Cody. If so, she was going to humiliate him right back and up the ante without any care as to what members of the public thought.

This was the *National Enquirer* fodder of its time, even if most newspapers had more kinship with the supermarket tabloid sensationalist publication back then anyway. It seems as if it has always been of great note and gossip to banner massive headlines on papers when the rich and famous are being torn down to size. Well, there was no one more famous in the world than Buffalo Bill Cody and here he was suffering with the same kind of troubles as the average man. Neither publicity wizard John Burke, nor the king-sized Wild West advertising budget that churned out those marvelous posters, could save him.

"For over twenty years, Mr. Cody had been contemplating a divorce," one researcher wrote, "but it was not easy in those days to secure one, especially if one party would not consent. He was willing to give up most of his fortune to gain his freedom and have peace and happiness in his remaining years."[1] Cody thought he had a quiet settlement going, giving

Louisa his North Platte, Nebraska, holdings and some in Cody, Wyoming, as well as cash, but she reneged on the deal and decided to fight to prevent the official breakup.

The courtroom scenario was uncomfortable, but followers of the case were most astonished when Buffalo Bill alleged his wife tried to poison him. Never mind the accusations of philandering and neglect, that charge by Cody was the showstopper. Testimony came from the wife of a former ranch manager at North Platte that, indeed, Mrs. Cody had tried to poison Mr. Cody at least three times. That pretty much stopped the clock. The woman, who also said Louisa swore like a sailor, drank like a fish, and treated others poorly, said there were at least three occasions when Louisa doused Buffalo Bill's coffee, tea, or whiskey with a substance that Mrs. Cody called "dragon's blood" obtained from a gypsy. Once, when Cody became very ill and she feared he might die, the woman said she threatened to call the police, and Mrs. Cody replied, "she did not care if he did die, that she would either rule or ruin him."[2]

That was one side of the woman's testimony. On cross-examination, besides saying Bill Cody was often drunk at home, she also pretty much massaged her damning comments by quoting Louisa as saying the substance applied to Cody's drinks was not poisonous, but essentially a love potion to make him love her more. Just like that, Louisa was transformed from an evil witch willing to kill off her husband to a pining woman of great empathy who only wanted from this life that her legally wedded husband give her more affection. Bill Cody was portrayed as a homewrecker. Louisa Cody was portrayed as a wonderful hostess, welcoming to all, and a kind and gentle mother.

Things went downhill from there for Buffalo Bill. The same woman and others talked about his infidelities, his girlfriends and lovers, bringing into the public domain much of what had been hidden, sometimes for years. It was a tricky defense attempt, but to counter Louisa's and others' testimony about how Buffalo Bill drank too much, another cowboy said Cody could hold his booze better than anyone he ever knew, including himself. "I was pretty good at that myself," a cowboy named Pony Bob said, "but he had me skinned a mile."[3]

Not everyone admired Cody's huge capacity for liquor, or even, in the case of Nate Salsbury, his chief partner in the Wild West exhibition, how he acted when he was sober. Salsbury had invested considerable time in eyeing Cody's behavior when drunk, and while he urged him to stay sober at critical moments, it turned out Salsbury was nursing a grudge on the issue. Indeed, it seemed, Salsbury had accumulated a series of grievances against Cody, and he wanted a divorce from Bill more than Louisa did.

Theirs had been a magnificently fruitful financial partnership, but time eroded the bonds between them. When Salsbury realized he was dying in 1901, he severed himself from Cody and wrote a private missive ranting about different aspects of Cody. They had worked brilliantly together for sixteen years to make the Wild West exhibition the most successful show of its kind. But Salsbury was not polite upon parting. He wrote:

> Cody makes a virtue of keeping sober most of the time during the Summer Season, and when he does so for the entire season he looks upon himself as a paragon of virtue and self-abnegation. [When he drinks,] he forgets honor, reputation, friend, and obligation in his mad eagerness to fill his hide with rot gut of any kind. He would keep at it until he fell so sick that he could not move, or, as he used to put it, "His liver flopped." When he sobers up a little, he is so conceited as to imagine he has had a perfect right to get drunk, no matter at what cost to his associates in business, and takes it for granted he is so great a man that all the world excuses him because he is a hero and an "Old Timer" who saved America from going back to the wilderness (as) Columbus found it.[4]

So there. It was a scathing venting of the soul for Salsbury, but it was certainly not a discourse that would help convince those in the dark that Cody was not much of a drinker. On and on Salsbury continued detailing anger and resentment toward Cody. He called him a "Tin Jesus on horseback" and criticized the then-new book about Cody written by his sister Helen Cody Wetmore. It was true the book pretty much made Cody out to be a demigod, but Salsbury basically implied the only truth contained in its pages may have been the title, *Last of the Great Scouts*. Of that, Salsbury stated, "A man may be a 'Great Scout, and a damned rascal at the same time."[5]

Compared to his relationship at the end with Salsbury, Cody's relationship with Louisa seemed swimmingly good. In a result unlikely to be seen today, the court in Cheyenne refused to grant the divorce, a repudiation of Buffalo Bill. What a mess it was. Everyone knew how lousy the Bill–Louisa marriage was if they knew them well. The basic result, demoralizing to Buffalo Bill, was that he was stuck. There was no suggestion he wanted out of the marriage at that time to marry someone else, but nonetheless, this unexpected turn meant he really was going to be married to Louisa until death did them part.

Once the tawdry episode was behind him, as was Salsbury by then, the only thing left to do was hit the road again with the Wild West exhibition, resume his role as showman-in-chief doing what he did best. In this case that meant a return to Europe, another sail across the Atlantic to pull the equipment out of storage on Barnum & Bailey property in England and ensure the show did go on and meet the schedule. He had an image to uphold as the man who appeared so straight and tall and sturdy in the saddle, and was king of the Wild West empire he presided over. If Cody's image was tarnished somewhat in the United States, especially among extreme moralists, as a direct result of the failed divorce trial, the Europeans did not care so much about that stuff, if they even followed the developments closely. The ticket buyers wanted to be entertained, and royal heads of nations wanted to see what the other kings and queens, princes and princesses raved about.

Cody may have been weighted down mentally by baggage, and certainly he had been bloodied in the courtroom, but as always, even though he was getting close to sixty in age, he made an impressive first impact on those who met him. They were predisposed in his favor anyway. He was taller than most of them, and when he swept into a room in his buckskins he was a living embodiment of the Old West, the in-the-flesh symbol of the Wild West exhibition they came to see.

Although this description of a first meeting with Cody took place years earlier when he was still scouting, it sums up the way many who knew of him merely by reputation were taken with his physical vibrance. "Tall and somewhat slight in figure," a cavalry general observed, "though possessed of great strength and iron endurance, straight and erect as an arrow, and with strikingly handsome features, he at once attracted to him all with whom he became acquainted, and the better knowledge gained of him during the days he spent with our party increased the good impression he made upon his introduction."[6] That was a bit unwieldly, but left the reader with the idea Cody had magnetism.

Back to work. Buffalo Bill's Wild West and Congress of Rough Riders of the World played Aberdeen in Scotland in late April of 1904 and was in Wales by May before stops elsewhere in England in early June prior to a heavy focus again in Scotland over the summer. By then, Charles Griffin, one of the Wild West exhibition's managers, had completed his tourism hiatus while overwintering in England. Griffin generally felt at home after spending so much time in England, but at the July 4 exhibition in York he did have a moment of homesickness. "The whole show was a mass of red, white and blue bunting in honor of our national holiday, the bands played patriotic airs, and the entire company sat down to a regular Yankee dinner, which almost made us forget, for the time being, that we were 'strangers in a strange land.'"[7]

There is little doubt the expansion of the riding corps of the Wild West exhibition, beyond the American Indians, who still commanded great fascination, was a boon to the operation. Spectators responded well to the Congress of Rough Riders, knowing participants were from the world over. John Burke had something positive to say about all nationalities, of course: "The Cossack of the Caucasian lines is by inheritance and inclination among the most fearless and graceful horsemen of the world," Burke wrote. "As picturesque, and more gaudy in appearance and trapping than either the Bedouin or the Cossack is the Vaquero of our neighboring Mexico. But of all these native-born and wonderful horsemen of land other than our own, perhaps the most complete, the most daring and dangerous in war, the most phenomenal trailer, the greatest pathfinder, is the wonderful Gaucho from llanos of the Argentine Republic."[8]

Scotland made a very favorable impression on Griffin. He repeatedly described campsites as being in beautiful parks with lakes and magnificent scenery for company. In Glasgow, in early August, the turnout was fantastic. Although Griffin said the several-day stopover was the best financial production the Wild West exhibition ever had outside of the World's Fair in Chicago, it is not clear if he was in position to possess that knowledge. He did call Glasgow "one of the grandest cities I have ever visited."[9] When the season again adjourned for winter, Griffin noted the Wild West exhibition had never left Great Britain and garnered tremendous crowds everywhere it traveled within a fairly confined space, one so much smaller than the United States. For the second straight off-season, 1904–1905, Griffin based himself out of London as most other Americans, including Buffalo Bill, headed home.

Although he was not a lawyer, perhaps Buffalo Bill should have retained his loyal Major John Burke as part of his team in the courtroom. William F. Cody's integrity and attitude would never suffer a moment's assault without Burke at the standby to soothe his ego with persuasive words over years with the Wild West exhibition. Burke seemed to take particular relish in leading the uninitiated through Buffalo Bill's life story and to shout from rooftops in every European capital just how wonderful Cody and the Wild West were. No one's perfect, and it had clearly been demonstrated in court Cody was not, but Burke did his best to plead the case the Wild West exhibition and its leader were as close to perfection as anything in the world. Burke wrote: "This man of many parts, this unique exemplification of the possibilities of human intellectual and physical development and progress had now passed through success, and with all truth it can be said, successful gradations, from the illiterate urchin of the rough cabin on the Plains, to a great practical educator, and the lessons taught in his magnificently illustrated lectures had for their object the welding together of human interests and the enlarging of the mutual sympathies of nations."[10]

The English translation of the English words would be that Cody was born into tough circumstances, raised himself to fame and fortune, and was now providing an educational experience to the world through his riveting Wild West exhibition. It is not likely anyone ever kept track of the tonnage of manure produced in Wild West camps by horses and buffalo, but Burke probably equaled it in words. And he was not hardly done. Burke continued: "I am aware that the selfish, captious and narrow-minded may see in the exhibitions and travels of the Wild West under Colonel Cody's leadership simply a scheme for personal aggrandizement and accumulation of great wealth." Not so, Burke added. Otherwise, all great inventors and adventurers might be subject to the same charge even as they brought news of fantastic feats to the public. Those who make such accusations "are unworthy of serious consideration."[11]

Interaction with Europeans was just so amazing, Burke said, in so many ways. Artists from many countries wished to paint and were invited to the camp. Rosa Bonheur extended her invitation to Buffalo Bill to have his portrait painted at her studio and then began visiting the show. The former queen of Spain rode in the Deadwood stagecoach. In Italy, authorities worried wild horses would trample spectators, so extra precautions were taken. In Venice, the troupe did everything but swim in the Grand Canal. A *New York Herald* dispatch quoted by Burke read, "No one can think them ordinary artistes after they have seen the gathering of different Indians in gondolas."[12] Just the local version of canoes.

Considerable time was spent in France in 1906, and Griffin decided to learn how to speak the language. He said he took twenty lessons, and that was good enough to get him by in his introductory speeches at the sideshow of "freaks" at the Wild West exhibition "Well, I got along pretty fair considering that I did not know the meaning of half the words I was saying," he said. "I honestly believe that more people came in the sideshow in Paris to hear and laugh at my 'rotten' French than anything else, and when I found that a certain word or expression excited their risibilities, I never changed it." If Griffin wished to learn other languages, all he would have to do is hang around camp where he said at least a dozen languages were spoken and the situation resembled "a polyglot school. Being in such close contact every day, we were bound to get some idea of the other's tongue."[13] Not that each member of the cast became fluent in several languages. More likely, some of the cowboys learned how to swear more efficiently.

The end for Griffin in Europe was the 1907 season, and the last country visited was Belgium. It had been an exciting, but also exhausting, four years abroad with Buffalo Bill. His ship docked in New York on October 20, and after all his time away, many things struck him as different in the big city. He had not heard that much English spoken on a regular basis in quite a while. Griffin concluded that "the people are more polite in Europe than in America. But these were only impressions of New York City, which is not America any more than London is England or Paris is France."[14]

When Cody finally got around to filing his divorce petition to dissolve his marriage to Louisa, it was long overdue. He had thought about it for twenty years and once come close to carrying through with his divorce plan. But when their daughter Orra died he had withdrawn. Their daughter Arta had long campaigned for reconciliation between her parents, though she tended to side with her mother. Once again, almost unbelievable in its timing, Arta passed away just as Cody was diving into the divorce effort. This was the third of four Cody children to pass away prematurely, before their parents. This time, though, the death of a child did not halt the proceedings. Buffalo Bill even reached out to Louisa, asking her to reconcile through Arta's funeral for the sake of the rest of the family. Rather than pacify her, the suggestion seemed to inflame her. Cody biographer Louis Warren reported Buffalo Bill's sister May Bradford Cody, who was with Louisa during this trying time, saying a distraught Louisa "wanted to send a telegram accusing William Cody of murdering their daughter by breaking her heart with the divorce petition. Relatives persuaded her to soften her language."[15]

Arta's body was transported by train through Chicago to Rochester, New York, where other family members were buried. Bill Cody and Louisa rode on the same train but in separate compartments and did not speak to one another on the trip. One can imagine the very upset Louisa stewing amid her tears, for she did not ease up on language aimed at Bill for long. She told others she planned to "denounce him as Arta's murderer from the grave of his dead child," and in Chicago even thrust a fist in the air and aimed a verbal barrage at May Cody, saying, "I will bring you Codys down so low the dogs won't bark at you."[16]

For all of his years in the public eye, even though he had clandestine affairs, Cody presented himself as a happily married man. It was talked up in the Wild West programs. The divorce trial collapsed that house of cards. Many willing fans of the man lost some faith as the case played out in newspapers.

When the trial ended with Cody still married, his reputation somewhat soiled, and no permanent financial settlement to clear him of obligations with Louisa, he had gained nothing and lost much. No wonder Europe looked good for a getaway, responsibilities and work volume aside.

18

Cody, Wyoming

There might never have been a Cody, Wyoming, if Buffalo Bill could have put a more secure stamp on North Platte, Nebraska. He had long before built his Scout's Rest Ranch, often used it as a home base in between his tours, and intended to make it his retirement home, if and when he ever retired from the road. Eventually, though, Scout's Rest became its own battlefield between Bill and Louisa. While at times various members of the Cody family, notably sister Julia and her husband Al, lived on the land and supervised the property, the comings and goings of Louisa, how the land became an object of contention between them, had to sour Cody somewhat on the concept that peace and quiet would ever prevail in Nebraska.

The idea for creating a new town in Wyoming's Big Horn Basin did not originate with Cody. There were businessmen who felt a community could thrive using the waters of the Stinking Water River (as local Native Americans called what was renamed the Shoshone River) to irrigate farmland. While the community came to bear the name of William F. Cody and does so today, there were other town founders in on a plan before he was. George Beck, H.C. Alger, Bronson Rumsey, Elwood Mead, and Horton Boal had discussions of how to invent a new town. Boal was Cody's initial connection to the group because he was married to daughter Arta. Mead was Wyoming's first state engineer and became the first commissioner of the Bureau of Land Reclamation.

Just when Bill Cody saw the Cody area of the Big Horn Basin for the first time is not clear. In Helen Cody Wetmore's book *Last of the Great Scouts*, she outlines a couple of potential visits that seem at odds with his schedule. Another source said many years earlier Cody had thought about checking out the region, perhaps for hunting. It is indisputable that Cody took a horseback tour of the area in 1894, which would be shortly in advance of the start-up plan for the new community.

Wyoming had only become a state in 1890, evolving from a territory, and state officials wanted to beef up the population, so they looked favorably on growth projects. In 1894, Wyoming Senator Joseph Carey ushered the Carey Act through Congress to aid western settlement. It was true settlers did not have much to fear from Indian attack by then, but much of the West was arid and not conducive to farming without access to water. As part of the overall Carey plan, the federal government could give land to states, and those states could sell water rights to private citizens to improve the land through irrigation. This is what Buffalo Bill and his partners were banking on to get them going.

Buffalo Bill grew excited about the prospect of being part of something new. Long before, he had attempted to found a town called Rome, Kansas, but that failed. Now he had scads of money and was looking for investments. The first thing the organizing group decided was that the name of the river had to go. How could you sell home lots next to water called the Stinking Water River? That would not do. So the name was changed to the Shoshone River. That alteration inspired the first proposed town name of Shoshone. However, that was rejected by the U.S. Postal Service because there already was a Shoshoni near what became the Wind River Indian Reservation. Although the name of the start-up project was called the Shoshone Irrigation Agency, the founding fathers decided to call the town Cody—something he pushed for. This is where name recognition paid off for Buffalo Bill. His name and face were so famous the businessmen felt they could use it to their advantage and sell homes and land. Thus, Cody, Wyoming, was born.

While the others may have thought it vain of Cody to campaign for his name on the town, and it was to an extent, it meant he was totally engaged in helping make the 1896 founding a success. Buffalo Bill was a great believer in the effort and put his money where his thoughts were. He also recruited other wealthy businessmen to invest, including Nate Salsbury, his Wild West exhibition partner, George Bleistein, who was not from the area at all but from Buffalo, New York, and Rumsey. When Cody previously invested himself in trying to start a town, the project fizzled because of the placement of railroad tracks elsewhere. This project succeeded. Indeed, in the 2000s, there are streets in and near downtown Cody named for Beck, Rumsey, Salsbury, and Bleistein.

The town site was located on twenty-eight thousand acres at the split in the now-Shoshone River, referred to as the North Fork and the South Fork. The elevation is 5,016 feet, nearly a mile high. The setting, surrounded by nearby mountains, can be breathtaking on sunny days. Buffalo Bill, as well as the others, felt Cody would become a gateway to Yellowstone National Park, which, from its rudimentary beginnings in 1872 as the world's first national park, would attract growing numbers of tourists to its east side. This also all came to pass. Cody, with Salsbury, invested in additional land between Cody and the park and did eventually build a hotel in present-day Wapiti. In that area, too, near the park entrance, was Pahaska Teepee, Buffalo Bill's hunting lodge. Buildings there are still in use, though the main lodge is open only for tourist visits.

The cornerstone of the series of developmental ideas was water. These could be very dry parts, and irrigation was mandatory. The very first step was to build the Cody Canal, and it took until 1910 for the Shoshone Dam to be constructed and opened. Still, it tamed the rushing waters of the river and diverted them to the Buffalo Bill Reservoir and to farmland. In 1946, the name of the 325-foot tall concrete dam was changed to the Buffalo Bill Dam.

One thing Buffalo Bill never lacked was energy, and he threw himself into the role of salesman for Cody. He called the acquisition of the land for Cody "the greatest land deal ever" and said it should be a great place to retire. "We will all have a big farm of our own that will support us in our old age and we can lay under the trees and swap lies."[1]

The show programs of the Wild West carried advertising and articles that helped sell land to spectators as the show toured the nation and the

After helping to found Cody, Wyoming, in 1896, Buffalo Bill Cody established a ranch called the TE on the outskirts of town (courtesy of Park County Archives).

18. Cody, Wyoming

world. That was a help, since it brought hundreds of thousands of sets of eyes to the project. This advertising began calling Cody Buffalo Bill's hometown. He did buy land and set up a ranch there. Cody was his new hometown. As one Wyoming writer who studied Cody's connection to the town bearing his name put it, a project brochure "essentially based its appeal on the fact that Bill Cody had chosen to live in this land, and therefore others should."[2]

During this time, in the 1890s, Cody was the owner of the *Duluth Press* newspaper in Minnesota, which was run by his sister Helen and her husband Hugh Wetmore. There were ads in that newspaper that urged people to think about relocating to this new paradise going up in Wyoming. Briefly, Cody also had the *Shoshone News*, and Buffalo Bill imported John Burke to run it. In 1899, Buffalo Bill brought in J.H. Peake, formerly of North Platte, as an editor for his new newspaper, the *Cody Enterprise*. It made its debut on August 31. The twice-a-week newspaper still serves the community, and there is an image of a Buffalo Bill sculpture adorning the front-page masthead.

While on paper and in energetic minds founding a town was exciting, the nitty-gritty work became more costly than anticipated. George Beck obtained $30,000 for a bond sale from Phoebe Hearst (he knew her late husband) in 1896 that helped the bankroll, although Buffalo Bill and Nate Salsbury also talked him into loaning $5,000 for the Wild West exhibition to start on time and did not pay Beck back for nine months.

It was also extremely useful that by 1901 the railroad ran to Cody. The automobile was just about to make its first big splash, but roads were rudimentary and no one could foresee the way cars would take over as families' primary modes of transportation as quickly as they did. Buffalo Bill wanted to run a stage line from Cody to Yellowstone. This vision was being aided by the federal government, which spent $50,000 to build a road between Cody and Yellowstone. If the other partners felt the employment of Cody's name was simply a gimmick at first, they may have been surprised at how much this very busy man threw himself into making the town a successful venture for all of them. Buffalo Bill energetically invested in oil wells, coal mines, and gold mines, throwing his money every which way, though receiving little financial return. He was always in there pitching, though. His heart and his bank account embraced Cody.

Salsbury marveled at Cody's acquisitions. "While you were about it," he said, "why didn't you make application to control all the air in the Basin? You seem to have pinched everything else in sight."[3] Buffalo Bill ended up with a 160-acre ranch (the TE) on the South Fork and 640 acres adjacent to Carter Mountain.

In no single more visible way did Cody commit to the new town than

Buffalo Bill Cody built a luxury hotel in Cody, Wyoming, in 1902 and named it after his daughter Irma. The hotel is still a thriving business (photograph by the author).

by building a luxury hotel, where he maintained an apartment. He already had constructed one in Sheridan, Wyoming, and it was managed by an old friend from North Platte. In 1902, the Irma, named after his daughter, opened for business. A hotel of major historical import and lavish in the care in which it was constructed, the Irma is the home to that cherrywood bar of some beauty, even if Queen Victoria never saw it, never mind gave it to Buffalo Bill. Buffalo Bill hired a quality chef and made sure furnishings were first class. He decorated the walls with lovely and dramatic western paintings.

18. Cody, Wyoming

The grand opening of the $80,000 hotel on November 18 of that year was conducted in typical Buffalo Bill fashion—with showmanship. Knowing he would be traveling often, Cody persuaded his sister, Julia Goodman, to become the on-site manager. Many Cody relatives were in attendance, though not Louisa. Irma's engagement to Lieutenant Clarence Armstrong Scott was announced simultaneously at the party. Among the one thousand invitations, many went to newspapermen Cody knew from all over the country through the Wild West exhibition. The hotel was the biggest and most visible business in town. Buffalo Bill hung out there, and the restaurant and bar became hangouts for other residents.

Cody, Wyoming, had become Buffalo Bill's primary residence. He occasionally visited North Platte, but now he was only passing through. While always a man on the go, a traveling salesman of the Wild West exhibition, but also now of real estate, Cody did not stay in one place very long. But as the 1890s shifted into the 1900s, the place he gravitated to most often was Cody. It was something special to go home to a community named after yourself.

One story goes that when the Sheridan Inn opened, the town was still so rustic Buffalo Bill was able to audition candidates for the Wild West exhibition riding and roping while he sat on the porch, boots up, relaxed, as they did their stuff. The same story clings to him in Cody, at the Irma. In Cody, it is recalled one potential rider was a little shaky in putting the brakes on his horse and crashed through a business's plate-glass window downtown on Sheridan Avenue. The crowning touch was that Buffalo Bill hired him. Maybe it happened. In any case, people did not travel long distances to visit with Beck, Alger, or Rumsey.

Buffalo Bill was so famous he not only knew the generals who were the top military leaders of the nineteenth century, he also became acquainted with presidents. There was a natural kinship through the outdoors between President Theodore Roosevelt and Cody. They certainly both saw themselves as men of action. Cody was even invited to the wedding of Roosevelt's daughter Alice on February 16, 1906. He was unable to attend because he was getting ready for another Wild West European tour. But he sent a magnificent and elaborate present—a silver inlaid saddle worth $2,000. The item was apparently so pretty Roosevelt wrote to Cody with gratitude, saying, "I appreciate it, I think, as much as she does, for I was particularly glad to have her wedding day remembered by you."[4] If nothing else, Cody's gesture was good public relations. Everyone would like to have the president of the United States on his side, especially if favors might be needed later.

In one of his many other ventures in and around Cody, Buffalo Bill established a hunting club in the early 1900s (Roosevelt was a member before becoming president). He began speaking out about game preservation and the need to protect other species since it was too late for the buffalo, and the need for local guides to become involved with visiting hunters. "Most of the eastern men who go to Wyoming for the shooting are strongly in favor of the rigid enforcement of the law," he said.[5] Cody seemed to be adopting fresh attitudes toward conservation. Perhaps Roosevelt was an influence. He had espoused such views dating back to the days of the founding of the Boone & Crockett Club.

Cody did not refrain from hunting. Periodically, when he was not with the Wild West exhibition, he brought friends to Pahaska Teepee, his base for major trips. George Beck once wrote of going on one. Iron Tail accompanied Buffalo Bill once or more. Wyoming remains one of the United States' hunting paradises, and it was probably even more so in the early twentieth century. Elk, deer, and perhaps bears were taken.

Certainly, one of the most famous hunts Cody was connected to, if not the most famous, considering the Grand Duke Alexis Russian buffalo hunt of years before, was the 1913 hunt featuring the prince of Monaco. Referred to as "The Royal Hunt," Monaco's Prince Albert I embarked on a hunt with Buffalo Bill near both Pahaska Teepee and Yellowstone National Park. This followed a hunt out of Meeteetse, Wyoming, about thirty miles from Cody, which then overshadowed the tiny new community although it is now home to only about 325 people. The organizer was A.A. Anderson, a prominent Wyoming citizen who was a renowned artist moved in from New York. Anderson had previously met the prince in Europe and served as the go-between. General Nelson Miles was present, as was Crow Chief Plenty Coups. A famous photograph was snapped that highlighted the prince and a few friends standing by a large tree.

A few-foot tall sign reading "Camp Monaco 1913" is showcased in the middle of the row of five men. The two-hundred-year-old tree was a landmark for decades, but during the 1988 Yellowstone National Park fires it was severely damaged. Still, five thousand pounds of surviving pieces were repatriated via helicopter to the Buffalo Bill Center of the West. The prince killed a bull elk and a black bear and had such a good time he kept delaying his departure from the woods. Rather remarkably, given the times, much activity was recorded on camera by Charles Kaufman. Film-making was in its infancy. Some footage at the camp was shot of Buffalo Bill chopping wood. Although most of his life predated film technology, Buffalo Bill can also be seen on grainy film inside the Buffalo Bill Center riding in Wild West exhibitions and heard introducing them.

In a surprising twist, as a demonstration of how much the hunt meant to Prince Albert, his great-grandson Albert II has made more than one visit to Cody, Wyoming, from Monaco, and in 2015 even visited the campsite of the original hunt. Also, the monarch endowed a $100,000 Camp Monaco Prize administered in Cody in connection with the Buffalo Bill Center. It is awarded every three years to someone creating new scientific and education initiatives supporting the environment.

Whether the proper word is "mellowing or not, as Buffalo Bill aged into his early sixties, he showed some indications of change in his outlook and personality. In 1907, something which was rare for him, he commented on religion. "I believe man gets closer to God in the big free West," he said. "You feel differently about your fellow man in the West. He's nearer to you and God is nearer to you. You are filled with a true religion and a bigger realization of life."[6] The one member of the Cody family who would not have been surprised by this statement was Bill's sister Julia. She was a very religious Christian woman and had lobbied him for years to get straight with God. In 1901, she wrote him a letter saying as much. He did not respond warmly to the suggestion then, but must have spent some time thinking about things because in 1905 he seemed to receive a wake-up call, which he wrote to her about. Cody said, "And it's in my old age that I have found God—And realize how easy it is to abandon sin and serve him. When one stops to think how little they have to give up—to serve God. It's a wonder so many don't do it. A person only has to do right."[7]

Cody also endorsed women's suffrage. Wyoming was still a territory when its government approved giving women the vote. In an interview, on tour, Cody was interviewed by a reporter and surprised her by saying he was a keen supporter.

It is only against a backdrop of a specific inner (religious?) peace can one imagine Bill Cody reconciling with Louisa. Their longstanding divisions, the publicly embarrassing divorce case, their long absences from one another's sight, their failure to communicate, would lead to the belief that a permanently ingrained bitterness would prevail forever. But Irma, the last of the couple's four children, and Cody Boal, Arta's son, conspired to bring them back together. The plot revolved around Easter of 1910 when Buffalo Bill was wooed back to North Platte. Neither he nor Louisa had a clue what their relatives intended until they ended up alone in a room at Scout's Rest Ranch. When they emerged they agreed to spend the rest of their lives together, at least technically, since Cody was not retiring from travel.

While development of the city of Cody was taking place and Buffalo Bill was captivated by it all, he was never more than one gigantic step in his fancy boots away from heading back on tour with the Wild West exhibition. This town stuff was fun and could well represent his retirement future, but the Wild West exhibition was the bread and butter, the business that provided for everything else. Cody was in no way ready to leave the road behind. Besides, he needed the money. He poured considerable funds into the town of Cody, had been burned by poor investments in Wyoming and in a mine in Arizona, and regularly helped his sisters and their families financially. However, the biggest blow may have been a growing indifference to the Wild West and the Old West being demonstrated by the American public. Ticket sales were declining while expenses were not. Nate Salsbury was no longer around to organize trips, and neither was James Bailey after 1907. He too had died.

Once, Buffalo Bill and Pawnee Bill had been close colleagues. Pawnee Bill, aka Gordon Lillie, had provided Pawnee scouts in the early days of the Wild West exhibition. When the men split, Pawnee Bill operated his own show. Now his attendance was also dropping. In 1909, the men made a truce and joined forces. No longer was Cody's exhibition called "Buffalo Bill's Wild West and Congress of Rough Riders of the World." The new title of the men's merged operation was "Buffalo Bill's Wild West and Pawnee Bill's Great Far East Combined." No longer could Buffalo Bill ride into an arena astride his great horse and intone, "Ladies and gentlemen, permit me to welcome you..." without modification.

When he committed to join forces with Lillie, Buffalo Bill said he would perform for two more years and then retire. This was a premeditated plan and thus began the billing of the show as a two-year farewell tour. A wiser man would have banked the proceeds, but Cody kept spending, using money earned to finance other investments. Buffalo Bill and

Several Buffalo Bill Cody descendants are buried in Cody, Wyoming, including William Garlow Cody (a.k.a. Bill Cody). His grave marker is in Old Trail Town, featuring buildings of the 1800s. Photograph by the author.

18. Cody, Wyoming

Pawnee Bill did well at first, but in 1911 bad weather was costly to the outdoor shows. What Cody discovered, although he truly was weary by then, was that he could not really afford to retire.

It may be that fans who wanted to see Buffalo Bill Cody in action one last time were used up, or there was merely a declining level of interest in such shows, but the Buffalo Bill–Pawnee Bill alliance experienced business setbacks in 1913. "The show business isn't what it used to be," Cody said.[8] Not for him, at least. Cody took a $20,000 loan from Henry Tammen, a Denver businessman, to help finance the 1914 season. But Tammen then told the world Buffalo Bill's Wild West was now affiliated with his Sells-Floto Circus. Blindsided, Lillie was furious at Cody, although Cody said he had not signed an agreement for that move. Cody and Lillie began the season, but sales were not good, and the six-month deadline for paying off Tammen loomed. On July 21, after Tammen consolidated other creditors and prevailed upon the sheriff's office to intervene, the Cody–Lillie operation closed its doors. This preordained plan resulted in all show assets being sold at auction, including Cody's beloved horse Isham. However, on that day, friends of Buffalo Bill made sure to win the bidding, and the horse was given back to him.

Cody was trapped. If he wanted to perform and could hold out any hope of running his own Wild West exhibition again, he had to participate in the Sells-Floto Circus. He did so, while also seeking to gain more traction financially by starting to film a series of movies. Alas, for him, this venture did not bear fruit, either. Tammen had so tied up Cody that when they parted after the 1915 season, Cody could not legally use the name "Buffalo Bill's Wild West" to start a new show. When he was affiliated with the Miller Brothers 101 Ranch for a short time in 1916, he was advertised as "Buffalo Bill (Himself)." When he came off the road at the end of that season, it marked the end of William F. Cody's days as a traveling showman. While he talked big about starting a fresh show, and was even seeking investors, the reality was he was seventy years old and his health was failing.

19

The Death of the Great Showman

If his health permitted, one might wonder how long Buffalo Bill Cody would have stayed in the saddle. One could ponder if he would have kept on performing in a western show of some kind with top billing for whomever ran the outfit. Even though he said he wished to retire, and certainly wife Louisa was in favor of that, Bill Cody was not one to go softly into that good night. His ego, his habits, his love of the applause and spotlight might well have overruled appeals to common sense.

He turned seventy years old on February 26, 1916, which by the standards of the time definitely made him an old man. Before the end of the year, he looked it. He was white-haired, though also somewhat bald to those who saw him without a cowboy hat. His goatee and mustache had turned white. He was not necessarily one who had to watch the parade continue to pass by in a rocking chair, but one whose body had taken some beatings, and he was definitely not as robust as he had once been.

Vanity alone would have spurred Cody on to do more shows. For someone who invented a genre that was wildly successful and made him millions of dollars over time, he had to reflect on where all the money had gone and how some fifteen years into the twentieth century he had lost his grip on audiences. Where were all of those adoring fans of past decades? Were they really all more worn out on the topic of the Old West than he was? Box office sales said that was true.

Even with his trusted stand-in son Johnny Baker by his side and loyal friend Iron Tail ready to go, and even if Buffalo Bill believed he had the strength and could find the backing for mounting one last profitable show, that was an unknown. In the end, his health refused to support such a venture.

Some of the old standbys that had made the Wild West exhibition so spectacular were long gone. Sitting Bull was a four-month shooting

19. The Death of the Great Showman

star. Annie Oakley and Frank Butler spent sixteen out of twenty-one years with the Wild West exhibition, but retired for good in 1901. Annie was seriously injured in a train accident. She suffered temporary paralysis and endured five back operations. That ended her touring days and performing trick shots from moving horses. The accuracy of Little Miss Sure Shot, though, was not affected. A woman very much ahead of her time, Oakley was said to provide firearms instruction to fifteen thousand women, and when World War I started, she said women should also engage in combat in support of the country. Oakley was sixty-six when she died in 1926.

As the years sped by, Buffalo Bill faced his tribulations, many of them financial near the end. There are contradictory reports and studies of whether or not he was very much bankrupt by 1917, personally so or just

Buffalo Bill Cody (left) in Colorado near the end of his life with Harry Tammen, who forced Cody into bankruptcy and conspired to keep Cody's body in Colorado (courtesy of Park County Archives).

short on cash. In any case, he had not saved his money or invested very wisely. His generosity in taking care of many relatives financially and as a soft touch with loans that turned into gifts all contributed. The last days with Pawnee Bill did result in show bankruptcy, and at various times Cody put up some of his major property holdings, including the Irma Hotel, as collateral. He lost all of those.

Cody fulfilled his obligation to Henry Tammen by appearing with the Sells-Floto Circus into the autumn of 1916, fully planning to start anew the next year. He stopped in Denver to visit his sister May, but then departed for his ranch outside Cody. Then he went back to Denver in early December. This was supposed to be a temporary stay before once again adjourning to Cody, Wyoming. Cody the man was tired from his travels with the tour, and his constitution seemed weakened. It was while back in Denver he contracted a bad cold he could not shake and which seemed to be developing into something more serious. It was obvious to May, and she sent word to Louisa and Irma they should come to her place in Denver to see Will. When the doctor looked him over, he said Cody's heart was not doing so well and he should cut back on smoking. Still, by the time Louisa and Irma arrived, he was no longer bedridden.

An idea was advanced that Cody should try taking the waters, as the expression went, in nearby Glenwood Springs, Colorado. Cody followed the advice on January 3, 1917. A photograph taken of Cody as he was traveling between Glenwood Springs and Denver showed a white-haired man wearing a rakish hat, a tie, and white shirt beneath an overcoat. It was the last known picture taken of the man who had had thousands upon thousands taken of him. Considering the state of his health, he looked sharp, if a bit slender.

Two days into Cody's stay in Glenwood Springs he suffered a collapse and returned to May's house in Denver. Doctors told Cody he probably had about thirty-six hours to live. The knowledge that the famed Buffalo Bill might be deathly ill became public January 8, and a vigil of sorts began. Fans congregated outside the house, but inside the home things were chaotic as well. Newspaper reporters were allowed in to conduct final interviews with the most famous man in the world as he lay dying. Relatives went in and out of the bedroom. Depending upon who is believed, this was when Cody supposedly informed Louisa he had changed his mind about being buried on the outskirts of the town named for him and instead preferred being interred in Golden, Colorado, some twenty miles from Denver.

What conversation truly took place, and what William F. Cody truly wanted, has been the subject of debate since. There are those who do not believe for one minute Cody had any affinity for Golden or had even been

19. The Death of the Great Showman

there. Many people believed Cody's heart was in Cody, Wyoming, until the end, and he would never have changed his mind. This situation engendered wild stories of just how it was Cody's funeral took place in Denver, not a city dear to him, and even whether his body was later secretly moved. More than a century later, there are contradictory beliefs about what may have transpired in that bedroom, why the funeral was in Denver, and just where Cody's remains are.

The vigil did not last long. Two days after the world was informed Buffalo Bill Cody had only a short time to live, he passed away in his sister's house in Denver. It was January 10, 1917, at five minutes past noon. The word spread quickly. Western Union, apprised of the situation, was holding an open telegraph line to speed the word around the nation and the globe. Rather astoundingly, since the United States and Germany were engaged in conflict in World War I, Kaiser Wilhelm even took time out to send condolences, clearly a message bespeaking of better times.

In those days, the *Cody Enterprise* front page was almost always a sea of gray, with no photographs. For a time it changed its name to the *Park County Enterprise*, and it was during that phase William F. Cody died. In testimony to how swiftly news spread about Cody's demise, the newspaper was printed the same day, January 10. Under the name plate it still referred to the newspaper as Bill Cody's baby with the words "Founded in 1899 by Col. W.F. Cody (Buffalo Bill) and Col. Peake." Smack in the middle

Directional sign to Buffalo Bill Cody's marked grave site in Golden, Colorado, on Lookout Mountain (photograph by the author).

of the front page was a fairly large, though not inordinately so, headline reading, "DEATH SUMMONS COL. W. F. CODY." In a deck below that, it read, "Famous Old Scout Passed Away at Noon in Denver—Funeral to be Held There Sunday."

The obituary followed, and in the midst of it was a graphic, a head and shoulders image of Cody, appearing as if it was a photograph of a framed photograph of him. It was the only picture on the page. The beginning of the obituary read this way:

> Col. W.F. Cody, "Buffalo Bill," better known perhaps than any other man in private life in the whole world, answered the last summons and quietly passed away at Denver today, at five minutes after noon. Facing death in the manner he faced it many times on the plains of our western country in the days when death stalked every white man who dared its perils and mysteries. Colonel Cody calmly awaited the end that respects no man, no difference what station in life he might have enjoyed. The famous scout, plainsman, educator, philanthropist, and empire builder for days awaited this last message bravely and unflinching, and now the noble visage is as calm and peaceful in the repose in death as though he were only sleeping.[1]

Given that Buffalo Bill Cody died in front of several witnesses and that he was in a controlled environment—in the bedroom of a family home in a major city—it is ironic that the fact of his death was one of the

A tribute to Johnny Baker, Buffalo Bill Cody's foster son, whose memorabilia made the creation of the Golden museum possible (photograph by the author).

19. The Death of the Great Showman

few events pertaining to his departure from this earth that was not controversial. His memorial service, his burial, and where his body was buried were all more controversial.

In the final days, and final hours, Louisa Cody was with her husband. So was his sister May. So was his daughter Irma. So was his grandson William Cody Boal. His sister Julia and son-in-law Fred Garlow had also come to Denver. Cody kept repeating, "I wish Johnny would come."[2] Johnny Baker was far away in New York City trying to raise money for the next season and could not reach the deathbed in time to pay his final in-person respects. Buffalo Bill had long made it clear he wished to be buried on Cedar Mountain overlooking Cody, Wyoming. It was contained in a will he wrote out. The citizens of Cody were surprised then, when it was revealed after Bill's death he changed his heart, and another will, apparently stating he wished to be buried on Lookout Mountain in Golden, Colorado.

Louisa testified to this change of desire. The Golden thing annoyed many. In a 1902 letter, Cody informed Julia of how he wished his burial site to be on Cedar Mountain. "I have got a mountain picked out big enough for us all to be buried on," he wrote.[3] He did reaffirm that idea in his will, writing:

> It is my wish and I hereby direct that my body shall be buried in some suitable plot of ground on Cedar Mountain. I further direct that there shall be erected over my grave, to mark the spot, a monument wrought from native red stone in the form of a mammoth buffalo, and placed in such a position as to be visible from the town ... that it may be a constant reminder ... that it was the great wish of its founder that Cody should not only grow to prosperity and become a populous and influential metropolis, but that it should be distinguished for the purity of its government and the loyalty of its citizens to the institutions of our beloved country.[4]

Strongly influenced by what Buffalo Bill had told them himself, and this document, written in 1906, Cody's friends in Wyoming and elsewhere felt his wishes were being thwarted not only because a grand funeral was conducted in Denver, not in the town named after him, but also because Colorado was going to keep the body. This is where the widow held sway. In his will, Cody stated his executioner should provide $10,000 toward the construction of the monument on Cedar Mountain. Aside from bankruptcy talk, there were other estimates he still had an estate of $60,000 or more and property Louisa had taken control of previously. However, another will, dated 1913, appeared, and in that Cody designated the responsibility for handling his burial and other death-related issues to Louisa.

Louisa reported her own description of the last days of Buffalo Bill in Cody. She said he was weak, but fighting for life and repeatedly said he was still alive if he had his boots on. "But as the days passed, in spite of the fact that he still 'kept his boots on,' he began to realize the last fight was ending—ending in spite of the fact that he was struggling against it with every fiber of his being." Some years earlier, Louisa said, Will told her of his wish to be buried on Cedar Mountain, and he told her while in Denver he had wanted to spend the end of his life in Cody. "But—it was on the day before the end came— he very quietly viewed the subject in a different light. 'I want to be buried on top of Mount Lookout. It's right over Denver. You can look down into four states there. It's pretty up there. I want to be buried up there—instead of in Wyoming."[5]

A view of Buffalo Bill Cody's headstone in Golden, Colorado, fenced with wrought iron and under twenty tons of concrete (photograph by the author).

Boal said he played cards with Buffalo Bill, and reporters were coming and going. Apparently, on January 9, in between those interviews, Buffalo Bill was baptized into the Roman Catholic Church. Yet previously persuaded by Julia's lobbying, he had told her he wanted to join her faith, Episcopalian. Several people noted Cody told his family to let the Elks and Masons take over the production of his funeral. The actual cause of William F. Cody's death, as listed on his death certificate, was uremic poisoning, stemming from kidney disease and kidney failure.

The somewhat nefarious Harry Tammen, who had plotted to split up Buffalo Bill and Pawnee Bill, entered the picture—supposedly. Right away it was said Tammen, co-owner of the *Denver Post* along with Frederick Bonfils, was at the bottom of another plot—to make sure William F. Cody's body remained in the Denver area as a tourist attraction. Some say he took advantage of a grieving Louisa and paid her $10,000 to stage the

19. The Death of the Great Showman 197

The modern-day view from the area of Buffalo Bill Cody's grave site, obstructed by communication towers—not the scenic view he sought for his repose (photograph by the author).

funeral in Denver and to then have the body buried in Golden. She did pay the bills, so some felt she had the right to decide where her husband was buried. Some speculated this was her way of cashing in for some of the aggravation she felt for complaints of the past against Buffalo Bill.

The entire scheme had appeal for some of Denver's elites, including then-mayor Robert Speer, who actually donated some of the land where Cody was to be buried in Golden. The *Denver Post* wasted no time indicating Buffalo Bill would be buried in Golden, although not until sometime in the spring when the ground thawed. The top of Lookout Mountain is at 7,379 feet. The *Post* also reported a splendid monument would be constructed at the site, something of course Buffalo Bill had requested in his will. Thus began a nationwide fundraising campaign focused on school children who donated pennies up to five cents (even possibly Iron Tail nickels) to the cause. That aspect of the program was fairly swiftly overshadowed, however, by the United States' entry into World War I later in 1917.

While the observation came much too late to change things, nearly three decades later, on what would have been Buffalo Bill's 100th birthday, *Time* magazine revisited the occasion of Cody's death, writing, "Denver's mayor, Robert W. Speer was out to claim him. Buffalo Bill, dead and enshrined, would obviously be a greater civic asset than Buffalo Bill alive with one foot on the Albany Hotel bar rail."[6] Speer played a part in the scheme all the way, but Tammen was likely the moving force.

The Elks and the Masons did oversee the funeral service, but they had some assistance turning it into an extravaganza. The date was set as January 14, with Cody's body allowed to rest in state inside the capitol rotunda for two hours, beginning at 10 a.m., so admirers could stream past. And they did, an estimated twenty-five thousand strong. It was an open casket. At noon, four days after Cody's death, the top was closed as family members, including Johnny Baker, gathered around. Since the line of mourners had not exhausted itself, people were allowed to pass the casket for an extended twenty minutes before a procession through the streets began. This included a rider-less white horse. It was at first said the horse was McKinley, the last in a long line of white horses Buffalo Bill favored. Then it became known the horse was merely borrowed from a stable for the occasion, a little white lie for the public to consume. Government officials and up to seventy cowboys also marched. Speeches were made, and Cody's body was taken to Olinger's Crown Hill Mortuary. There it was to be embalmed, preserved, and, if not literally, put on ice to await spring burial.

Meanwhile, despite the massive amount of attention paid to their friend and founder, people in Cody, Wyoming, were disappointed about how this entire scenario played out. For the longest time there were rumors a group of avengers gathered in a bar drinking in liquid courage planned to extricate Cody's body from enemy hands. Then, it was said, they reached the border with Colorado and the courage ran out. Many years later, Dr. Jeremy Johnston, currently curator of the Buffalo Bill Museum in the Buf-

19. The Death of the Great Showman

falo Bill Center of the West, investigated this claim and discovered no evidence this happened. As someone who was raised in nearby Powell, just twenty miles from Cody, and who had been weaned on many Buffalo Bill myths, he wanted this story to be true, but instead ended up debunking it.

Yet another story lingers that would explain how Buffalo Bill was body-snatched from his protective Denver hosts and his remains deposited exactly where the wanted them to rest all along—on 7,890-foot Cedar Mountain in Wyoming. This tale would make for a marvelous movie, a story both gripping and daring and possibly fanciful, even if the tellers so ardently want it to be true. The proselytizer and true believer at the root, at least in the present day, is Bob Richard, currently in his early eighties, and a long-time Cody resident, whose descendants go way back in Buffalo Bill's community.

Richard said he was fourteen years old when his grandfather, Fred Richard, told him how he, Ned Frost, and John Vogel, who at the time was Cody's funeral home director, made a stealth road trip to Denver and stole Cody's body. Then they buried Buffalo Bill on Cedar Mountain. "The grave site sits on Cedar Mountain looking up to the North Fork and looking out over Cody," Bob Richard said in 2017 and has said many times before and since to anyone interested in listening. "Fred took me up there and showed me where they buried him."[7]

A winding, rocky road, fit only for four-wheel drive travel or perhaps horseback, leads to the summit. The road is steep and climbs past some telephone cell towers on a privately owned patch of land and past Bureau of Land Management land.

Bob Richard, in his eighties, said when he was fourteen, his grandfather told him how he and two others stole Buffalo Bill Cody's body from a Denver, Colorado, funeral home (photograph by the author).

The scenic view looking out at Wyoming from the summit of Cedar Mountain where Buffalo Bill Cody said he wished to be buried (photograph by the author).

A life-sized bison placed at the summit of Cedar Mountain overlooking Cody, Wyoming (photograph by the author).

19. The Death of the Great Showman

There is one well-marked grave site at the top, too, belonging to a man named Breck Moran, who was a big booster of Cody the town. The ashes of a well-known Buffalo Bill imitator were spread there, too.

Paul Fees, former curator of the Buffalo Bill Museum, said he was told directly by Dick Frost, a descendant of Ned Frost, that the body caper was true and that Fred Cody Garlow, Jr., Buffalo Bill's grandson, said yes, Cody's body was taken from Denver and delivered to Cedar Mountain. However, Fees doubts the veracity of the story, saying "Buffalo Bill is on Lookout Mountain." Also, "He never said he wanted to be there."[8]

The mayor of Cody at the time of Buffalo Bill's death was Jacob Schwoob. He said he was contacted by Louisa from Denver saying Denver had pledged a substantial amount of money for "a $10,000 funeral. Can Cody match that?" Richard said the way his grandfather told him the story, two men, Tammen being one, took Louisa to breakfast, each laid $10,000 on the table as a body negotiation, and "she opened her big purse, pulled it in and said of Buffalo Bill's body, 'It's yours.'"[9]

Ned Frost, shown here, was said to be one of three men who snatched Buffalo Bill Cody's body from a Denver, Colorado, funeral home and buried it on Cedar Mountain (courtesy of Park County Archives).

For the time being after the funeral, the body was Olinger's. Many months would pass before a grave site could be blasted into the hard ground on Lookout Mountain. In the immediate aftermath of Cody's death, the nation mourned, and dignitaries reached out with telegrams, letters, and notes to the family, expressing condolences and mentioning what a great and influential man William F. Cody had been. Among some of the comments received, collected, and now preserved by the Buffalo Bill Center of the West were these: From President Woodrow Wilson to May Cody Decker, "May, I express my sincere sympathy with you in the death of Colonel Cody"; from General Nelson Miles to Louisa Cody, "Please accept for yourself, family and relatives my deepest sympathy and condolences in this hour of sad bereavement. Colonel Cody was beloved and is now mourned by many millions."[10] To them and others, acknowledgment and thank you cards were sent: "Mrs. William F. Cody, Mrs. Irma Cody Garlow, Mrs. Julia Cody Goodman, Mrs. May Cody Decker desire to express their sincere thanks and appreciation for your kind expressions of sympathy in their deep bereavement."[11]

While most of the activity surrounding Bill Cody's death was centered in Denver, the plot of which Bob Richard spoke was hatched in Cody, Wyoming. Soon after Buffalo Bill's death, an older cowboy who worked for a ranch on the outskirts of Cody passed away and was brought to Joe Vogel's funeral home. It was said the man had no living relatives to notify. Vogel made the man presentable for burial and then noted, "He looks just like Bill." Ned Frost and Fred Richard agreed with this assessment, Bob Richard said he was told. The are-you-thinking-what-I'm-thinking idea was discussed. The trio of Cody men loaded the stranger into a rubber body bag and put him into a car. Then the four of them drove to Denver. The three living members of the quartet entered Olinger's. Vogel knew the proprietor and asked George Washington Olinger if they could take a look at their old friend Bill Cody in repose in a back room, preserved well enough as he waited for spring. They supposedly said, "Yep, that's Old Bill" and left.[12]

They had not made the five-hundred-mile drive just to confirm it was Bill Cody's body. They had no doubt of that. What they did was case the joint. They returned late at night when the last light had been extinguished in the funeral home. Finding the door to the mortuary unlocked, they quietly carried in the dead rancher and placed him in the coffin, then shifted Buffalo Bill to the rubber bag, and made good their getaway. They drove back to Cody, and without any fanfare brought Cody's body to the summit of Cedar Mountain and buried it without placing a marker.[13] Bob Richard's narrative was straightforward, no inflection of drama other than reporting what he was told were the facts.

19. The Death of the Great Showman

Deed done, the trio set up to create a smokescreen. This could be where the story Johnston had always heard originated. It was said the men who had already stolen the body went around to drinking establishments and stirred up feelings over the wrong done to the town of Cody and to the man Cody, leading to a posse being formed, but it was rebuffed at the Colorado border by the National Guard. If this happened, it would stand to reason newspapers would have made a big deal over it. But no such news clips are known to exist.

On June 3, 1917, as summer approached and as the weather warmed, it came time to bury Buffalo Bill. A service was conducted in Golden with some three thousand people turning out. There was an open coffin. No matter what wonders Vogel may have worked to transform the ranch hand into a Buffalo Bill look-alike, it would seem someone would have put up a fuss if the man in the coffin was not the man they came to see. On the other hand, Buffalo Bill, embalmed or not, had been moldering for six months. Also, was Buffalo Bill really under guard twenty-four hours a day, seven days a week the entire time he lay at Olinger's? "There's a lot you can do with makeup," said Bruce Eldredge, retired CEO of the Buffalo Bill Center. "Was there someone there with him every second?"[14]

Still, Eldredge is not a strong believer that Buffalo Bill was absconded with and returned to Cody. Those in Golden mightily resent the mere idea such a thing could have happened. Storytellers do sometimes point to the fact that a tank was rolled onto the grounds to protect the grave from assault. However, in reality, the tank was put in place as an advertisement to sell war bonds during World War I, not as a strong-arm symbol of protection for Buffalo Bill. There is a plaque on the premises that can still stir up anger today in Cody, Wyoming. One phrase refers to Buffalo Bill's choice to be buried in Golden, and it reads, "By His Own Request." "It's all baloney," Fees said. "That's a story later developed by the (Colorado) boosters."[15]

When Louisa Cody died in 1921, she was also buried in Golden, said to be right next to her husband. Johnny Baker, who idolized Buffalo Bill and did love him like a father, donated his collection of Buffalo Bill memorabilia to the people in Golden, and his materials formed the foundation for the museum collection on the premises. It was said Baker was the impetus for pouring twenty tons of concrete at the grave site of Buffalo Bill and Louisa so no one would even think of ever digging up the body.

However, in 1927, family members did begin a campaign lobbying Washington, DC, figures to exhume the body from Golden and rebury Buffalo Bill in Arlington National Cemetery in Virginia. General John "Blackjack" Pershing, the famed World War I officer, supported the move.

However, under the law, the custodians of the body had to agree to a transfer. Those were the Golden individuals, and they refused to consider the overture.

For a time, with no additional proof as to Buffalo Bill's true resting place one way or another, a sign rested on top of Cedar Mountain stating that was where Buffalo Bill was really buried. Some years ago, Michael Johnson, who then owned a business called Cody Trolley Tours, ventured to Denver to see the house where Buffalo Bill died. After making the trip and wishing to see the place where the hero passed away, Johnson said he chickened out when it came time to ring a stranger's doorbell to check out the scene. "The rational brain says the body is in Denver," Johnson said. "But the conspiracy theorist in me thinks he is on Cedar Mountain."[16]

There are a core group of believers who maintain that Buffalo Bill Cody rests atop Cedar Mountain. The story is perpetuated by a small number of people, even if they have not pushed for the ground to be dug up and remains given DNA testing.

In his 2019 novel *Land of Wolves,* Wyoming author Craig Johnson, creator of the Longmire series, has his well-known character Walt Longmire, a county sheriff, tell a story to a passenger visiting from outside the state. Longmire regales the visitor with a variation of the stolen body tale, gussied up a little more. The woman goes, "What?" when he mentions Buffalo Bill's body being taken and says, "They [someone else besides the threesome Bob Richard speaks of] went down and tried to steal the body? But they didn't?" Walt replies, "There's a lot of conjecture on that."[17]

Depends on who you ask, he might have said.

20

Buffalo Bill's Legacy

Those feeling the brunt of the wind, and those who knew the words (not so many since the tune was a top forty hit around 1864), sang "Tenting on the Old Campground," William F. Cody's favorite song. The wind was blustery on January 10, 2017, in Golden, Colorado, howling at about forty miles per hour, making the air cold enough that unless one was bundled heavily, a chill was felt. The mourners carried lanterns, flashlights, cell phone lights, or candles hard to keep lit. It did not take long to hurry through the informal outdoor service. The Buffalo Bill Museum and Grave was closed to regular customers for the day, and darkness surrounded the buildings. It was windy enough to blow cowboy hats the twenty miles to Denver. Few wished to linger, and it was suggested quickly moving inside made sense.

Lights of the city could be seen in the distance. Much has changed at the summit of Lookout Mountain since the idea of placing Buffalo Bill's body in that location was advanced. If he supposedly (though doubtfully) said the view would be unobstructed for miles, that is no longer true. Only a short distance down the hill, in the line of sight, are communications towers. Hardly a grand view of nature. Before everyone scuttled indoors, a former politician and holy man (at least for the night) named Dennis Gallagher sprinkled holy water on Buffalo Bill's grave, saying this recognized Cody's deathbed conversion to Catholicism. Gallagher said his grandmother told him stories of seeing a drunk Cody, so he expected this holy water to quickly turn into whiskey.[1]

In a small snack bar for museum visitors, appropriately named Pahaska Teepee, same as the hunting camp near the east entrance of Yellowstone National Park, about thirty people gathered to pay tribute to William F. "Buffalo Bill" Cody. It was the 100th anniversary of his death, and this wake was called to memorialize the hero of the Old West. The wind raised the question of whether perhaps Buffalo Bill was feeling restless that day, was maybe reaching out to these hardy fans in some way.

Leaning in a corner on a small table was a framed photograph of Cody, circa perhaps 1913, judging from the white hair and white goatee visible from beneath his black hat. A lit candle burned in front of the picture, an homage. Given that the corpse was at least claimed to be buried just outside the door, it was a gathering to pay respect. Yet also like the man in question, organizers, led by Steve Friesen, then the director of the museum, brought a sense of showmanship to the early evening activity as well.

Some dressed in all black. One such figure was Theodore Roosevelt. It was okay to call him Mr. President, or even Theodore, but he frowned at any shorthand references of Teddy. After admonishing anyone who was so casual, Mr. President lightened up and offered to share from his plate of onion rings. Annie Oakley, too, was appropriately adorned. In period military dress was Lieutenant Charles King of the Fifth Cavalry, who witnessed scout William Cody taking "the first scalp for Custer." Mostly, it was a convivial collection of Colorado and other admirers. However, when Friesen introduced a visitor representing the *Cody Enterprise* newspaper from Cody, Wyoming, that individual was booed. He had to remind the crowd—in case observers were unaware of it—Cody himself founded the paper. Proof was nearly demanded that no pick axe or shovel had invaded the premises.

The graves marked for Bill and Louisa are rimmed in rocks behind wrought iron fencing, and twenty tons of concrete poured to prevent grave robbing remains rigidly in place. Though they waited until going back indoors, President Roosevelt and Annie Oakley did speak highly of Buffalo Bill, as if they were providing eulogies from 1917. Annie, however, did not attend Buffalo Bill's funeral, although when asked, she gave him favorable reviews, regularly extolling his generosity. That was common knowledge among those who knew Cody well. If he had been a more determined builder of his savings, he would have retained much more of his money at the end. "Goodbye, old friend," this Oakley said. "The sun setting over the mountain will pay its tribute to the resting place of the last of the great builders of the West, all of which you loved, and part of which you were."[2]

Only a couple of days after the memorial, some of the same people and more gathered in Denver for a Buffalo Bill wake and banquet. The uniqueness of the location was the Lola Coastal Mexican Restaurant, housed in the same building at 1575 Boulder Street where Olinger's mortuary once did business and where Buffalo Bill's body once rested in a coffin awaiting burial in Golden (and maybe from where his body was removed by the Wyomingites). On this given night, the room was not available to see. It was only in use for liquor storage by the present owners, though it could be noted it was a storage corner a hundred years ago, too. Maybe Buffalo Bill had been the only tenant, or maybe not.

There were two guests of honor that night. One was a Buffalo Bill mannequin reposing in an open casket. Ordinarily, this mannequin lived at the Golden museum, overlooking the gift shop. The other was a Buffalo Bill real live imitator named Buzz Baker, dressed out in the same type of buckskins the genuine article wore in the Wild West performances. Baker said this was not unusual garb for him. "I always dress like this," he said, perhaps an indicator he might well have wished to ride in the Wild West, or even in the Old West.[3]

The dinner menu included five courses: fried oysters, braised bison cheeks, huevos rancheros, carved bison roast, and a dessert called donuts but described as spiced apple compote with 1921 Crema Tequila Chantilly. The preparers mixed up some peculiar liquid refreshments, including one drink called "Corpse Reviver," another called "Embalming Fluid," and another more basic "Buffalo Bill."[4] When it came time to toast Buffalo Bill, drinks imbibed were varied.

Friesen, the organizer of this festival, as well as the service at Lookout Mountain, presided over a Buffalo Bill trivia quiz. There were fifteen questions, and all were woven from Buffalo Bill's personal history. The right answers for several were relatively easy, referring to Iron Tail as Buffalo Bill's best friend and Sitting Bull as a star attraction. Harry Tammen was the answer as to the identity of the man who forced Buffalo Bill into bankruptcy. Then came the final question. This was as provocative as possible for a Denver audience. It read, "Where is Buffalo Bill really buried?" There were hoots and hollers from the Colorado crowd, but two bold individuals shouted out that his body was on Cedar Mountain in Cody. One specifically called out Cody to annoy Friesen. The other said he formerly lived in Cody. Neither one were awarded any points for choosing a non–Golden option.[5]

In an intriguing twist, just as Buffalo Bill originally wrote in his will about desiring a large buffalo be erected on Cedar Mountain, such a statue was placed on the summit adjacent to where he is, or is not, buried. The bison figure was placed on a platform in 1968 and faces out with an unhindered look at the sky and the Absaroka Mountains. Cody thought such a buffalo should stand a hundred feet tall. This buffalo is merely life-sized, which is large enough. It is commonly said this bison has nothing to do with Buffalo Bill and was erected on its own merits.

Bob Richard, the purveyor of the body-stealing story, said he visits the summit a couple of times a year. It is a rough ride, even in a four-wheel drive truck at five to ten miles an hour. He calls this area on top of the mountain where William F. Cody wanted to be buried "a spiritual place.

The reason Bill Cody said he wanted to be buried here is because he could see in all directions."[6] That is still true, unlike Lookout Mountain, where the view has been hemmed in. There is little doubt Cody did ride a horse to this spot, just as there is complete doubt that he ever did to the top of Lookout Mountain, despite the solo testimony of someone who later said she rode up there with him.

Where the bison stands, there is a sign-in box. Visitors write notes on what is the equivalent of a summit diary, jotting impressions. At one point a sign was placed on the spot where the friendly grave robbers allegedly buried Buffalo Bill. It read, "Buffalo Bill's Burial Place." Ned Frost can be seen standing next to the sign in an old photograph snapped by Jack Richard, Bob's father.

In 1969, a reporter for the *Cody Enterprise* visited the buffalo at the summit and had a mock conversation with the ersatz animal. The thrust of it was the buffalo's complaint that people had no respect, and he urged her to help halt vandals shooting holes in him with .22-caliber bullets. "It's ALWAYS open season on me," the buffalo lamented.[7]

Caroline Lockhart (left) with Buffalo Bill Cody in Cody, Wyoming. Lockhart was the first president of the Buffalo Bill Cody Stampede Rodeo and owned the *Cody Enterprise* newspaper (courtesy of Park County Archives).

20. Buffalo Bill's Legacy

The mystery of where Buffalo Bill is buried remains. But his memory has otherwise been honored in many, many ways. One notable way in his adopted hometown of Cody was the creation of the Buffalo Bill Cody Stampede Rodeo in 1919. It was intended as a one-time thing, but in 1920 became formalized. A chief supporter was a woman named Caroline Lockhart. Although not as famous as Buffalo Bill during her lifetime, Lockhart was the most famous woman of her time in Cody.

Lockhart was born in Illinois in 1874. A talented writer and feminist of the first order, Lockhart became a newspaper reporter in Philadelphia and Boston. By happenstance, she met Buffalo Bill and wrote a feature article about him. She traveled to Cody in 1904 to write about Native Americans and made that her home. Lockhart wrote several popular western novels, and some were made into early movies. In 1920 she bought the *Cody Enterprise*, which she ran through 1925.

A colorful figure in town, Lockhart was not above serving drinks during Prohibition, speaking her mind so plainly she made enemies, but also making clear how proud she was of the community. She had a wildcat for a pet, owned a ranch outside town (now on the National Register of Historic Places), as well as a good-sized house in town that remains a boardinghouse under the name the "Lockhart Inn," and believed she was as tough as any man around. She once declared she wanted to be the

Buffalo Bill Cody on the deck of his Pahaska Teepee hunting lodge near Yellowstone National Park in 1904 (courtesy of Park County Archives).

most famous woman west of the Mississippi River. Her writings, which included a stint as a columnist with the *Denver Post*, may not have carried her that far, but in her own mind she may have thought she reached that exalted status.

In life, Lockhart, who never married but had a series of affairs, and Cody were friends but not love partners. After he died, and after the first remembrance rodeo, as a booster running the newspaper, she campaigned heavily to make the rodeo a permanent fixture. When the meeting of an official rodeo committee concluded, Lockhart was the first president of the Stampede. Lockhart wielded a sharp pen, could duel in sarcasm with the best of them, and had two positions of power as the editor of the local newspaper and, for six years, as president of the rodeo. One of Lockhart's promotional missives about the Cody Stampede read like this: "The Old West, with its sports and feats of daring, has almost passed. Nearly everywhere the honk of the scissor-bill's tin lizzie has replaced the yip of the cowboy. Yet some of that Old West that we love can hold a little longer, if we make the effort. And surely there is no more fitting place in America for exhibitions of cowboy skill and valor than right here in Buffalo Bill's town at the foot of the Rockies."[8] Such a theme, of course, was very much like what Buffalo Bill spent all of those years following at the helm of the Wild West exhibition as it traveled the world.

The Buffalo Bill Cody Stampede Rodeo kept expanding, and in the era of Professional Rodeo Cowboys Association leadership and its $400,000 purse, the rodeo has become iconic. During the stretch of time surrounding July 4 each year, which is known as Cowboy Christmas, Cody is a must-stop for the best. In 2019, the town and its governing committee celebrated the 100th anniversary of its founding. The holiday was the biggest day of the year in town, and in coincidental timing, the rodeo and rodeo committee were inducted into the Professional Rodeo Hall of Fame in Colorado Springs, Colorado.

It should not be very surprising that since Buffalo Bill went everywhere and lived many places, there are little pieces of his history scattered around the United States from towns that wish to claim him. Immediately after he died in Denver, it was not merely that city, plus Cody, Wyoming, that sought his body, but North Platte, Nebraska. North Platte was his former home by 1917, though. He had spent many years in that community, and his Scout's Rest Ranch remains as a mini-museum. Also noted is his introduction of rodeo the way we know it there in 1882. And there is also a gift shop called Fort Cody. It contains one rather enticing item. There is a hand-carved recreation of the Wild West exhibition in few-inch tall figures that is regularly jump-started by electricity with all its moving pieces to make a performance unfold. While the original was life-sized, if not bigger than life, this replica version is almost too large to grasp with a single sweep of the eye, too.

A guidebook was even published to tell the curious where to stop and visit if they have interest in Buffalo Bill. It is called *The Great Plains Guide to Buffalo Bill: Forts, Fights & Other Sites*, and hints at the outings possible when exploring Buffalo Bill's life. A driver could spend an entire summer on the nation's highways just checking out Buffalo Bill's haunts, from his Iowa boyhood home, to the family's abode in Kansas, to Pony Express territory, places where he scouted and hunted, and, of course, Cody, Wyoming, and Denver and Golden, Colorado. The author, who had produced such a guide to General George Armstrong Custer's travels, said he was debating what his next subject would be in a like-minded project. "I found my winning subject at—of all places—a Leavenworth hotel," wrote Jeff Barnes. "After checking into my room for the night, I found a large image of Buffalo Bill Cody hanging on the wall. The motel apparently had a famous 'Leavenworth residents' theme, but I took it as a sign to get started on Cody."[9]

Buffalo Bill was both idolized and sometimes vilified during his life. At times he drove his wife Louisa crazy and exasperated his partner Nate Salsbury. But he was a man of many talents who did extraordinary things, although some hated it when he got drunk in their presence. To many,

A collection of Buffalo Bill Cody memorabilia in a window of a Cody, Wyoming, post office store (courtesy of Park County Archives).

Buffalo Bill Cody's friend, Caroline Lockhart, was also a well-known western novelist (photograph by the author).

Buffalo Bill was a hero. To others, he was simply a showman. There is no doubt he was a man of many parts and symbolized many different things to many people. The more Barnes investigated Cody's life, the more he came to enjoy his connections to all of those well-known Old West sites and many more where the Wild West exhibition played.

Barnes seemed to be very struck by the tales told by people like Annie Oakley of Cody's wide-ranging generosity. This belief in Cody as the man who coveted little and gave away much was formed for him in a story he heard about a Buffalo Bill stay in a hotel in Omaha, Nebraska, in 1889. He set up shop to provide gifts to family and friends. "He took a suite at a hotel and passed out diamond jewelry, advertising in the *Omaha Herald* for any he missed to call on him at the hotel. I loved that story, and over the course of putting together the book I came to love Cody. Unquestionably, the man had flaws, but that's what makes him human. It's the places and the stories they tell that keep him alive today."[10]

20. Buffalo Bill's Legacy

Those may or may not include discussions of ghost sightings of Buffalo Bill. One story goes that sometimes at around 2 a.m., Buffalo Bill and Caroline Lockhart can be seen dancing together in the living room of the Lockhart Inn in Cody, but it is basically impossible to find anyone to say they witnessed such an occurrence. It is one of those marvelous, fanciful notions fun to gab about, even if a group of ghost hunters did once investigate the premises and declare it was chock full of paranormal indicators. Likewise, many say Buffalo Bill's ghost wanders the hallways of the Irma Hotel sometimes. But there are no snapshots of such doings. The most ghostlike visual of Buffalo Bill in Cody is actually a hologram reproduction at the entranceway to the Buffalo Bill Center of the West's Buffalo Bill Museum. The reenactor, who resembles Buffalo Bill enough to pass for posterity more than a hundred years after Buffalo Bill's death, Pete Simpson's "Ladies and gentlemen" greeting is as close as we can get to the real thing.

As a young newspaper feature writer in Philadelphia and Boston, Caroline Lockhart wrote about Buffalo Bill Cody and subsequently moved to Cody, Wyoming (photograph by the author).

During his lifetime, Bill Cody saw incredible change. He is identified with the Pony Express, fought in the Civil War, was a stirring figure on the Plains during buffalo hunting days and westward expansion, fought in the Plains Indians Wars, made a reputation as a scout, and was awarded the Medal of Honor. He invented a new realm of show business that defined an era in American history, helped build a new city, and trailed legends that academics and historians still debate.

In August of 2017, in its own observance of the 100th anniversary of his death, and as a way to both recognize Buffalo Bill's accomplishments and explore his connections to twentieth and twenty-first century life, the Buffalo Bill Center of the West oversaw a massive event called the "Buffalo Bill Centennial Symposium." It was organized by Dr. Jeremy Johnston and brought together some forty speakers who lectured virtually nonstop, straight through lunches and dinners, about different aspects of Buffalo Bill's life. There were authors and historians, academic researchers and professors, one by one seeking to make sense of all that Buffalo Bill achieved, what he really did and what was too mixed up with mythology to straighten out. To some extent it was dizzying. To some it was exhilarating. To all it was amazing in the sense that entire volumes were written about single aspects of Cody's life. There was seriousness and touches of whimsy.

One who defied many conventions, Caroline Lockhart is seen here with her pet bobcat (photograph by the author).

Specialists investigated Wild West visits to England and throughout Europe. Others spoke about his relationship with Native Americans, the military, and his family, and there was a large share of chuckles when exploring what the dime novelists made of Cody. Emily Burns, the Auburn University professor, called Buffalo Bill the "symbol of rough masculinity." Another speaker contended Buffalo Bill was "simultaneously himself and playing himself." Someone noted writer Ned Buntline once said, "It's been the thrill of my life to have invented you."[11]

Call it offbeat, peculiar, difficult to believe, or plowing new ground, but one speaker's outlook stood out as offering a perspective perhaps no one else ever thought to check out. Ch. Didier Gondola, chair of the history department and professor of African history at Indiana University–Purdue University, Indianapolis, made the contention that Buffalo Bill Cody influenced the outcome of the Congo's rebellion against Belgium in the 1950s and 1960s.

Gangs of young men, building upon images they saw in western American movies, which added on to Buffalo Bill and his Wild West, called themselves the "Bills" as they agitated in the independence movement.

Gondola makes this case in a book called *Tropical Cowboys: Westerns, Violence, and Masculinity in Kinshasa*. These young people of Kinshasa, Gondola said, "became enamored with the idea of the West. Action is what mattered to them, not the dialogue. Those young people dubbed themselves the 'Bills.' The Bills rooted for the cowboys, although like the Indians, they were oppressed. Indians were the losers. Cowboys were the winners."[12]

Danielle Haque of Minnesota State-Mankato, whose area of focus was Arab participation in the Wild West, nonetheless made some universal observations about how Buffalo Bill's persona influenced western movies and how those movies in turn spoke to people not necessarily considered cowboy fans. "Films about Buffalo Bill did not go away," she said. "The two magic words, 'Buffalo Bill,' led to many from other countries calling the West 'Buffalo Bill's land.'"[13]

During Prohibition, Caroline Lockhart had her own bar going in her house to serve illegal booze (photograph by the author).

William F. "Buffalo Bill" Cody shaped the land with his exploits and his western adventures that formed the basis for the Wild West exhibitions. He shaped the lives of those close to him with his generosity, honesty, and straight-shooting, not with a pistol or rifle so much as in his professional dealings. He shaped the mindset of Americans even more so with his acting and his performances, his storytelling ingraining a romantic image of the Old West so deeply that more than a hundred years after his death, his vision of the way things were remains the dominant public viewpoint.

Buffalo Bill died only months after Iron Tail passed away. John Burke died at around the same time as well. Cody's last child, Irma Cody Garlow, and her husband both died in the worldwide flu epidemic a year after Buffalo Bill died. Garlows and Codys survived, but those most intimately connected to Cody passed from the scene comparatively soon after his own death. Irma is buried in Riverside Cemetery in Cody.

Born in 1846, even before covered wagons made their way across the Plains for settlers, Cody lived until 1917, when the automobile was just beginning to come into fashion and the airplane had made it off the ground. Cody saw it all and was part of it all as America grew up. He changed with society. He transformed from an unsophisticated boy on the frontier who participated in numerous Indian battles into a man who stood up for Native Americans and provided jobs when no one else would hire them.

As author Jeff Barnes recognized, it is not difficult to come across properties, statues, and totems of Buffalo Bill throughout the West. Nowhere is that more so than in Cody, Wyoming. The Buffalo Bill Center of the West is a major museum. Hanging out front of the Cody Country Chamber of Commerce is a sign featuring Buffalo Bill's face. There is lodging named Buffalo Bill Cabins in town. The tall Irma Hotel sign is a notable feature downtown.

Buffalo Bill Cody as he often appeared in his buckskins (courtesy of Park County Archives).

Buffalo Bill is a built-in marketing tool. In 2018, the Park County Travel Council, seeking fresh ways to advertise the area and community, came up with a slogan that went like this: "Our town's founder could beat up your town's founder."[14] Or at the very least shoot the whiskey glass out of his hand.

Of course, there is the rodeo, the Buffalo Bill Cody Stampede, which brings the finest cowboys in the country to town each July. Held concurrently with the rodeo in 2019 was the International Cody Family Association reunion. Some sixty-four members of the group, with links back to Buffalo Bill, attended, some marching in the Independence Day parade. They also visited the museum named after the patriarch and the rodeo, too.

"When you have the last name Cody and come to Cody, people look at you funny," said Allan Cody, president of the association, whose great-grandfather was Buffalo Bill's first cousin.[15]

Coming to Cody often means stopping at the Buffalo Bill Center of the West, a museum outsized for its location in terms of its programs, collections, and reach. When Buffalo Bill died in 1917, a Buffalo Bill Memorial Association was created immediately, and its initial log cabin quarters were far from imposing. In 1924, Gertrude Vanderbilt Whitney donated her $50,000 dramatic Cody sculpture called "The Scout," which looms on an imposing perch next to the museum today.

Over the decades, the museum kept expanding to encompass far more than artifacts and memorabilia related to Buffalo Bill. There are five separate museums under one roof today: the Buffalo Bill Museum, the Plains Indian Museum, the Whitney Western Art Museum, the Draper Natural History Museum, and the Cody Firearms Museum. Also included is the Harold McCracken Research Library, a depository of vast amounts of Buffalo Bill minutia and western history.

When Buffalo Bill died, there were grand proclamations and announcements of grand plans to honor him with great and mighty structures. Denver was fast on the bandwagon with such ideas. Golden did have Johnny Baker on its side, and it was his personal collection of Buffalo Bill memorabilia that started the museum there. But as World War I captured the country's attention, Cody residents emerged as possessing more hunger and energy to establish a larger monument to Buffalo Bill. Buffalo Bill hoped someday the town he helped found would become a major crossroads and destination in the West like Denver. That did not happen. Cody's year-round population is slightly less than ten thousand. Denver's most recent count was 620,000. "Denver has all the advantages," said Johnston, the Buffalo Bill Museum curator. "It's amazing. But Cody wins the war. We lost the body. Denver lost the war. Cody was the underdog, but was sneaky and crafty."[16]

A key player in making the Buffalo Bill Center what it became, and in making Cody, Wyoming, the fundamental museum honoring Buffalo Bill, was Mary Jester Allen, Cody's niece. Her mother was Cody's sister Helen Cody Wetmore. Allen was visiting her uncle and always recalled his statement to a group of friends of how he hoped there would be a brick and mortar building basically encompassing the history and stories he felt he was spreading with the Wild West exhibition. "On Decoration Day of

1916," Allen said, "an idea was born. My uncle, Colonel William F. Cody, spent the day with me in Seattle, Washington. With many old friends gathered around the hearth we lived again in song and story those colorful days of the Old West. An old Army comrade asked the Colonel in what way he would like his memory kept fresh for posterity. Like a flash came Uncle Will's reply, 'Teaching the youth by seeing history.' Those present pledged to carry out the plans."[17] Allen took to heart Cody's little speech. Although the memorial association was founded in 1917, it was not until July 4, 1927, that a large log building followed. For thirty-four years, Mary Jester Allen, Buffalo Bill's loyal niece, served as the director, a trustee, or curator in critical roles that grew the museum.

It may comfort some to believe Buffalo Bill Cody is buried on Cedar Mountain in proximity to the scenery he so loved. But it might well have been more important to him that his dreams and spirit lived on, his story inspiring lovers of the Old West, those fascinated with all that he accomplished and saw.

There has never been anyone else quite like William F. Cody, a man who defined his era, a man who strode through historical turbulence in the eye of a hurricane and walked out nearly dry in his gleaming buckskins, telling us all about it. He could wink at truth or consequences without blushing and make everyone he met like him and make everyone he had not met yet wish they had. He was so American.

Chapter Notes

Chapter 1

1. Russell, Don, *The Lives and Legends of Buffalo Bill* (Norman: University of Oklahoma Press, 1960), 106.
2. Carter, Robert A., *Buffalo Bill Cody: The Man Behind the Legend* (New York: John Wiley & Sons, Inc., 2000), 92.
3. Russell, 89.
4. Carter, 93.
5. Cody, William F., *Buffalo Bill's Life Story, An Autobiography* (New York: Skyhorse Publishing, 2010 edition, originally published 1879), 172.
6. Cody, William F., *Buffalo Bill's Life Story*, 172.
7. Cody, William F., *Buffalo Bill's Life Story*, 173.
8. Cody, William F., *Buffalo Bill's Life Story*, 174.

Chapter 2

1. Cody, William F., *Buffalo Bill's Life Story, An Autobiography* (New York: Skyhorse Publishing, 2010 edition, originally published 1879), 17.
2. Cody, William F., *Buffalo Bill's Life Story*, 17.
3. Wetmore, Helen Cody, *Last of the Great Scouts* (New York: Grosset & Dunlap, 1899), 1.
4. Warren, Louis, *Buffalo Bill's America: William Cody and the Wild West Show* (New York: Alfred Knopf, 2005), 10.
5. Warren, 10.
6. Cody, William F., *Buffalo Bill's Life Story*, 50.
7. Cody, William F., *Buffalo Bill's Life Story*, 51.
8. Cody, William F., *Buffalo Bill's Life Story*, 62.
9. Cody, William F., *Buffalo Bill's Life Story*, 63.
10. Wetmore, 60.

Chapter 3

1. Carter, Robert A., *Buffalo Bill Cody: The Man Behind the Legend* (New York: John Wiley & Sons, 2000), 24.
2. Cody, William F., *Buffalo Bill's Life Story, An Autobiography* (New York: Skyhorse Publishing, 2010 edition, originally published 1879), 70.
3. Clavin, Tom, *Dodge City: Wyatt Earp, Bat Masterson and the Wickedest Town in the American West* (New York: St. Martin's Press, 2017), 85.
4. Cody, William F., *Buffalo Bill's Life Story*, 72.
5. Cody, William F., *Buffalo Bill's Life Story*, 72.
6. Pony Express 1860 advertisement reproduction.
7. Bradley, Glenn Danford, *The Story of the Pony Express* (Chicago: A.C. McClurg & Co., 1913), 25.
8. DeFelice, Jim, *West Like Lightning: The Brief, Legendary Ride of the Pony Express* (New York: William Morrow, 2018), 271.
9. Majors, Alexander (Prentiss Ingraham, ed.), *Seventy Years on the Frontier* (New York: Rand McNally and Publishers, 1893), 177.
10. Majors, 243.
11. Majors, 243.
12. DeFelice, 101, 103.

13. Cody, William F., *Buffalo Bill's Life Story*, 91.
14. Cody, William F., *Buffalo Bill's Life Story*, 105.
15. Russell, Don, *The Lives and Legends of Buffalo Bill* (Norman: University of Oklahoma Press, 1960), 50.
16. Majors, 245.
17. Majors, 174.

Chapter 4

1. Cody, William F., *Buffalo Bill's Life Story, An Autobiography* (New York: Skyhorse Publishing, 2010 edition, originally published 1879), 125.
2. Cody, Buffalo Bill, *True Tales of the Plains* (New York: Empire Book Company, 1908), 40.
3. Cody, William F., *Buffalo Bill's Life Story*, 135.
4. Cody, William F., *Buffalo Bill's Life Story*, 135.
5. Cody, Buffalo Bill, 41.
6. Wetmore, Helen Cody, *Last of the Great Scouts* (New York: Grosset & Dunlap, 1899), 125.
7. Wetmore.
8. Cody, William F., *Buffalo Bill's Life Story*, 136.

Chapter 5

1. Cody, Buffalo Bill, *True Tales of the Plains* (New York: Empire Book Company, 1908), 95.
2. Cody, Buffalo Bill, 96.
3. Cody, Buffalo Bill, 97.
4. Cody, Buffalo Bill, 99.
5. Cody, Buffalo Bill, 99.
6. Cody, Buffalo Bill, 101.
7. Carter, Robert A., *Buffalo Bill Cody: The Man Behind the Legend* (New York: John Wiley & Sons, 2000), 86.
8. Russell, Don, *The Lives and Legends of Buffalo Bill* (Norman: University of Oklahoma Press, 1960), 101.
9. Clavin, Tom, *Wild Bill: The True Story of the American Frontier's First Gunfighter* (New York: St. Martin's Press, 2019), 78.
10. Russell, 112.
11. Warren, Louis, *Buffalo Bill's America: William Cody and the Wild West Show* (New York: Alfred Knopf, 2005), 135.
12. Warren, 135.
13. Scott, Douglas D., Bleed, Peter, and Damm, Stephen, *Custer, Cody, and Grand Duke Alexis: Historical Archeology of the Royal Buffalo Hunt* (Norman: University of Oklahoma Press, 2013), 41.
14. Scott, Bleed, and Damm, 51.
15. Germain, David, "Army May Have Made a Grave Error When It Buried Custer: Remains at West Point May Not Be Famous Soldier Killed at Little Bighorn, Historians and Anthropologists Say," *Associated Press/Los Angeles Times*, September 15, 1991.
16. Germain.

Chapter 6

1. Cody, William F., *Buffalo Bill's Life Story, An Autobiography* (New York: Skyhorse Publishing, 2010 edition, originally published 1879), 141.
2. Cody, William F., *Buffalo Bill's Life Story*, 141.
3. Cody, William F., *Buffalo Bill's Life Story*, 142.
4. Cody, Louisa Federici, *Memories of Buffalo Bill* (Miami: HardPress Publishing, 1919), 6.
5. Carter, Robert A., *Buffalo Bill Cody: The Man Behind the Legend* (New York: John Wiley & Sons, 2000), 122.
6. Carter, 122.
7. Cody, Louisa Federici, 113.
8. Cody, Louisa Federici, 110.
9. Cody, Louisa Federici, 111.
10. Cody, Louisa Federici, 136.
11. Cody, Louisa Federici, 222.
12. Foote, Stella, *Letters From Buffalo Bill* (Cody, WY: Shoshone Distributing Co., 1954), 13.
13. Cody, William F., *Buffalo Bill's Life Story*, 215.
14. Russell, Don, *The Lives And Legends Of Buffalo Bill* (Norman: University of Oklahoma Press, 1960), 257.

Chapter 7

1. Clavin, Tom, *Wild Bill: The True Story of the American Frontier's First Gunfighter* (New York: St. Martin's Press, 2019), 74.
2. Cody, William F., *Buffalo Bill's Life Story, An Autobiography* (New York: Sky-

horse Publishing, 2010 edition, originally published 1879), 263.
3. Monaghan, Jay, *The Great Rascal: The Life and Adventures of Ned Buntline* (New York: Little Brown & Co., 1952), 7.
4. Monaghan, 15.
5. Monaghan, 20.
6. Monaghan, 28.

Chapter 8

1. Freedman, Lew, "Buffalo Bill Was Awarded Medal of Honor," *Cody Enterprise*, July 4, 2017.
2. Cody, William F., *Buffalo Bill's Life Story, An Autobiography* (New York: Skyhorse Publishing, 2010 edition, originally published 1879), 314.
3. Cody, William F., *Buffalo Bill's Life Story*, 314.
4. Cody, William F., *Buffalo Bill's Life Story*, 314.
5. Carter, Robert A., *Buffalo Bill Cody: The Man Behind the Legend* (New York: John Wiley & Sons, 2000), 174.
6. Freedman, "Buffalo Bill..."
7. Freedman, "Buffalo Bill..."
8. Freedman, "Buffalo Bill..."
9. Freedman, "Buffalo Bill..."
10. Dominy, Charles E., Letter, Department of the Army to Wyoming Senator Alan Simpson, July 6, 1989. This letter can be viewed at the Buffalo Bill Center of the West in the McCracken Research Library.
11. Dominy.
12. Russell, 134.
13. Russell, 143.
14. King, Major General Charles, "The Battle of War Bonnet Creek," The William F. Cody Archive, Buffalo Bill Center of the West, Cody, Wyoming.
15. Russell, 220.
16. King.
17. King.
18. Russell, 226.
19. Russell, 226.
20. Russell, 226.
21. Russell, 230.
22. Cody, Louisa Federici, *Memories of Buffalo Bill* (Miami: HardPress Publishing, 1919), 259–260.
23. Cody, Louisa Federici, 260.
24. Cody, William F., *Buffalo Bill's Life Story*, 343–344.

25. Cody, William F., *Buffalo Bill's Life Story*, 347.
26. Wetmore, Helen Cody, *Last of the Great Scouts* (New York: Grosset & Dunlap, 1899), 219.

Chapter 9

1. Sell, Henry Blackman, and Weybright, Victor, *Buffalo Bill and the Wild West* (New York: Oxford University Press, 1955), 127.
2. Miller, Darlis A., *Captain Jack Crawford: Buckskin Poet, Scout, Showman* (Albuquerque: University of New Mexico Press, 1993), 75.
3. Sell and Weybright, 130.
4. Sell and Weybright, 130.
5. Warren, Louis, *Buffalo Bill's America: William Cody and the Wild West Show* (New York: Alfred Knopf, 2005), 232.
6. Freedman, Lew, "Stampede Rodeo Has Storied History," *Cody Enterprise*, Summer 2019, Special Section.
7. Fredriksson, Kristine, *American Rodeo: From Buffalo Bill to Big Business* (College Station: Texas A&M University Press, 1985), 140.
8. Sell and Weybright, 133.
9. Sell and Weybright, 133.

Chapter 10

1. Foote, Stella, *Letters From Buffalo Bill* (Cody, WY: Shoshone Distributing Co., 1954), 20.
2. Foote.
3. Wetmore, Helen Cody, *Last of the Great Scouts* (New York: Grosset & Dunlap, 1899), 260–261.
4. Wilson, R.L., and Martin, Greg, *Buffalo Bill's Wild West: An American Legend* (New Jersey: Chartwell, 2004), 47.
5. Knappe, Stephanie Fox, "Art Perpetuating Fame: The Posters of Buffalo Bill's Wild West" (Ph.D. diss., University of Kansas, 2013).
6. Wilson and Martin, 47.
7. Knappe.
8. Knappe.
9. Warren, Louis, *Buffalo Bill's America: William Cody and the Wild West Show* (New York: Alfred Knopf, 2005), 233.
10. Kasson, Joy S., *Buffalo Bill's Wild West: Celebrity, Memory and Popular

History (New York: Hill and Wang, 2000), 52.
11. Kasson, 53.
12. Warren, 212.
13. Wilson and Martin, 137–138.
14. Wilson and Martin, 138.

Chapter 11

1. Bridger, Bobby, *Buffalo Bill and Sitting Bull: Inventing the Wild West* (Austin: University of Texas Press, 2002), 315.
2. Sell, Henry Blackman, and Weybright, Victor, *Buffalo Bill and the Wild West* (New York: Oxford University Press, 1955), 145–147.
3. Freedman, Lew, "Sitting Bull's Grandson Shares Lakota Culture," *Cody Enterprise*, June 28, 2017.
4. Sell and Weybright, 147.
5. Sell and Weybright, 147.
6. Sell and Weybright, 147–148.
7. Bridger, 320.
8. Carter, Robert A., *Buffalo Bill Cody: The Man Behind the Legend* (New York, John Wiley & Sons, 2000), 289.
9. Stillman, Deanne, *Blood Brothers: The Story of the Strange Friendship between Sitting Bull and Buffalo Bill* (New York: Simon & Schuster, 2017), 215.
10. Stillman, 223.

Chapter 12

1. Sell, Henry Blackman, and Weybright, Victor, *Buffalo Bill and the Wild West* (New York: Oxford University Press, 1955), 141.
2. Sell and Weybright, 143.
3. Sell and Weybright, 143.
4. Russell, Don, *The Lives and Legends of Buffalo Bill* (Norman: University of Oklahoma Press, 1960), 371.
5. McMurtry, Larry, *The Colonel and Little Missie* (New York: Simon & Schuster, 2005), 13–14.
6. Bricklin, Julia, *America's Best Female Sharpshooter: The Rise and Fall of Lillian Frances Smith* (Norman: University of Oklahoma Press, 2017), 33.

Chapter 13

1. Cody, Louisa Federici, *Memories of Buffalo Bill* (Miami: HardPress Publishing, 1919), 277.
2. Cody, 288.
3. Enss, Chris, *The Many Loves of Buffalo Bill* (Guilford, CT: Twodot/Globe Pequot Press, 2010), 45.
4. Enss, 55.
5. Enss, 58.
6. Enss, 67.
7. Warren, Louis, *Buffalo Bill's America: William Cody and the Wild West Show* (New York: Alfred Knopf, 2005), 345.
8. Warren, 501.
9. Enss, 100.
10. Enss, 105.
11. Johnston, Jeremy, interview, August 23, 2019.
12. Houze, Lynn, interview, August 23, 2019.
13. Carlson, Peter, "Encounter: Buffalo Bill at Queen Victoria's Command," *American History Magazine*, December 2015.
14. Correspondence Diary, 1887, Buffalo Bill Center of the West Archives, Harold McCracken Research Library, Cody, Wyoming.
15. Fees, Paul, interview, August 29, 2019.

Chapter 14

1. Carter, Robert A., *Buffalo Bill Cody: The Man Behind the Legend* (New York: John Wiley & Sons, 2000), 302.
2. Carter, 312.
3. Carter, 312.
4. Carter, 313.
5. Carter, 313.
6. Carter, 314.
7. Carlson, Peter, "Encounter: Buffalo Bill at Queen Victoria's Command," *American History Magazine*, December 2015.
8. Cody, William F., "The Wild West In England," in Christianson, Frank (ed.), *The Papers of William F. Cody* (Lincoln: University of Nebraska Press, 2012), 72.
9. Cody, William F., "The Wild West In England," 74–75.
10. Cody, William F., "The Wild West In England," 77.
11. Cody, William F., "The Wild West In England," 90.
12. Cody, William F., "The Wild West In England," 92.
13. Wilson, R.L., and Martin, Greg, *Buffalo Bill's Wild West: An American Legend* (New Jersey: Chartwell, 2004), 56.

14. Wilson and Martin, 79.
15. May, Karl, *Winnetou* (Pullman: Washington State University Press, 1989 edition, originally published in 1892), xiv.
16. Sell, Henry Blackman, and Weybright, Victor, *Buffalo Bill and the Wild West* (New York: Oxford University Press, 1955), 184.
17. Kasson, Joy S., *Buffalo Bill's Wild West: Celebrity, Memory and Popular History* (New York: Hill and Wang, 2000), 55.
18. Kasson, 61.
19. Freedman, Lew, "Buffalo Bill Was the Ultimate Showman," *Cody Enterprise*, August 1, 2017.
20. Freedman, "Buffalo Bill..."
21. Freedman, Lew, "Cody Remembered in Many Ways," *Cody Enterprise*, August 22, 2017.
22. Freedman, "Cody..."
23. Bell, Bob Boze, "Wild West Fever Proves Deadly; The Narrow Path," *True West Magazine*, March 2016.
24. Serrano, Richard A., *American Endurance: Buffalo Bill, the Great Cowboy Race of 1893, and the Vanishing Wild West* (Washington, D.C.: Smithsonian Books, 2016), 192.
25. Serrano, 194.
26. Serrano, 196.
27. Serrano, 196.
28. Warren, Louis, *Buffalo Bill's America: William Cody and the Wild West Show* (New York: Alfred Knopf, 2005), 419.
29. Freedman, "Cody..."

Chapter 15

1. Burdette, Roger, *Renaissance of American Coinage, 1909–1915* (Great Falls, VA: Seneca Mill Press, 2007), 224.
2. Berry, Chris, "Chief Iron Tail: Star of the Wild West Show," *Collectors Weekly*, 2012.
3. Augherton, Tom, "Buffalo Bill Cody's Ambassador Was Immortalized in Nickel," *True West Magazine*, December 11, 2014.
4. Freedman, Lew, "Iron Tail Was Buffalo Bill's Right-Hand Man," *Cody Enterprise*, June 6, 2019.
5. Freedman.
6. Harvey, Ian, "Photos of Native Americans Who Performed in Buffalo Bill's Wild West," *The Vintage News*, November 29, 2016.

7. Kasson, Joy S., *Buffalo Bill's Wild West: Celebrity, Memory and Popular History* (New York: Hill and Wang, 2000), 109–110.
8. Friesen, Steve, and Chladiuk, Francois, *Lakota Performers in Europe: Their Culture and the Artifacts They Left Behind* (Norman: University of Oklahoma Press, 2017), xi.
9. Friesen and Chladiuk, 18.
10. Friesen and Chladiuk, 22.
11. Friesen, Steve, "Buffalo Bill & His 'Blood-Thirsty Indians,'" *True West Magazine*, July 24, 2017.

Chapter 16

1. Russell, Don, *The Lives and Legends of Buffalo Bill* (Norman: University of Oklahoma Press, 1960), 370.
2. Fees, Paul, "Wild West Shows: Buffalo Bill's Wild West," Buffalo Bill Center of the West, https://centerofthewest.org. (No date).
3. Russell, 371–372.
4. Russell, 372.
5. Griffin, Charles Eldridge, *Four Years in Europe with Buffalo Bill* (Albia, IA: Stage Publishing Co., 1908), 21.
6. Griffin, 28.
7. Griffin, 29.
8. Griffin, 30.
9. Griffin, 31.
10. Griffin, 37.
11. Grant, Richard, "Buffalo Bill and the Wild, Wild West," *The Elks Magazine*, February 1985.
12. Freedman, Lew, "Wake Held to Honor Buffalo Bill," *Cody Enterprise*, February 7, 2017.
13. "At a Mexican Restaurant," *New York Sun*, December 18, 1886.
14. "William Sweeney: Buffalo Bill's Cowboy Band," Buffalo Bill Center of the West Archives (no date), Cody, Wyoming.

Chapter 17

1. Foote, Stella, *Letters from Buffalo Bill* (Cody, WY: Shoshone Distributing Co., 1954), 60.
2. Foote, 60.
3. Foote, 61.

4. Warren, Louis, *Buffalo Bill's America: William Cody and the Wild West Show* (New York: Alfred Knopf, 2005), 495.
5. Warren, 495.
6. Russell, Don, *The Lives and Legends of Buffalo Bill* (Noman: University of Oklahoma Press, 1960), 171.
7. Griffin, Charles Eldridge, *Four Years in Europe with Buffalo Bill* (Albia, IA: Stage Publishing Co., 1908), 44.
8. Burke, John, *Buffalo Bill: From Prairie to Palace* (Lincoln, NE: Bison Books, University of Nebraska Press, 2012), 43–44.
9. Griffin, 45.
10. Burke, 249.
11. Burke, 249.
12. Burke, 259.
13. Griffin, 56.
14. Griffin, 87.
15. Warren, 503.
16. Warren, 503.

Buffalo Bill (Miami: HardPress Publishing, 1919), 323–324.
6. Yost, 403.
7. Freedman, Lew, "100 Years Later: Where's Bill? A Century After the Western Icon's Death, Legend of Cedar Mountain Gravesite Persists," *Cody Enterprise*, January 10, 2017.
8. Freedman.
9. Freedman.
10. Buffalo Bill Center of the West Archives, Cody, Wyoming.
11. Buffalo Bill Center of the West Archives, Cody, Wyoming.
12. Freedman, Lew, "Buffalo Bill Remains in Cody, at Least in Spirit," *Cody Enterprise*, January 12, 2017.
13. Freedman, "Buffalo Bill..."
14. Freedman, "Buffalo Bill..."
15. Freedman, "Buffalo Bill..."
16. Freedman, "Buffalo Bill..."
17. Johnson, Craig, *Land of Wolves* (New York: Viking, 2019), 156.

Chapter 18

1. Warren, Louis, *Buffalo Bill's America: William Cody and the Wild West Show* (New York: Alfred Knopf, 2005), 472.
2. Bonner, Robert E., *William F. Cody's Wyoming Empire: The Buffalo Bill Nobody Knows* (Norman: University of Oklahoma Press, 2007), 77.
3. Bonner, 157.
4. Bonner, 211.
5. Bonner, 231.
6. Friesen, Steve, *Buffalo Bill: Scout, Showman, Visionary* (Golden, CO: Fulcrum Publishing, 2010), 115.
7. Friesen, 116.
8. Friesen, 131.

Chapter 19

1. "Death Summons Col. W.F. Cody," *Park County Enterprise*, January 10, 1917.
2. Carter, Robert A., *Buffalo Bill Cody: The Man Behind the Legend* (New York: John Wiley & Sons, 2000), 444.
3. Yost, Nellie Snyder, *Buffalo Bill, His Family, Friends, Fame, Failures and Fortunes* (Chicago: Sage Books, 1979), 401.
4. Yost, 401, 403.
5. Cody, Louisa Federici, *Memories of*

Chapter 20

1. Freedman, Lew, "Colorado Town Marks Passing of Buffalo Bill," *Cody Enterprise*, January 24, 2017.
2. McMurtry, Larry, *The Colonel and Little Missie* (New York: Simon & Schuster, 2005), 229.
3. Freedman, Lew, "Wake Held to Honor Buffalo Bill's Death," *Cody Enterprise*, February 7, 2017.
4. Buffalo Bill Dinner Menu, January 12, 2017, Denver, Colorado.
5. Freedman, "Wake..."
6. Freedman, Lew, "The Perfect Spot for Buffalo Bill," *Cody Enterprise*, August 28, 2018.
7. Loge, Carole, "Non-Buffalo Buffs 'Pot Shoot' Buffalo," *Cody Enterprise*, August 27, 1969.
8. Clayton, John, *Cowboy Girl: The Life of Caroline Lockhart* (Lincoln: University of Nebraska Press, 2007), 148.
9. Barnes, Jeff, *The Great Plains Guide to Buffalo Bill: Forts, Fights & Other Sites* (Mechanicsburg, PA: Stackpole Books, 2014), xi.
10. Barnes, xiii.
11. Buffalo Bill Centennial Symposium, August 4, 2017, Buffalo Bill Center of the West, Cody, Wyoming.

12. Gondola, Ch. Didier, Lecture, Buffalo Bill Centennial Symposium, August 4, 2017, Buffalo Bill Center of the West, Cody, Wyoming.
13. Haque, Danielle, Lecture, Buffalo Bill Centennial Symposium, August 4, 2017, Buffalo Bill Center of the West, Cody, Wyoming.
14. Freedman, Lew, "Competition for Cody's New Slogan," *Cody Enterprise*, December 23, 2017.
15. Bartel, Evan, "Cody Family Comes Together," *Cody Enterprise*, July 16, 2019.
16. Freedman, Lew, "Women Key in Starting Museum," *Cody Enterprise*, February 4, 2017.
17. Freedman, "Women..."

Bibliography

Books

Barnes, Jeff. *The Great Plains Guide to Buffalo Bill: Forts, Fights & Other Sites*. Mechanicsburg, PA: Stackpole Books, 2014.
Bonner, Robert E. *William F. Cody's Wyoming Empire: The Buffalo Bill Nobody Knows*. Norman: University of Oklahoma Press, 2007.
Bradley, Glenn Danford. *The Story of the Pony Express*. Chicago: A.C. McClurg & Co., 1913.
Bricklin, Julia. *America's Best Female Sharpshooter: The Rise and Fall of Lillian Frances Smith*. Norman: University of Oklahoma Press, 2017.
Bridger, Bobby. *Buffalo Bill and Sitting Bull: Inventing the Wild West*. Austin: University of Texas Press, 2002.
Burdette, Roger. *Renaissance of American Coinage, 1909–1915*. Great Falls, VA: Seneca Mill Press, 2007.
Burke, John. *Buffalo Bill: From Prairie to Palace*. Lincoln, NE: Bison Books, University of Nebraska, 2012.
Carter, Robert A. *Buffalo Bill Cody: The Man Behind the Legend*. New York: John Wiley & Sons, Inc., 2000.
Clavin, Tom. *Dodge City: Wyatt Earp, Bat Masterson and the Wickedest Town in the American West*. New York: St. Martin's Press, 2017.
Clavin, Tom. *Wild Bill: The True Story of the American Frontier's First Gunfighter*. New York: St. Martin's Press, 2019.
Clayton, John. *Cowboy Girl: The Life of Caroline Lockhart*. Lincoln: University of Nebraska Press, 2007.
Cody, Buffalo Bill. *True Tales of the Plains*. New York: Empire Book Company, 1908.
Cody, Louisa Federici. *Memories of Buffalo Bill*. Milwaukee: HardPress Publishing, 1919.
Cody, William F. *Buffalo Bill's Life Story, An Autobiography*. New York: Skyhorse Publishing, 2010 edition, originally published 1879.
Cody, William F. "The Wild West In England." In Christianson, Frank (ed.). *The Papers of William F. Cody*. Lincoln: University of Nebraska Press, 2012.
DeFelice, Jim. *West Like Lightning: The Brief, Legendary Ride of the Pony Express*. New York: William Morrow, 2018.
Enss, Chris. *The Many Loves of Buffalo Bill*. Guilford, CT: TwoDot/Globe Pequot Press, 2010.
Foote, Stella. *Letters from Buffalo Bill*. Cody, WY: Shoshone Distributing Co., 1954.
Fredriksson, Kristine. *American Rodeo: From Buffalo Bill to Big Business*. College Station: Texas A&M University Press, 1985.
Friesen, Steve. *Buffalo Bill: Scout, Showman, Visionary*. Golden, CO: Fulcrum Publishing, 2010.

Bibliography

Friesen, Steve, and Chladiuk, Francois. *Lakota Performers in Europe: Their Culture and the Artifacts They Left Behind.* Norman: University of Oklahoma Press, 2017.
Griffin, Charles Eldridge. *Four Years in Europe with Buffalo Bill.* Albia, IA: Stage Publishing Co., 1908.
Johnson, Craig. *Land of Wolves.* New York: Viking, 2019.
Kasson, Joy S. *Buffalo Bill's Wild West: Celebrity, Memory and Popular History.* New York: Hill and Wang, 2000.
Knappe, Stephanie Fox. "Art Perpetuating Fame: The Posters Of Buffalo Bill's Wild West." Ph.D. dissertation, University of Kansas, 2013.
Majors, Alexander (Prentiss Ingraham, ed.). *Seventy Years on the Frontier.* New York: Rand McNally and Publishers, 1893.
May, Karl. *Winnetou.* Pullman: Washington State University Press, 1989 edition, originally published in 1892.
McMurtry, Larry. *The Colonel And Little Missie.* New York: Simon & Schuster, 2005.
Miller, Darlis A. *Captain Jack Crawford: Buckskin Poet, Scout, Showman.* Albuquerque: University of New Mexico Press, 1993.
Monaghan, Jay. *The Great Rascal: The Life and Adventures of Ned Buntline.* New York: Little Brown & Co., 1952.
Russell, Don. *The Lives and Legends of Buffalo Bill.* Norman: University of Oklahoma Press, 1960.
Scott, Douglas, Bleed, Peter, and Damm, Stephen. *Custer, Cody, and Grand Duke Alexis: Historical Archeology of the Royal Buffalo Hunt.* Norman: University of Oklahoma Press, 2013.
Sell, Henry Blackman, and Weybright, Victor. *Buffalo Bill and the Wild West.* New York: Oxford University Press, 1955.
Serrano, Richard A. *American Endurance: Buffalo Bill, the Great Cowboy Race of 1893, and the Vanishing Wild West.* Washington, DC: Smithsonian Books, 2016.
Stillman, Deanne. *Blood Brothers: The Story of the Strange Friendship between Sitting Bull and Buffalo Bill.* New York: Simon & Schuster, 2017.
Warren, Louis. *Buffalo Bill's America: William Cody and the Wild West Show.* New York: Alfred Knopf, 2005.
Wetmore, Helen Cody. *Last of the Great Scouts.* New York: Grosset & Dunlap, 1899.
Wilson, R.L., and Martin, Greg. *Buffalo Bill's Wild West: An American Legend.* New Jersey: Chartwell, 2004.
Yost, Nellie Snyder. *Buffalo Bill, His Family, Friends, Fame, Failures and Fortunes.* Chicago: Sage Books, 1979.

Newspapers

Cody Enterprise (Wyoming)
New York Sun

Magazines

American History Magazine
The Elks Magazine
True West Magazine

Online Sources

https://centerofthewest.org (Buffalo Bill Center of the West)
http://thevintagenews.com (The Vintage News)

Personal Interviews

Paul Fees, August 29, 2019
Lynn Houze, August 23, 2019
Jeremy Johnston, August 23, 2019

Lectures

Buffalo Bill Centennial Symposium, Buffalo Bill Center of the West, August 2017, Cody, Wyoming.

Archival Files

Buffalo Bill Center of the West, Harold McCracken Research Library (Correspondence), Cody, Wyoming.
Papers of William F. Cody, Buffalo Bill Center of the West, Cody, Wyoming.

Ephemera

Pony Express 1860 advertisement reproduction.

Index

Numbers in **_bold italics_** indicate pages with illustrations

Aberdeen, Scotland 176
Academy of Music (New York) 73
The Adventures of Huckleberry Finn 144
The Adventures of Tom Sawyer 144
Alaska 91
Albany, New York 75
Albany Hotel (Colorado) 198
Albert, Prince (England) 138, 141
Albert I of Monaco, Prince **_57_**, 186
Albert II of Monaco, Prince 186
Albright, Emmett 150, 151
Alexandrovich, Grand Duke Alexai (Russia) 56, 59, 60, 186
Alger, H.C. 180
Allen, Colonel Alvaren 115, 117, 118
Allen, Mary Jester (niece) 217, 218
America's Best Female Sharpshooter 128
Anderson, A.A. 185
Appomattox 40
Arapaho Indians 51, 55
Argentina 165, 177
Arizona 188
Arkansas River 48
Arlington National Cemetery 203
Arthur, President Chester 117
Astoria Hotel (New York) 134
Atkins, John D.C. 116
Atlantic Ocean 15, 140
Auburn University (Alabama) 157
Australia 104
Austria 91
Ayer, Edward E. 36

Bad Bear 159
Bailey, James 100, 146, 147, 163, 188
Baker, Buzz 207
Baker, Johnny 82, 125, 126, 127, 130, 145, 150, 190, **_194_**, 195, 198, 203
Barnes, Jeff 211, 212, 216

Barnum, P.T. 92, 100, 103, 163
Barnum & Bailey Circus 101, 146, 175
Barnum's American Museum 101
Battle of Summit Springs 85
Battle of the Little Bighorn (Custer's Last Stand) 47, 56, 60, 61, 85, 86, 88, 110, 112, 114, 119, 145, 153, 154, 157, 160, 170
Battle of the Washita River 54, 55
Beadle, Erastus 70
Beadle, Irwin 70
Beadle and Adams 135
Beck, George 180, 183, 186
Belgium 91, 178, 214
Bennett, James Gordon 72, 73
Benteen, Captain Frederick 55
Berry, John 150, 151
Bierstadt, Albert 58, 59
Big Horn Basin, Wyoming 180, 183
Billy the Kid 7
Birmingham, England 143
Bismarck, North Dakota 115
Black Elk 142
Black Fox, Joe 159
Black Heart 161
Black Hills, South Dakota 60
Black Horn, Chief 162
Black Kettle, Chief 54, 55
Bleistein, George 181
Boal, Horton 180
Boal, William Cody (grandson) 187, 196
Bogardus, Captain Adam H. (and family) 108, 125
Bonfils, Frederick 196
Bonheur, Rosa 146, 178
Boone & Crockett Club 186
Borgia, Lucretia (gun) 7, 10, 79
Borgia, Lucrezia (woman) 7
Boston 75, 168, 209
Bricklin, Julia 128

231

Brigham (horse) 7, 10, 13
Brink, Doc 38
Bristol, England 167
Bronx Zoo 155
Brule Lakota Indians 58
Brussels, Belgium 162
Buckingham Palace 137
Buckskin Joe 83
Buffalo, New York 118, 181
Buffalo Bill Cabins 216
Buffalo Bill Center of the West (and sub-museums) (Wyoming) 1, *2*, 4, 15, 18, *46*, 77, 81, 91, 136, 145, 149, 152, 155, 164, 169, 186, 187, 198, 202, 203, 212, 214, 216, 217
Buffalo Bill Cody Homestead 16
Buffalo Bill Cody Stampede Rodeo 208, 209, 210, 216
Buffalo Bill Dam (Shoshone Dam) 182
Buffalo Bill: King of the Border Men 72, 169
Buffalo Bill Memorial Association 217
Buffalo Bill Museum (Iowa) *17*, *18*, *19*
Buffalo Bill Museum and Grave (Colorado) 3, 82, 92, 161, 171, 194, 205, 207
Buffalo Bill Ranch State Historical Park 68, *95*, *96*
Buffalo Bill Reservoir 182
Buffalo Bill's Cowboy Band (and band leader William Sweeney) 171
Buffalo head nickel (Indian head nickel) 154, 155, 156, 157
Bull Bear, David 162
Buntline, Ned (Edward Zane Carroll Judson, Sr.) 70, 71, 72, 73, 74, 75, 92, 110, 112, 153, 169, 214
Burke, John 92, 95, 96, 98, 99, 105, 106, 107, 110, 111, 112, 113, 116, 117, 118, 119, 125, 126, 130, 136, 138, 140, 144, 145, 147, 150, 151, 163, 165, 176, 177, 178, 215
Burlington Inn 15
Burns, Dr. Emily 157, 214
Burroughs, Edgar Rice 72
Butler, Frank 124, 125, 126, 129, 191

California 18, 26, 29, 31, 128, 132
California Gold Rush 31
California Trail 32
Camp Alexis 58
Camp Monaco 186
Camp Monaco Prize 187
Campbell, Senator Ben Nighthorse (Colorado) 155
Canada 15, 91, 114, 119, 140, 144, 157
Canadian River 54
Carey, Senator Joseph (Wyoming) 181

Carr, General Eugene 53, 54, 83, 84, 85, 86, 116
Carson City, Nevada 32
Carter Mountain (Wyoming) 183
Carver, Dr. A.W. 99, 100, 102, 104, 105, 106, 108
Cash, Johnny 91
Cashman Greever Garden 15
Cedar Mountain (Wyoming) 195, 196, 199, *200*, *201*, 202, 204, 207, 218
Center of the American West 152
Central Overland and Pike's Peak Express Company 31
Chadron, Nebraska 149
Charging Thunder 159
Cheyenne, Wyoming 86, 92, 172
Cheyenne Indians 51, 54, 55, 83, 86, 87, 89
Cheyenne River 86
Chicago 26, 73, 74, 75, 116, 134, 147, 140, 150, 151, 170, 179
Chicago Burlington and Quincy Railroad 15
Chicago Elevated train 148
China 143
Chrisman, George 34, 35
Cincinnati 75, 124, 125
Civil War 2, 5, 11, 16, 21, 40, 41, 42, 45, 46, 48, 50, 62, 71, 80, 104, 123, 173, 213
Claire, John 135
Clark, Ben 55
Clear Creek, Wyoming 33
Clemmons, Katherine 134, 135
Cleveland 23
Cleveland, President Grover 117, 119
Cobb, Ty 81
Cody, Allan (descendent, cousin of Buffalo Bill) 217
Cody, Arta (daughter) 1, 2, 66, 67, 68, 134, 135, 143, 179, 180
Cody, Charley (brother) 16, 18, 19
Cody, Elijah (uncle) 21
Cody, Eliza (sister) 16
Cody, Fred Garlow (grandson) 82
Cody, Irma (daughter) 134, 135, 192, 195, 202, 216
Cody, Isaac (father) 5, 16, 19, 20, 21, 22, 23, 26, 40
Cody, Julia (sister) 16, *20*, 21, 42, 68, 96, 103, 180, 185, 187, 195, 196, 202
Cody, Kit Carson (son) 66, 67, 68, 69, 70, 82, 109, 127
Cody, Laura (sister, also Nellie, Helen Jester and Helen Wetmore) 16, 18, *20*, 24, 34, 43, 49, 89, 90, 94, 175, 183, 217
Cody, Louisa Frederici (wife) 12, 45, 62,

Index 233

63, 64, 65, 66, 67, 68, 69, 88, 96, 97, 109, 130, 131, 132, 133, 134, 135, 171, 172, 173, 174, 179, 180, 187, 190, 192, 195, 196, 201, 202, 203, 206, 211
Cody, Martha (sister) 16, 24
Cody, Mary (sister, May) 16, *20*, 179, 192, 195, 202
Cody, Mary Ann (mother) 5, 16, 22, 26, 40, 42
Cody, Orra (daughter) 68, 109, 131, 179
Cody, Samuel (brother) 16, 19
Cody, William F. (Buffalo Bill): buffalo hunting 5–14, 56–60, 186–187; cavalry scouting/Indian wars 48–54, 77–90; Civil War involvement 41–44; Cody, Wyoming, creation 180–185; fame and stage 70–76; health, decline and death 192–204; love affairs 131–137; marriage 62–69, *63*, 173–175; Pony Express involvement 31–39; relationship with Native American employees 153–162; Wild West exhibition 91–96, *99*–111, *100*, *101*, *104*, *106*, *107*, 112–122, 138–148, 163–172, 176–179; youth 15–25
Cody, William Garlow (descendant, Bill) *188*
Cody, Wyoming 3, 4, 15, 46, 77, 91, 118, 136, 150, 164, 171, 174, 180, 181, *182*, 183, 185, 186, 187, 188, 192, 193, 198, 199, 202, 203, 206, 210, *211*, 212, 216, 217
Cody Canal 182
Cody Country Chamber of Commerce 3, *6*, 216
Cody Enterprise (Park County Enterprise) 183, 193, 206, 208
Cody Trail 19
Cody Trolley Tours 204
Cody's Creek 53
The Colonel and Little Missie 127
Colorado 3, 82, 195, 203, 207
Colorado National Guard 203
Colorado Springs, Colorado 210
Comanche Indians 41, 51
Comstock, Billy 11, 12, 13, 51, 67
Coney Island, New York 103, 105
Confederate Army 43, 44
Congo (Kinshasa) 214, 215
Cooke, Lt. L.W. 53
Cossacks *107*, 176, 177
Crawford, Captain Jack 93, 94
Croatia 91
Crook, General George 85, 86, 115, 168
Cuba 148, 164
Custer, Elizabeth 52, 55

Custer, Gail-Kelly 55
Custer, General George Armstrong 3, 46, 47, 48, 49, 52, 54, 55, 56, 59, 60, 61, 85, 86, 88, 92, 112, 114, 118, 119, 145, 157, 170, 211
Custer, Tom 55, 170
Custer: The Controversial Life of George Armstrong Custer 55
Cut Nose, Chief 89

Daily Conservative (Leavenworth, Kansas) 8
Deadwood, South Dakota 28
Declaration of Independence 141
DeFelice, Jim 34
Denmark 141, 142
Denver 1, 3, 5, 36, 106, 107, 109, 132, 152, 188, 192, 193, 194, 196, 197, 199, 201, 202, 204, 205, 206, 207, 210, 211, 217
Denver Post 196, 198, 210
Dominy, General Charles E. 83
DuBois, Pennsylvania 156
Duluth, Minnesota 18
Duluth Press (Minnesota) 183
Dunn, Charles 21

Edison, Thomas 145
Egan, Howard R. 36
Eldredge, Bruce 1, 2, 203
Elks 196, 198
Elliott, Major Joel 55
Emancipation Proclamation 40
England 3, 91, 129, 134, 140, 142, 144, 146, 162, 164, 165, 166, 167, 175, 176, 178, 214
Enss, Chris 133
Etruria 166
Europe 91, 134, 138, 146, 151, 161, 162, 163, 164, 168, 175, 178, 179, 185, 214
Evansville, Wyoming 92

Fees, Paul *81*, 82, 136, 201, 203
Feller, Bob 123
Fifth Cavalry 6, 53, 83, 84, 87, 206
Flying Hawk, Chief 156, 159
Forrest, General Nathan Bedford 43, 44
Fort Bridger 30
Fort Cody (Gift Shop) *93*, *101*, 210
Fort Hays, Kansas 6, 8, 9, 11, 48, 51, 52, 53, 65
Fort Kearney 23
Fort Laramie 27, 86
Fort Larned 48, 49, 50, 51, 52
Fort McPherson 66, 70, 72, 78, 83
Fort Riley 47

Index

Fort Sumter 40
Fort Wallace 11
Fort Yates 117
France 2, 91, 141, 144, 146
Fraser, James Earle 154, 155, 158
Fraser, Thomas 154
Friesen, Steve 82, *161*, 171, 206, 207
The Frontier Rodeo (Prescott, Arizona) 98
Frost, Dick 201
Frost, Ned 199, *201*, 202, 208
Fry, Johnny 33

Gallagher, Dennis 205
Garlow, Bill (great-grandson) 83
Garlow, Bill Cody (grandson) 188, 201
Garlow, Frederick H. (son-in-law) 195
The Garryowen 56
George III, King (England) 143
Germany 91, 144, 146, 165, 193
Ghost Dance Movement (Wovoka) 121
Gillespie, John 151
Gilmore Garden 108
Glenwood Springs, Colorado 192
Golden, Colorado 3, 92, 161, 192, *193*, *196*, *197*, 198, 203, 204, 205, 206, 211
Golden, Nat 43
Gondola, Ch. Didier 214, 215
Gonzalez, Isadore 167
Goodman, Al (brother-in-law) 103, 180
Gordon, James 37
Gothenburg, Nebraska *37*, *38*
Grand Opera House (Brooklyn) 97
Grange, Red 1
Grant, General and President Ulysses S. 46, 47, 58, 115
Gray, Bee Ho 154
The Great Cowboy Race 149, 151
Great Plains 5, 30, 55, 56, *57*, 62, 76, 77, 89, 105, 106, 110, 112, 119, 120, 131, 151
The Great Plains Guide to Buffalo Bill: Forts, Fights & Other Sites 211
Greece 142
Griffin, Charles Eldridge 166, 167, 168, 176, 178
Gwin, Senator William McKendree 31

Hamilton, William 32
Haque, Danielle 205
Harpers New Monthly Magazine 71
Harpersfield, New York 70
Harris, Mayor Carter (Chicago) 147
Harrison, President Benjamin 122
Hartford, Connecticut 110
Hartford Daily Courant 107
Haslam, Bob 36, 37

Hawaii 91, 164
Hazen, General William B. 51, 53
Hearst, Phoebe 183
Hickok, Wild Bill 3, 27, 28, 29, 33, 37, 38, 41, 45, 52, 53, 54, 65, 71, 76, 92, 93
Hoffman House (New York) 134
Holland 165
Houze, Lynn 81, 82, 136
Hungary 91
Hutchinson, James 101
Hyatt, Mary 22

Illinois 104
Indian Wife and White Hunter 70
Indiana University–Purdue University, Indianapolis 214
Innocents Abroad 144
International Cody Family Association 217
Iowa 1, 19
Irma Hotel *136*, 137, *184*, 212, 216
Iron Hail, Chief (Dewey Beard) 157
Iron Tail, Chief 153, 154, 155, 156, 157, 158, 163, 166, 186, 190, 198, 207, 215
Isbell, Bessie 134
Isle of Jersey 15
Italy 91, 143, 144, 146, 153
It's a Mad, Mad, Mad, Mad World (movie and cast) 169

Japan 164
Jefferson, President Thomas 154
Jester, Alexander (brother-in-law) 18
Johnson, Craig 204
Johnson, Michael 204
Johnson, Walter 123
Johnston, Jeremy 77, 78, 136, *149*, 198, 214, 217
Jordan, Michael 10
Junction City, Kansas 52

Kansas 19, 20, 24, 40, 41, 42, 44, 48, 51, 52, 65, 72, 211
Kansas Pacific Railway 5, 7
Kasebier, Gertrude 155, 156
Kaufman, Charles 186
Kentucky 125, 133, 134, 140
Kentucky Fried Chicken 140
King, Lieutenant Charles (and imitator) 86, 87, 206
Kiowa Indians 41, 51, 52, 55
Knappe, Stephanie Fox 107

Lamar, Lucius Q.T. 115, 116
Land of Wolves 204
LaPointe, Ernie 118

Last of the Great Scouts 18, 49, 175, 180
Leavenworth, Kansas 8, 15, 24, 30, 41, 62, 65, 94, 211
LeClaire, Iowa 15, 16, *17*, 18, 19, 26
Lee, General Robert E. 45, 47
Liddle, Bruce 61
Life on the Border 92
Lillie, Gordon (Pawnee Bill) 100, 156, 188, 189, 192, 196
Limerick, Patty 152
Lincoln, President Abraham 36, 40
Little, Amos 159
Little Bighorn, Battle of (Custer's Last Stand) 47, 56, 60, 61, 85, 86, 88, 110, 112, 114, 119, 145, 153, 154, 157, 160, 170
Little Rock, Chief 55
Liverpool 165, 166
Livingstone, David 72
Lockhart, Caroline ***208***, 209, 210, ***212***, ***213***, ***214***, ***215***
Lockhart Inn (Cody, Wyoming) 209, 213
Lola Coastal Mexican Restaurant 206
London 137, 141, 142, 151, 153, 161, 167, 178
Lone Bear 162
Lone Bear, Sammy 159, 162
Lonesome Dove 127
Longmire, Walt 204
Lookout Mountain (Colorado) 193, 195, 196, 198, 201, 202, 205, 207, 208
Louisiana 47
Louisville 125
Luxembourg 91

Madison Square Garden 138, 147, 155, 171
Madsen, Chris 87
Major League Baseball 10
Majors, Alexander 31, 34, 36
Manchester, England 143, 166
Masons 196, 198
Massachusetts/Massachusetts Bay Colony 15, 16
May, Karl 145
McCanles, David 37
McCausland, Iowa 16
McConnell, Evan 61
McCreight, Alice 157
McCreight, Major Israel 156, 157, 158
McKinley (horse) 198
McLaughlin, James 115, 117, 120, 121, 162
McMurtry, Larry 1, 127
McNeil, General John 45
McPherson Station 78
Mead, Elwood 180
Meador, Fred 72, 74
Medal of Honor 2, 78, 79, 80, 81, 82, 83, 213

Medicine Woman 55
Meeteetse, Wyoming 186
Meinhold, Captain Charles 79
Memories of Buffalo Bill 64
Memphis 42
Mexico 164, 170, 171, 176
Midway Plaisance 148, 151
Miles, General Nelson 81, 82, 115, 121, 122, 186, 202
Miller Brothers 101 Ranch Wild West Show 156, 158, 189
Minnesota 115, 118, 154
Minnesota State–Mankato 215
Mississippi 42
Mississippi River 15, 17, 106, 171, 210
Missouri 21, 31, 40, 41, 42, 132, 167
Monaco 3
Monahsetah, Princess 55
Montana 47, 61, 85
Moran, Breck 201
Morlacchi, Giuseppina 76
Mormon Trail 32
Mormons 27, 30
Moses, Mollie 133, 134, 135

National American Indian Memorial (Staten Island, New York) 154
National Basketball Association 140
National Enquirer 173
National Hockey League 140
National Register of Historic Places 16
Native Americans 6, 8, 27, 29, 85, 104, 112, 113, 118, 140, 141, 153, 154, 157, 158, 159, 160, 161, 164, 216
Nebraska Game and Parks Commission 68
Nebraska National Guard 48, 140
Nebraska Territory (state) 33, 58, 93, 95, 96, 97, 99, 102, 150, 164, 170, 171, 180
Nevada 121
New England 15
New Orleans 109, 110, 125
New York 31, 32, 50, 58, 72, 73, 75, 100, 102, 108, 138, 143, 151, 154, 166, 178, 195
New York Herald 72, 73, 178
New York Sun 170, 171
New York Weekly 72
New York World 75
Newberry College (Chicago) 36
Nixon, Jim 74
Nixon, President Richard 143
Normandy 15
North, Frank 71, 72 84, 100, 110
North, Luther 8, 110
North Dakota 114

North Platte, Nebraska 56, 58, 68, 69, 71, 93, **94**, **96**, **97**, 98, 101, 121, 128, 132, 133, 134, 146, 174, 180, 183, 184, 185, 187, 210
North Platte River 29
Northern Pacific Railroad 115

Oakley, Annie (Phoebe Ann Mosey) (and imitator) 1, 111, 115, 118, 123, **124**, 125, 126, 127, 128, 129, 130, 140, 141, 142, 145, 157, 163, 165, 166, 191, 206, 212
Obama, President Barack 169
Ohio 123
Old Glory Blowout (Buffalo Bill Rodeo) 98, 171
Old Shatterhand 145
Olinger, George Washington 202
Olinger's Crown Hill Mortuary 198, 201, 202, 203, 206
Omaha, Nebraska 58, 101, 103, 212
Omaha Herald 212
Omohundro, Texas Jack 74, 75, 76, 78, 95
Ontario 144
Oregon Trail 32
Ostrich Man (Alfonso) 167

Pahaska Teepee 182, 186, 205, **209**
Palmer, General Joel 58
Palmquist Ernie 100, 101
Palmquist Virginia 100
Paris 144, 151, 153, 178
Park County Travel Council 216
Park Theatre (Brooklyn) 97
Pawnee Indians 83, 84, 100, 110, 112, 159
Peake, J.H. 183, 193
Pecos Rodeo (Texas) 98
Pennsylvania 15, 40, 70
Penrose, General William H. 54
Perry Hotel 65
Pershing, General "Black Jack" 203
Philadelphia 75, 100, 139, 150, 158, 209
Philippines 164
Piccadilly Circus 168
Pine Ridge Indian Reservation 158, 160
Plains Indians 3, 7, 47, 50
Plant's Station 33
Plenty Coups, Chief 186
Pony Express 2, 5, 26, 31, 32, 33, 34, 35, 36, **37**, **38**, 39, 40, 44, 46, 66, 102, 104, 110, 211, 213
Powder River, Wyoming 33
Powell, Wyoming 199
Prairie Wolf 95
Price, Captain George 84
Price, General Sterling 45
Proctor, Alexander Phimister 158

Professional Rodeo Cowboys Association 210
Professional Rodeo Hall of Fame 210
Prussian Guard 165

Quebec 144

Rawlins, Wyoming 92
Reconstruction 45, 47
Red Cloud, Chief 33
Red Cloud Agency 86, 89
Red Shirt 137, 142
Red Willow Creek 58
Republican River (Frenchman Fork) 59
Revolutionary War 141
Richard, Bob **199**, 202, 204, 207, 208
Richard, Fred 199, 202
Richard, Jack 208
Riverside Cemetery 216
Rochester, New York 67, 68, 87, 109, 179
Rock Creek Station 33, 37, 41
Rock Springs 92
Rocky Mountain Prairie Expedition 105
Rocky Mountains 1, 144, 210
Roman Catholicism 196, 205
Roman Colosseum 144
Rome, Kansas 65, 181
Roosevelt, Alice 185
Roosevelt, President Theodore (and imitator) 148, 165, 185, 186, 206
The Royal Buffalo Hunt 59
Royall, Major William 6, 7, 53
Rumsey, Bronson 180, 181
Russell, Don 36
Russell, William 31, 35
Russell, Majors and Waddell (freight company) 23, 26, 27, 31, 32, 33, 41
Russia 58, 59, 91, 165
Rutgers University–Camden (New Jersey) 150
Ruth, Babe 1, 11, 81

Sacramento 31, 32
St. Joseph, Missouri 31, 32, 33, 36, 38
St. Louis 11, 45, 62, 63, 64, 66, 75, 120, 133
Saline River 51
Salsbury, Nate 97, 100, 102, 104, 105, 109, 110, 111, 113, 127, 130, 138, 144, 147, 148, 151, 160, 163, 164, 174, 175, 181, 182, 183, 188, 211
Salsbury's Troubadors 104
Salt Creek 22
Salt Creek Squatters Association 21
Salt Lake City, Utah 23 32
Salt Valley 21

Index

San Francisco 31, 128
Sanders, Harland 240
Satana, Chief 52, 53
Schwoob, Mayor Jacob (Cody, Wyoming) 201
Scotland 91
Scott, Lieutenant Clarence Armstrong (son-in-law) 185
Scott County, Iowa 19
The Scout 217
Scouts of the Plains 92
The Scouts of the Plains 73
Scout's Rest Ranch 58, 68, **94**, **96**, 97, 121, 180, 187, 210
Seattle 218
Seibert, Peter 2
Sells Brothers Circus 125
Sells-Floto Circus 189, 192
Seneca, Kansas 33
Seventh Cavalry (U.S.) 47, 52, 55, 56, 61, 85, 92, 112, 154, 160
Seventh Cavalry Kansas/Red-Legged Scouts 41, 42
Sheridan, General Philip 47, 51, 52, 53, 54, 56, 58, 59, 60, 72, 80, 86, 115
Sheridan, Kansas 11
Sheridan, Wyoming 92, 184
Sheridan Avenue (Cody, Wyoming) 185
Sheridan Inn (Sheridan, Wyoming) 185
Sherman, William Tecumseh 46, 59, 116
Shoshone News (Wyoming) 183
Shoshone River (Stinking Water River) 180, 181
Shoshoni, Wyoming 181
Sierra Mountains 32
Sikes, Olive Logan 135
Simpson, U.S. Senator Alan (Wyoming) 82, 83, 213
Simpson, Lew 28, 29, 30
Simpson, Governor Milward (Wyoming) 213
Simpson, Pete 4, 213
Sioux (Lakota) Indians 51, 85, 112, 114, 118, 120, 142, 153, 157, 159, 162, 164, 167
Sistine Chapel 144
Sitting Bull, Chief 3, 47, 112, **113**, 114, 115, 116, 117, 118, 119, 120, 121, 122, 123, 130, 153, 155, 157, 159, 162, 163, 190, 207
Sitting Bull's Voice 118
Smith, General Andrew J. 42, 43, 44
Smith, Lillian 128, 129, 141, 145
Snow, Clyde 61
Solomon River 51, 83
Son of the Morning Star 61
South Bend, Indiana 158

South Dakota 60, 114, 120, 158, 160
South Platte River 84
Spain 91, 146, 178
Spanish-American War 148
Speer, Mayor Robert (Denver) 197, 198
Sporting Life 142
Spotted Tail, Chief 58, 59, 60
Standing Bear, Chief (wife Laura) 167
Standing Bear, Luther 162
Standing Rock Agency 114, 115, 116, 120, 121
Stanley, Henry Morton 72
"Star Spangled Banner" 171
State of Nebraska (ship) 140
Staten Island, New York 147
Sully, General Alfred 51
Summit Springs 71
Summit Springs, Battle of 85

Taft, President William Howard 154
Takes Enemy 159
Tall Bull, Chief 83, 84, 85, 86
Tammen, Henry (Harry) 189, **191**, 192, 196, 201, 207
Tarzan 72
Tate, Naoma 150
TE Ranch **182**, 183
Tennessee 31, 40, 42
Tenth Cavalry 50, 51
Tenting on the Old Campground 205
Terry, General Alfred 115
Texas 47, 135
Texas Panhandle 54
Thayer, Governor John M. (Nebraska) 140
Third Infantry 53
Thompson, M. Jeff 32
Time magazine 198
Topeka 52
Toronto 15
Transcontinental Railroad 31
Tropical Cowboys: Westerns, Violence and Masculinity in Kinshasa 215
True West 82, 150
Turner, Frederick 160
Tutt, David 71
Twain, Mark 144

Union Army 2, 42, 43, 44, 46, 48, 55, 71, 104
United States (and government agencies) 1, 7, 15, 31, 40, 45, 50, 51, 58, 60, 78, 80, 82, 83, 91, 105, 112, 114, 115, 116, 134, 138, 140, 142, 153, 154, 158, 159, 160, 162, 165, 167, 168, 169, 171, 176, 180, 193, 198, 199, 209, 210

University of Colorado 152
Utah 24, 27
Ute Indians 10

Van Gogh, Vincent 150
Vatican (City/Pope) 144
Venice, Italy 178
Victoria, Queen (England) 128, 136, 137, 138, 141, 142, 146, 161, 184
Virginia 40, 47, 203
Vogel, John 199, 202, 203

Waddell, William 31
Wales 91, 141, 142, 143, 176
Wallen, Rick 169
Wallop, Malcolm 82
Wanamaker's Department Store *139*
Wapiti, Wyoming 182
Wapsipinicon Valley, Iowa 16
War Bonnet Creek (Hat Creek) 87
War of 1812 141
Warren, Louis 50
Washington, George 143
Washington, D.C. 32, 50, 58, 85, 115, 117, 121, 154, 203
Washita River, Battle of 54, 55
Wellman, Horace 37
Wert, Jeffry D. 55
West, George Ward Nichols 71
West Chester, Pennsylvania 67, 80
West Point 47, 50, 61
Weston, Missouri 21
Westport, Missouri 41
Wetmore, Hugh (brother-in-law) 18, 183
Whirling Horse 159
White Beaver 95
White Buffalo Man 162
White House 141
Whitney, Gloria Vanderbilt 217
The Wigwam 156, 158

Wild West (Buffalo Bill's exhibition/Congress of Rough Riders) 3, 9, 39, 58, 59, 60, 66, 69, 77, 85, 91, 92, 94, 96, 97, 98, 99, 100, 101, 102, 103, 104, 105, 106, 107, 108, 109, 110, 111, 112, 113, 115, 116, 117, 118, 119, 120, 125, 126, 127, 128, 129, 130, 131, 132, 133, 134, 135, 136, 137, 138, 140, 141, 142, 143, 144, 147, 148, 149, 150, 151, 152, 153, 155, 156, 157, 158, 159, 160, 161, 162, 163, 164, 165, 166, 167, 168, 169, 170, 171, 172, 174, 175, 176, 177, 178, 181, 182, 183, 186, 187, 188, 189, 190, 191, 207, 210, 214, 215, 217
Wilhelm II, Crown Prince (Germany, Kaiser) 127
Wilhelmina, Queen (Holland) 165
Willoughby, Jim 129
Wilson, President Woodrow 202
Wind River Indian Reservation 181
Windsor Castle 137, 141, 143
Winnetou 145
Wood, George 30
Wood, "Smoky" Joe 123
Woods, James 37
Woodside, Martin 150
World War I 127, 165, 191, 193, 198, 203
World War II 162
World's Columbian Expedition (World's Fair) 147, 148, 149, 151, 164, 169
Wounded Knee 157, 160
Wyoming 1, 4, 6, 33, 57, 82, 85, 92, 180, 186, 195, 196, 199, 200, 204

Yellow Hair (Yellow Hand) 87, 89, 93, 132
Yellowstone National Park 15, 169, 181, 183, 186, 205, 209
Young, Cy 10

www.ingramcontent.com/pod-product-compliance
Ingram Content Group UK Ltd.
Pitfield, Milton Keynes, MK11 3LW, UK
UKHW041942140426
5217IPUK00014B/611